Fear or Freedom

A Woman's Options in Social Survival and Physical Defense

by

Susan E. Smith

Published by Mother Courage Press

Mother Courage Press
1533 Illinois Street
Racine, WI 53405

Acknowledgments

Thanks to my mother, Elaine E. Smith, who has always been supportive. She participated in the major portion of the phone work in the four-part study and was an excellent interviewer.

I thank my sisters, Priscilla Smith and Deborah Powell, for supporting my efforts in so many ways. Priscilla conducted part of the study in Portland, Oregon, and was always ready for long-distance brainstorming.

I am grateful to Margie Peper who generously donated her time, expertise and considerable intellect to design and run the computer program for the four-part study; to J. Scott Oancea and Susan Friedman for research services; to Wendy Crow for trying to make the best out of a disastrous word-processing situation at a secretarial service; and to Beth Nieman for editing consultation and for finally unscrambling the manuscript.

Gratitude to Sargent John Humphries of the Phoenix Police Department for recognizing and supporting my efforts in social change and crime prevention. He involved me in one of his crime prevention talks where he introduced me to Judy Hille, a reporter for the *Arizona Republic* in Phoenix. Judy wrote an intelligent and sensitive attention-getting feature article about women's self-defense, my school and Sargent Humphries' well placed comments on self-protection.

Thanks to Dave Phillips for photography and to Sensei Michael Wall of the Paradise Valley School of Karate in Phoenix for volunteering his considerable skill as a model and martial artist to pose for the photographs that Donna Atwood used for the illustrations in the basics and technique sections.

Special thanks to Chief Ruben B. Ortega and Captain Harold L. Hurtt of the Community Relations Bureau of the Phoenix Police Department for information on home security and to Gregory Bowen for the illustrations in the home security section.

I am grateful to my current instructor Sensei Michael Wall for teaching and challenging me and to all my formal and informal instructors. Special recognition to Shifu D. G. Isch, an independant thinker, instructor and innovator in the martial arts.

My gratitude to all the women who participated in the study and shared so honestly of themselves and their experiences.

To all the women who accepted me as their instructor at the school, I can only say thank you collectively for trusting and believing in me and in yourselves. You challenged me and I encouraged and needed that challenge. We grew together and this book is ours - a reflection of our discoveries and experiences. You helped me to go on with a lighter heart because it was so clear that we could make a difference.

And finally thanks to Barbara Lindquist and Jeanne Arnold of Mother Courage Press who had the same vision, recognized mine and responded so positively to my proposal and the manuscript. With their efforts and attention to detail, organization and editing, we completed the circle. This book is dedicated to their courage and to the courage of all women.

Fear or Freedom

A Woman's Options in Social Survival and Physical Defense

by

Susan E. Smith

Illustrated by Donna Atwood

Table of Contents

Self-Defense For Women:
A Positive Social Trend And an Opportunity for Personal Growth

Woman must not depend on the protection of man
but must be taught to defend herself.
Susan B. Anthony, 1871

Chapter 1

Self-Defense for Women:

A Positive Social Trend

and an Opportunity for Personal Growth

How many times have you hopefully read a women's self-defense book or an article on the subject and have been slapped with staggering statistics and assaulted by lists of behavior "rules" or "avoidance" techniques that women are expected to perform compulsively so that they won't "incite" attacks? How many times were you left hanging on the ominous statement, "It Could Happen to You!" or "Any Woman Could Be a Victim!"

Everywhere you look are articles about women dealing with violence and from every source comes the well-intended warnings about the prevalence of violence. Education and knowledge are powerful forces for social change, but in the area of women and violence, damaging social attitudes and messages distort the known facts about men, women and violence.

Women have been increasingly empowered by social advancements and by recent media efforts to expose violence against women. Across the nation, women now are speaking out and fighting back through legal and social channels. Yet, on a private level, their questions linger and their fears prevail. Every woman wants to know, "What can I do to prevent becoming a victim?" or "What should I do if I were ever attacked?"

Women today are rapidly gaining economic independence, personal freedom and physical fitness, yet there is one area that is obscured by misinformation, doubt, fear and ineptitude. That weak spot is their ability to defend themselves effectively.

As women search for answers, they often end up dazed and confused by all the conflicting opinions of self-defense instructors. Hundreds of martial arts styles and specialized self-defense courses are surfacing all over the country. Books, courses and institutions - military, law enforcement, firearms training - are designed to teach survival and defense. The basic principles of defense and the elements of confrontation are almost universally agreed upon and understood, yet no one can agree on what **women** should do in their defense.

1

> **"Self-defense skills add to personal growth with life expanding implications. Recognizing women's need for self-defense is a positive sign of social progress."**

In general, society has utilized scare tactics or the "boogyman" approach to motivate women to learn about self-defense. However, this is a deceptive and fragmentary approach. Women do not need self-defense merely because "there's a lot of weirdos out there." Self-defense skills add to personal growth with life-expanding implications. Recognizing women's need for self-defense is a positive sign of social progress. Fear tactics and emphasis on the negative aspects of women's self-defense have been generally ineffective in motivating them to learn essential self-defense skills.

Even worse, women are lured into self-defense programs with high hopes of learning to live more effectively and actually learning to be physically assertive. Instead they are indoctrinated with more fear and social and behavioral rules based on "limitations" of women. I believe that women should act and react within the entire range of possibilities taking into account situational factors, environmental advantages and physical and psychological variables which will be explained fully in the chapter on "Degrees of Threat/Degrees of Resistance: Application of Strategy."

Self-defense instructors remain divided on one of the central issues of self-protection: whether or not a woman should physically resist an attacker. That this aspect of defense is considered controversial is a sad comment on how deeply ingrained social prejudice is against women. That it **remains** the raging question within the programs designed to help women clearly demonstrates unresolved conflicts about women and their abilities.

Self-defense skills encompass **all** areas of social interaction. Women will be confronted in a range of situations from mild social aggravation to extreme degrees of violence. Their actual circumstances will be as diverse as the people themselves. A responsible self-defense program must teach defenses to assault in addition to communication techniques to reduce the risk and probability of violence. Self-defense training should provide options to passive victimization should an attack occur, not merely provide an arsenal of physical techniques.

Whether a woman should resist physically is not a question to be answered by self-defense instructors or crime experts. Women should be made aware of known elements of successful resistance based on recent extensive research and decide for themselves. They should know a few simple principles which apply to nearly all defensive techniques.

I have reduced the techniques in this book to incorporate in six major principles. These techniques were designed for women but their principles are based on solid fundamentals. They are covered in detail in the Technique Chapter.

An instructor's job is to synthesize and disseminate information based on the current research pertaining to this issue, provide students with as many options as possible and encourage students to trust their own judgment and abilities.

Women have been encouraged to be passive, compliant and even "nice" to a rapist. This attitude coincides with female socialization practices and attitudes in our society which define women's natures and personalities by so-called "feminine" behaviors.[1] In most cases, women are directly taught these behaviors and are influenced by all forms of cultural communications.

The exaggerated characteristics of femininity result in a diminished ability to adjust and to survive in our society. Although this personality distortion occurs in varying degrees in almost all women, two extreme examples are anorexia and agoraphobia. Anorexics are reacting to the cultural obsession with female body size and the demand to be thin. Ninety-five percent of anorexics are female.[2] Agoraphobics are excessively fearful and will rarely, if ever, leave their homes. The majority of agoraphobics are women.[3]

Based on their socialized assumptions about women, many self-defense instructors promote distorted ideas about "psychological" defenses which are supposedly effective for women. Current research in one study has shown that physical resistance is effective, especially in the initial encounter.

"... in the final analysis, a woman must develop a deep belief in her own worth and her right to physical integrity."

I differ with women's self-defense experts on another major point. I do not confine the concept and practice of self-defense to physical reactions and/or psychological ploys. My concept of resistance is an internal commitment not merely an external set of reactions. This commitment should be encouraged, but in the final analysis, a woman must develop a deep belief in her own worth and her right to physical integrity. In any case, a woman deserves a choice of weapons. When a resistor believes she has a choice, she retains psychological control, even if she chooses temporary compliance or apparent submission. Many self-defense instructors psychologically slaughter their students in a misguided attempt to "reduce the risk" of injury or "prevent assault" when they teach women they have no other option but cooperative and submissive behavior.

My message is a very simple, fundamental truth about human existence.

We cannot influence social and personal change by reinforcing the negative aspects of self-defense for women. We need to maintain a basic integrity about our ability to survive.

Appeals to fear are most commonly used to convince women they need self-defense, yet it is a well-documented fact that such low-reassurance communications are the least effective means of influencing attitude change.[4] Once a woman makes a commitment to self-defense, she often faces indoctrination about her physical and social "limitations" and must be psychologically defeated before she can truly accept these messages.

Instructors also resort to issuing long lists of do's and don't's about female behavior which are supposed to be less likely to inflame male rage. This is a misguided attempt to make sense out of senseless violence.

This negative focus strips women of choice and self-esteem and describes the psychological model of "learned helplessness." Women are taught both covertly and overtly that danger is everywhere and that in the event of an attack, assertive behavior **is** futile and even harmful for the victim.

Learned helplessness has been studied in actual crime victims who, in the course of an attack, had experiences which caused them to believe that responding was futile. However, responding was often successful and, even when it was not, different people had extremely varied reactions. Some people became angry and motivated to change; others accepted helplessness as inevitable in future situations. When helplessness is viewed as inevitable, the result is emotional numbing and maladaptive passivity.[5]

On a large scale, even women who may never be physically victimized experience the same effect of learned helplessness from these prevalent and damaging messages. In effect, all women are victims

3

of social belief systems even if they never experience physical assault. A woman who believes in "future response futility" **on any level** is less equipped to live effectively **on every level**.

If society is so committed to protecting women, why then are women so effectively discouraged from taking the very steps that would change their lives? How can we then ultimately change the foundations of a society which promote the fear and helplessness that inhibit women's lives?

Self-defense for women seems to be the last frontier which society and the "experts" and the instructors have failed to consider rationally. How can they, in good conscience, exploit women's fear and encourage them to believe more deeply in their physical weakness and their lack of individual judgment?

Why would we assume that an assailant who commits a high degree of violence was driven to it or totally externally controlled by the behavior of his chosen target? A. Nicholas Groth, author of *Men Who Rape: The Psychology of the Offender*, has shown in his research that the degree of violence and type of assault are a result of the offender's needs and motivations, not merely a response to the actions or reactions of his chosen target.

Why continue to promote the idea that resistance is impossible and unnatural for women when all the current research refutes this social myth?

What of the woman who struggles wildly or fights and escapes unhurt?

What of the woman who escapes an attack, even with injuries, but gains a sense of victory and an increased feeling of control over future safety as a result of this victory?

What of the woman who cooperates to avoid injury, is severely beaten, and perhaps even led to her death? Serial murderers need a cooperative victim and a safe place to carry out the crime; they cannot act out their violent fantasies without safely procuring a relatively passive, naive victim and ensuring a safe location. What kind of logic assumes that consistently uncommitted self-protection measures will decrease risk?

"Then there is the final question. Who will protect us from our protectors? The majority of violence against women is inflicted by known assailants, often a husband, boyfriend or relative."

Then there is the final question. Who will protect us from our protectors? The majority of violence against women is inflicted by **known assailants,** often a husband, boyfriend or relative. One of my primary objectives is to expose the circumstances of known-assailant assault, which represents the majority of attacks on women.

In these situations, I offer alternatives to submission which, in these cases, is never the best solution.

There are many theories about violence against women. These theories include the fear of women, historical cultural practices, their economic exploitation, women as the "weaker sex," male's uncontrollable biological drives, and, most recently, media exploitation and the surrogate victim theory in which the rapist or murderer is acting out hatred of a specific woman or women in general on any available female.

Certain gender-specific social expectations and behavioral norms are the foundations of common rape theories such as rape precipitating behavior, "She asked for it!" or "Her behavior incited rape." Female violation of gender rules endorse the male to act as the enforcer and upholder of "social laws." "She shouldn't have been **there,**" which translates to **anywhere** without a valid male protector. "I wanted to teach her a lesson" is a common rationalization of rapists. This rationalization affirms the feminist definition of rape as a form of social control.

The issue of violence is innundated with cultural misconceptions about men and women. One of these issues is the anthropological or biological viewpoint of male violence. Explained briefly, this viewpoint depicts men as superficially controlled by a repressive society, almost sub-human creatures barely able to control their violent impulses and sexual urges. This viewpoint places the responsibility on women to inhibit their lifestyles and behaviors to avoid "inciting" men to rape and assault. In this theory, rape and assault are seen as a natural biological inevitability. According to anthropologist Beryl Lieff Benderly, "Rape is not an unavoidable fact of human nature. There are cultures in the world where it is virtually unknown."[6]

"I would like to assist in making this a culture where rape and violent assault are virtually impossible through teaching self-defense techniques as well as exploding social myths that maintain the status quo."

I would like to assist in making this a culture where rape and violent assault are **virtually impossible** through teaching self-defense techniques as well as exploding social myths that maintain the status quo. I believe this education will ensure that women can no longer be victimized either by socially encouraged or self-imposed physical "weakness" or by a false belief that somehow they deserve this violent, dehumanizing treatment.

To make rape and assault impossible, it must be exposed and confronted on every level. We must stop dividing men and women by rigid gender definitions and creating antagonism because **neither** gender can live up to sex-role demands. We must not glorify violence as a means of gratifying personal power needs, especially since women are so frequently exploited as the easiest means by which men gain illusory power. The closing line in a *Chicago Tribune* review of Susan Brownmiller's book, *Against Our Will: Men, Women and Rape*, stated the case succinctly: "Men do not rape their equals."[7]

A responsible self-defense program must not attempt to preserve the status quo by condoning, trying to maintain, and even **encouraging** women's socialized "weakness." It must concentrate on women's strengths, nearly all of which are disguised by learned helplessness and socialized weakness. It must address all levels of verbal and physical interaction. A realistic self-defense program must incorporate the current research on human communication; the known facts about crime, violence and victimization; and identify and expand students' options for deterrents and defense, awareness and recognition. This process should not be confined and limited by the instructor's fears and doubts. A woman who learns and expresses **healthy** aggression in a self-defense class is unlikely to leave the class like a walking time bomb, waiting to explode at the slightest provocation with either misplaced or ineffectual aggression.

In addition to building confidence and recognition of a variety of defense options, self-defense and the study of the martial arts should also inspire a recognition of higher values and respect for life. Unfortunately, many women must actually be convinced that their lives are worth defending; yet these same women would stop at nothing to defend their loved ones.

A basic human value must be respect for one's own life. How does society damage or destroy the foundation for self-respect in women?

Every woman has been affected by the demands of femininity, either by suffering from the restrictions it imposes or by suffering ridicule for refusing to comply with society's expectations. When these demands rob a woman of survival skills, the right to freedom, mobility, self-esteem, personal and physical integrity, they must be challenged.

"Violence diminishes a human being. It is the last resort of all communication possibilities."

Women need to understand the insidious messages of female socialization. This is largely why they have difficulty facing responsibility for their own physical safety. Women today need "remedial" training to discover their repressed strength and self-assertiveness. Women need viable answers to their questions about self-defense, not superstitious, frightening admonitions.

I will not waste space on the typical avoidance rules which encourage women to perform bizarre rituals to "avoid" attack. These avoidance rules prevent freedom for women while allowing men free exercise of social dominance through the threat of violence. This threat is effective because women have been encouraged to cultivate "weakness," euphemistically called "femininity." This social conditioning has been so effective that many women believe they are innately weak. Physical powerlessness and learned helplessness eventually become the choiceless reality for many women. According to Peterson's and Seligman's 1983 study, *Learned Helplessness and Victimization*, "Learned helplessness and victimization responses are partly brought about by a generalized belief about future response futility."[8]

Encouraging women's human needs for self-assertion and physical integrity and recognizing women as central, not peripheral, to all levels of social interaction

should be the larger goal of self-defense training beyond learning physical survival skills.

If the positive aspects of self-defense training are not recognized, there is no way to prevent women from viewing self-defense as a frightening series of losses and sacrifices, especially since self-defense is inadvertently promoted from this point of view. This negative focus is often applied with the best of intentions, yet intentions do not necessarily produce the desired results.

Educators who present self-defense merely as a means to avoid negative events cheat their students of the many positive effects of self-defense training, such as increased freedom, control and self-discovery. These educators are teaching the right things, but for the wrong reasons, and they are trying to reach positive goals through a negative focus.

Men in our society learn self-protection and confrontation skills in the natural course of growing up. In contrast, when women are introduced to these concepts, it is usually a negative experience, isolated from their past conditioning.

Assertion, aggression and the mental and physical skills to back up these qualities are encouraged and integrated into men's lives from birth as the natural order of things. This is basically a healthy attitude if it is not over-emphasized or distorted.

In its most productive form, masculine socialization prepares men to accept aggression as a natural part of themselves, a dynamic ability of self-expression and a controlled force to influence others and protect others as well as themselves. In its distorted form, masculine socialization succeeds in promoting the idea that if aggression is effective and manly then violence must make an even bigger man. In this case, more is not better.

Violence diminishes a human being. It is the last resort of all communication possibilities.

To learn to be an effective human being, you must be reasonably assertive and confident of your ability to communicate effectively and survive with dignity. This is why I see the recent demand for women's self-defense as a positive social trend as well as an indicator of the growth of a positive value system for women. The recent demand for these programs, even in their present state of confusion, is both a product and a cause of women's higher social status.

I look at the issue from a panoramic viewpoint. Self-defense skills are not a scary little bag of tricks that women shamefully and fearfully hide behind their feminine facades. They are part of the fabric of a woman's daily existence and essential to her as an independent, integrated human being.

I favor a comprehensive viewpoint which defines the larger issue of self-defense as a process of multilevel social integration. It is a way of telling women, "You have the right to move freely in this society. Your presence in any situation does not justify violence against you. You are physically capable and perceptually adept at fine discrimination and exercising good judgment. **You Have a Right to be Here--Welcome to the World!"**

Our society is deeply confused about violence and aggression. This is most clearly demonstrated by the fact that women even fear the **word** "aggression." In our attempts to live more effectively, we have utilized "assertiveness training," learned "how to say 'No' without guilt," and have used various encounter techniques to encourage effective self-expression while scrupulously avoiding "aggression."

Aggression is an active, creative and communicative force. Think about the birth of a child. Giving birth, in its natural form, is an aggressive act of nature. The tiniest child will bellow at the top of her lungs, aggressively asserting her existence and

needs. Is this violence or communication?

Have you ever seen a tender little plant break through cement or asphalt? Is this violence or a creative life force asserting its will to live?

Until we resolve the myth that violence and aggression are basically the same and that aggression is a dirty word to women, our efforts towards a more peaceful society will remain fragmented.

Violent behavior, not to be confused with aggressive behavior, is a passive force because it is a **reaction** to a sense of powerlessness. Reacting and moving towards random action because one feels out of control is not the same as acting because of an aggressive, creative movement within, a feeling of control which can be directed.

"You have the right to move freely in this society. Your presence in any situation does not justify violence against you. You are physically capable and perceptually adept at fine discrimination and exercising good judgment. You Have a Right to be Here-- Welcome to the World!"

Consider violence a little further: when a crowd erupts in mass hysteria, are any of these people in control? Are they feeling individual responsibility? Do they each make a conscious decision to act? No. As individuals, they have lost control and are passively carried, powerless to act independently, compelled to react collectively.

I hope that women will accept and understand the concept of aggressive self-preservation. Aggressive self-preservation means facing life with the conviction that you have a right to a full life and to all forms of productive self-expression. The need to protect your bodily integrity and assert your constitutional right to life and liberty is the foundation of aggressive self-preservation.

I agree with Jane Roberts, author of *The Nature of Personal Reality*, who says, "You confuse violence with aggression and do not understand aggression's creative activity or its purpose as a method of communication to prevent violence."[9]

"I hope that women will accept and understand the concept of aggressive self-preservation. Aggressive self-preservation means facing life with the conviction that you have a right to a full life and to all forms of productive self-expression."

As a society and as individuals, we need to resolve our conflicts about women and aggression. Aggression is used as a disparaging term only when it is used to describe women who do not conform to feminine standards. Certain feminine standards, such as passivity, prevent effective living which, in turn, prevents personal success. Yet when women fail, their failure is likely to be attributed to biological inferiority - not learned ineptitude.

Aggression is also viewed as a negative concept because it is confused with violence. An understanding of the concept of aggressive self-preservation could reduce the alienation between men and women and help women integrate aggression as a healthy form of communication and creativity as it is for most men.

Increased confidence and self-esteem among women is essential in removing the stigma that women are easy, reliable targets. Women lack confidence and self-esteem because they face continuous pressure to relinquish control over their lives and bodies. Nathanial Branden, author of *The Psychology of Self-Esteem*, explains, "Self-esteem has two interrelated aspects: it entails a sense of personal efficacy and a sense of personal worth. It is the integrated sum of self-confidence and self-respect. It is the conviction that one is competent to live and worthy of living."[10]

Women are encouraged to be physically helpless and ultimately not in control of their lives, which is dangerous to both physical well-being and psychological health.

I have been challenged for asserting that a normal expression of aggression is healthy, **especially** because I am writing for women. Our entire society has absorbed the belief that female aggression is both unnatural and impossible for psychologically healthy women. Media depictions of "aggressive" women overstep healthy aggression and present distorted images of bloodthirsty, vengeful, female savages.

In *The Nature of Personal Reality*, Jane Roberts clarifies "normal" aggression this way. "Normal aggressiveness is basically a kind of natural communication, particularly in social orders; a way of letting another person know that in your terms they have transgressed, and therefore a way of preventing violence - not causing it."[11]

The martial arts is a system of ritualized aggression and is widely acclaimed for the health-giving and life-affirming benefits of inner peace, confidence, strength and the learned ability to **ward off aggression**. This is not some mysterious event that occurs within a martial arts practitioner who reaches a certain rank. It happens when a person alters his or her internal beliefs and this change is reflected in his or her bearing and approach to life. Yet addressing belief systems is the most frequently ignored aspect of self-defense programs and martial arts training. For a martial arts practitioner, the internal change often happens through meeting frequent physical challenges which slowly alter the person's self-image and perceptions. In a self-defense program limited by time, belief systems must be addressed in conjunction with physical challenge. The only major difference in a "women's" self-defense program that should distinguish it from any responsible program is that more time must be spent on dispelling irrational ideas and fears extending beyond the normal degree of caution and fear which serve as survival mechanisms.

Many researchers and popular forms of media have taken on the social responsibility of dispelling irrational ideas and myths regarding sexual violence. Debunking rape mythology is the latest social concern sometimes producing an unexpected, unproductive outcome.

Although "rape myths" have been published in practically every major magazine and newspaper in the country, these are often little more than disclaimers preceding some prejudice-riddled "rules for behavior" or "safety precautions" for women. I do not encourage anyone to take foolish or unnecessary chances, but the efficacy of some of these behaviors we are supposed to adopt in "defense of ourselves" is, at best, questionable and, at worst, ridiculous and demeaning.

To "prevent" rape, we are told to vary the times when we leave our homes, take alternate routes home to avoid being followed, to travel in packs, to always tell someone where we're going and when we expect to be home, never to go **anywhere** alone at night, never to park our cars in a dark parking lot, never to walk close to shrubs and bushes, to sit behind the bus driver if we have to take public transportation, never to enter an elevator if we see a suspicious-looking person in it, never to leave an elevator if a suspicious-looking person is lingering in the hallway, never to flirt with strangers, and always to "dress appropriately" to name but a few.

In the event that an attack is imminent, women have been told to defecate, urinate, fake homosexuality, say they have venereal disease or a contagious virus, drop to the ground on all fours and babble insanely, start eating grass or stick their fingers down their throats and vomit. All of these "methods" have been reported to work at some time to a "self-defense authority" and are thereafter cited as an intelligent option of defense for women in an attack situation. Although I disagree with over-emphasis on "psychological ploys," any attempt to defend yourself or escape an attacker, even accidental reactions, could work.

One woman in my research reported that she reflexively vomited from fear as soon as the attacker grabbed her. He did release her, but she had not had time to stick her finger down her throat. It was a sudden attack and restraint so when she vomited, it was completely involuntary.

In any case where an attacker is going to stand dumbly while you take the time to induce yourself to vomit, you would probably be able to run away just as easily. The latest suggestion is to tell an attacker you have AIDS. This ploy was successful for a woman attacked by two men in January of 1986.

Remember, just about any action or reaction could be successful, but placing all your hopes on one particular response or ploy is like treating a cancer patient with a band-aid. All strategies for defense and escape should be considered and exploited if necessary or possible.

Most of these suggestions are based on erroneous beliefs about the nature of rape and violence against women. Many suggestions assume that if you make yourself "vulgar, unattractive, and unfeminine," an attacker will lose interest in you. This assumption is based on the false idea that rape is an expression of sexual desire on the part of the attacker. In fact, rape is an expression of a need for power over another human being. The rapist really doesn't care what you look like, how old you are or anything else. If you are someone over whom he thinks he can exercise power, he will try it regardless of whether you are 18 or 80, wearing a bikini or a bathrobe.

Other "helpful suggestions" imply that if women would control **their** behavior, men would stop attacking them. As you can see, this idea puts the burden of responsibility completely on women's shoulders. **Anything** a woman does could be interpreted as enticement. This is akin to telling a mugging victim that he had no business walking around in broad daylight with a $10 bill in his pocket and that anyone would think he was just **asking** to be mugged.

"Anything a woman does could be interpreted as enticement. This is akin to telling a mugging victim that he had no business walking around in broad daylight with a $10 bill in his pocket and that anyone would think he was just asking to be mugged."

There are additional problems with "avoidance rules," however well-intended they may be. Women must make decisions based on necessity and individual judgment. If you must be on the job at 7 a.m., you can't vary the time you leave your home. There will always be times when we are alone--sometimes just because we **want** to be! There will always be dark parking lots, and I hope there will always be shrubs and bushes. Women should be able to live their lives with safety and integrity while taking reasonable precautions. Even men have to lock up their homes and automobiles. Social and physical survival does not require that a woman perform demeaning behavioral acrobatics! It is a matter of learning and exercising all available options of surviving with personal and physical integrity.

Women can learn self-defense techniques and take control of their lives, but it must not stop there. It must be made difficult for these crimes to even be considered a possibility. On a personal level this can be done by refusing to believe in myths about female weakness and refusing to subscribe to the idea that female physical and social subordinance are desirable. On a social level this can be done by utilizing legal action, working through social service agencies, doing research, educating and becoming educated.

Through an independent research project on rape, assault, mugging and successful resistance stories, I was able to begin to answer some of the important questions that every woman seeking answers about self-defense would want to know.

I asked what type of approach the assailant used and his initial means of physical restraint or coercion. I asked women how they were treated by friends, family, police and authority figures. I asked many subjective questions and got the responses in which other women who have been victimized will see themselves and realize they are not alone.

Armed with this information, I planned a physical course that would deal with the highest risk restraints first. Defensive techniques utilizing 1) the opponent's proximity, 2) quick evasive action utilizing the opponent's momentum, and 3) realistic restraint escape techniques are the basis of the physical part of my course. The other major aspect is communicating information on sociological studies, feminist essays, psychological studies, studies on rape and resistance, and information on verbal assertiveness and non-verbal behavior.

The scientific basis and meaning of non-verbal behaviors have powerful implications for women's self-defense. This is why understanding non-verbal behavior is important in self-defense training. Women's non-verbal behavior is the most common justification for increasing a woman's risk of rape and violence.

Human beings subconsciously transmit non-verbal messages that are almost universally understood and interpreted. Women are especially adept at non-verbal behavior and interpreting such behavior. Biological scientists assert that these attributes are both a function of physiology and brain organization as well as being powerfully reinforced and encouraged by sex-role socialization. This ability should be brought into focus and fine tuned as a self-defense tool for women.

If submissive, "seductive" non-verbal behavior on the part of a woman is the most frequently cited justification for rape, why shouldn't more powerful non-verbal behavior be a deterrent?

The major elements of non-verbal behavior are the control of space and the projection of power. In our culture an established "social zone" is four to twelve feet and the "intimate zone" is six to eighteen inches.[12] If women learn to recognize encroaching and intrusive behaviors while also learning to project more power and protect their space, they will face fewer confrontive approaches. The elements of non-verbal behavior are explained more fully in Chapter IV, Attack Deterrents.

Today, stories of private violence -child abuse, parental abuse and male or female spouse abuse - and "sex crimes" of every nature are rampant in the media. As a society, we are learning more about violence, have more social service agencies to help victims and rehabilitate offenders, and we are less likely to blame victims or believe they were responsible for the crime. Yet experts feel that anywhere from one in ten to one in twenty-five rapes are reported, from one to six million children are abused annually and nearly six million women are being abused by their husbands. Authorities report that gang rapes and the rape of children and men are increasing.

Women's self-defense programs are often viewed as a shameful sign of the breakdown of society. Yet in the past several decades, social consciousness regarding many previously repressed, ignored or unrecognized human issues has advanced. There are hundreds of organizations dedicated to preventing violence of every kind. There are now over 700 rape crises centers nationwide and 800 shelters for battered women. Twenty years ago there were none; yet many social theorists feel that violence against women, child abuse and sexual victimization of both men and women may now be just coming to light; however, it has always been a social problem.

"Women can learn self-defense techniques and take control of their lives, but it must not stop there. It must be made difficult for these crimes to even be considered a possibility."

There is nothing wrong with presenting the "facts" about violent crime as we know them. In order to confront the problem, we must know the facts. But does this social consciousness movement represent merely an evolution of negative life changes from an increasingly violent society? My approach to women's self-defense is not reactionary; my methods not confined to women's over-exaggerated physical limitations. Comprehensive, responsible self-defense training for women is part of a positive social trend in a society where being female does not require a sacrifice of socially valued traits such as strength, assertion, aggression, athletic performance, intelligence and ambition, all of which are **survival skills.**

Not long ago society knew little about rape and the motivations of offenders. Rape was thought to be a means of gratifying uncontrollable sexual desires. A woman was warned that lurking in every

11

man is his "point of no return" and if he ever reaches it, she is to blame. Rape was regarded as the inevitable outcome of male/female interaction.

Now rape is widely recognized as a crime of violence and power. The motivation for rape is amost invariably cited as "anger directed at women" and "hatred of women." Although dubious, this is an advancement in the general social understanding of a prevalent violent crime in which women have been the primary targets.

Why should the admission of hatred of women be an advancement? Because it suggests an emotional instead of a biological basis for the act of rape; it implies there is some reasonable solution. By a "reasonable" solution I do not mean endorsing the common policy of "being nice" to a rapist. Women are targets of male rage and immature emotions in the same way children are victims of emotionally immature parents. Yet children are relatively powerless to change their life circumstances and do not understand the forces which dominate their lives until much later. As adults we can understand, we can change our internal values and fight for our rights.

Women do not have to remain easy targets for the raging immaturity of men, not in their private lives or in the larger society. One solution lies in attacking the foundations of social beliefs that make rape a means of degradation and encourages men to exploit women for personal power needs.

Women are making advancements within the vast range of human possibilities on an unprecedented scale. Women still face all degrees of social prejudice, but the fact remains that we are a moving force in society and there is no going back. We did not turn our backs on a better time nor foolishly destroy the fairytale existence in which we were protected and provided for. We did not inadvertently knock over our pedestals as we surged forward to claim

our equal rights as promised under the Constitution of a free country but which were denied us by society. Women have been struggling for centuries to reveal that the protection was an illusion; the provisions were a reward for conformity and that to be denied human rights and to remain unprotected under the law, to exist as wards of even a benevolent keeper, is not a privilege. It is bondage. This does not imply that women and men cannot assume different roles and duties, that men cannot be homemakers and women cannot earn wages. It has meant they could be assumed interchangeably. Women have fought to be recognized as contributing members of society and as individuals **no matter what they choose to do**. We have fought for choice and fought to throw off the stigma of inferiority and second-class status. Now that we are realizing these dreams, are we going to be driven back into seclusion by the last wall we have yet to scale? Will our unresolved conflicts about aggression and the threat of violence stop us from achieving our full potential as human beings?

"Women do not have to remain easy targets for the raging immaturity of men, not in their private lives or in the larger society."

This is the scope of the issue as I see it. Self-defense cannot be served up as a fragmentary concern that only some women who work or live in "high risk" situations are forced to face. It is the next natural step in our social evolution and integration.

It is important to stress that although this book evolved out of the lack of positive programs and focus in existing women's self-defense instruction, it is based on positive social progress and individual growth. I utilize a personal, confrontational approach as well as a panoramic concept of multi-level social integration. I ask women to take a hard look at themselves and at the society which shaped them. I ask women to determine which behaviors are the result of socialized femininity and which are honest expressions of true preference. A man could benefit from this type of self-confrontation as well.

I will not sign off with the dreary, overused message, "We Are All Potential Victims," and hope to motivate you through fear. In reality, **we are all survivors.** I hope to motivate you with the positive implications of self-defense for women and decrease the fears that prevent women from growing and experimenting with their physical skills.

Consider this logically for a moment. Any woman, even untrained and unprepared, has a fifty-fifty chance of escaping unharmed from an attacker or of preventing rape if sexual assault is the attacker's goal. I hope to improve the odds through education with the goal of inspiring continuing practice through women's groups, self-defense organizations and/or martial arts schools.

I am not encouraging complacency. I am only stating a plain truth: chance alone will abort half of all violent incidents. In addition, there are other variables you can manipulate in your favor which are explained at length in this book.

This brings us to the most important message, which is woven throughout this book. What you **believe** is even more important than what you know or what you **do.** What you believe will determine your degree of commitment to self-protection. A strong belief in your basic human rights will increase your chances of preventing violence and escaping should an attack occur.

Finding the strength to overcome socialized limitations is an important step in personal evolution for both sexes. For both men and women it is a journey back to themselves. Self-defense training is a powerful experience for women because it

confronts fears, exposes the inner depth of femininity training, provides a sharing experience in which honesty is possible, and finally, provides an experience of relief. Women truly realize that their fears and victimization experiences are not unique and they did not cause them because of some dark character defect that no other woman has.

We have all been hunted; we have felt physically powerless; we have fought and have been surprised when all the pervasive myths about female resistance didn't come true. We were told men "go out of control sexually" and that resistance would "make him really mad." We kept silent about the violence in our lives, yet we rarely shared our successful resistance stories because women were told that we "shouldn't get ourselves" into these positions.

Women today are less afraid to confront socialized vulnerability; we are not as likely to remain silent about victimization. Women have fought for social change and much has been achieved. We have experienced glimpses of what our lives could be if they were based on human values rather than gender divisions and life-negating, limiting belief systems. Self-defense for women is part of this evolution of social consciousness and individual empowerment. I hope this book will provide some guidance in this little understood area of women's lives, and that you can find in these pages the reinforcement and encouragement to reach out to other women, confront your fears, realize your existing strengths and claim your rights as a human being.

"This brings us to the most important message, which is woven throughout this book. What you believe is even more important than what you know or what you do."

Social Mythology:
Common Myths

Popular opinion is the greatest lie in the world.
Carlyle

Chapter 2

Social Mythology:

Common Myths

MYTH: Rape is a woman's problem.

Rape is not just a "women's problem." It is an attempt to create physical and social dominance. It can occur in any situation when violence is eroticized and physical dominance is valued as a means to enforce a social hierarchy. Violence and dominance, as ingrained cultural values, both create and reinforce a social power structure that is destructive and life-negating to all human beings.

It is in the sub-culture of the male prison system that this is most clearly demonstrated. A comment by Peter L. Nacci, Ph.D., director of the U. S. Department of Justice's Federal Prison System Staff Training Center in Atlanta, is particularly revealing. "The likelihood of a male inmate of a federal correctional institution being raped (sodomized) appears to be approximately that of a non-imprisoned female older than 12 being raped in a major metropolitan area."[1] Based on current statistics, rape is far more likely in heavily populated areas, and women between the ages of 12 and 24 are at the greatest risk of rape.

Susan Brownmiller, author of *Against Our Will: Men, Women and Rape,* writes, "Homosexual rape in the Philadephia prisons turned out to be a microcosm of the female experience with heterosexual rape."[2] This quote is in reference to the results of a comprehensive study of rape in the Philadelphia prison system conducted by Alan J. Davis, the chief assistant district attorney in charge of the investigation. Davis reported that sexual assault in Philadelphia prisons was "epidemic."

In any situation where brute strength reigns or where social power through the control of resources is the ultimate value, the possibility of rape exists regardless of whether or not females are present.

MYTH: Rape is a sex crime.

Modern social theorists have made great progress toward desexualizing rape. A. Nicholas Groth, author of *Men Who Rape: The Psychology of the Offender*, defines rape as "a sexual act in service of non-sexual needs."[3] All forms of violence can serve as a method of social control or physical dominance; rape could be most accurately defined as an attempt to create illusory power through violence or the threat of violence.

Groth clearly explodes the notion that rape is an expression of sexual passion when he says in his lectures, "Rape is the sexual expression of aggression, not the aggressive expression of sexuality."

"Rape is a complex and multidetermined act," he writes. "It serves a number of psychological aims and purposes. Whatever other needs and factors operate in the commission of such an offense, however, we have found the components of anger, power and sexuality are always present and prominent . . . Rape then is a pseudosexual act, a pattern of sexual behavior that is concerned much more with status, hostility, control and dominance than with sensual pleasure or sexual satisfaction."[4]

MYTH: Rape and violent assault are most likely to happen at the hands of a stranger.

In the study completed for *Fear or Freedom*, out of 209 subjects, 83 reported they knew the assailant. This was the largest group of women out of the four categories of attack. The four categories are Known-Assailant, Random-Attack, Successful-Resistance and Assaults-not-Involving-Rape.

In Diana E. H. Russell's study of "The Prevalence of Rape and Assault," 78.4 percent of 932 incidents were attempted or completed by known assailants.[5]

Robert Prentky, the director of research (sex-crime unit) at the Massachusetts Treatment Center in Bridgewater, states that the largest group of rapists are the "exploiters," whom he describes as "predatory acquaintance rapists."[6]

MYTH: All men are violent or potential rapists.

When people learn the truth about known-assailant rape and private violence, they start to look around suspiciously. A more accurate portrayal of rape and violence is that regardless of the social dynamics, the potential for violence exists in every imaginable situation, every second of our lives. This becomes less frightening when you consider how infrequently random violence actually occurs in relation to the ever present potential, and yet random violence is what we are taught to fear.

Observe crowds, such as those at ball games, concerts or shopping malls. Considering the number of people, heightened emotions, group activity or group proximity and the elements of crowd psychology, incidents of violence are rare. When the nature of violence as an expression of powerlessness is understood, and when the ever-present yet rarely actualized potential for violence is acknowledged, the threat of violence loses its mystery and therefore its power to create fear.

Violent behavior is a manifestation of fear. Violence against women and children, or anyone who is perceived as especially vulnerable, is an abuse of manipulated power, and the **need** to abuse power in social interaction or through physical violence is an attempt to establish dominance to alleviate the fear of losing control or of never having control.

MYTH: The most important concern of self-defense training for women is to prevent rape.

The focus on self-defense for women as merely a program of "rape prevention" is misleading. Rape is not the only concern of self-defense training for women. The entire spectrum of violence and subjugation, physical and social, must be addressed. The issue is not limited to

18

physical violence against women and children. Violence and dominance as an attempt to create illusory power is carried out by manipulating, then abusing physical, emotional, social and situational advantages. This abuse could occur in degrees in any situation regardless of age group, social or gender dynamics.

We cannot "prevent rape" by this nearly pathological insistence that it is an isolated incident totally removed from our life experience. Rape is an act of violence and subjugation occurring at the extreme end of a continuum of social, sexual and physical violence that both men and women could be victims of, if the circumstances permit.

According to social psychologists, a dimensional view of rape should be adopted. A survey administered to 3,862 university students supported a dimensional view of sexual aggression and victimization. Researchers Mary P. Koss and Cheryle J. Oros state, "In this framework, rape represents an extreme behavior, but one that is on a continuum with normal male behavior within the culture."[7] As long as we consider excessively dominating behaviors ranging from conversational politics right through sexual assault to be "normal" male behavior, especially in relation to females, we will have a violent society.

Self-defense is a much larger issue and cannot be viewed as merely "rape prevention." We must address the issues of self-responsibility and examine damaging socialization practices which maintain inequality and endanger women's lives and well-being. We must do everything possible to promote effective interaction and communication.

Self-defense is another step in development and self-realization for women. It is based on a positive value system of physical integrity, self-esteem, mutual respect, exercise of reason, transcending limitations and confronting personal and social inequities. Women need physical and mental techniques

designed for their abilities and needs with emphasis on the most common type of rape and assault which is known-assailant attack or social rape.

Self-defense is also a process of social survival and integration. As we express our freedom, we must also have the means to protect it on a personal level. We cannot rely totally on social institutions, political forces and legal protection. The revolution to a better society must take place on an internal, individual level as well as on an external, collective level.

MYTH: Women are more likely than men to be targets of violence in society.

Men are more than twice as likely to be victims of violent crime and property crimes, yet women are consistently viewed as victims. Socialized sex roles define masculine and feminine as opposing concepts. This logic implies that if the male is a natural protector and aggressor, then a woman must be in need of protection and a natural victim. The male as victim does not coincide with the ideal image of masculinity, yet men are far more likely to be attacked, mugged or involved in violent incidents.

MYTH: The FBI crime reports and police blotter files contain accurate representations of violence against women. This is the best place to obtain information in order to find out the circumstances of violent crime so we can effectively plan defenses.

In preparing a self-defense program for women, I was thwarted in my attempts to find out the actual circumstances of attacks on women and the methods-of-attack approaches, especially from a woman's point of view. This information is not available in police blotter files or the FBI crime reports, which are frequently cited in self-defense publications.

Statistics reveal very little about actual

19

circumstances of violent crimes against women. According to dozens of sources, rape is the most under-reported of all crimes. In Russell's study, "The Prevalence of Rape and Assault," involving 932 subjects, she found that "only 10 percent of the incidents of attempted or completed rape resulted in a police report."[8]

Known-assailant assault is even less reported than stranger-rape. Low reporting rates make information on this type of rape nearly impossible to get through traditional channels. Women's self-defense programs must address the issue of private violence and known-assailant attack, yet this has been nearly ignored. This information can only be obtained by independent surveys and library research.

MYTH: If you don't cooperate with a rapist, you are likely to be murdered.

Rape-murder does not even begin to represent the majority of violent attacks on women. According to Susan Brownmiller in *Against Our Will: Men, Women and Rape,* rape-murder represents only about two-tenths of a percent of **reported** incidents (according to speculative calculations).[9] Experts agree that only about 10 percent of all rapes and assaults are reported or end up in police files and would be even lower if based on actual incidents. In fact, the fear of mutilation and death contributes to successful raping. In Dr. Pauline Bart's research, "A Study of Women Who Both Were Raped and Avoided Rape," women who believed they would be murdered or mutilated if they didn't cooperate were more likely to be raped.[10]

MYTH: Women can't physically resist assault because they are weaker than men.

The foundation of the belief that a woman cannot effectively resist is based on **strength** vs. **weakness**. This is only one aspect of a confrontation. The other aspects include time, place and

environmental escape routes, barriers, objects, other people, and the assailant's degree of commitment and physical and mental state. Defense techniques themselves should not depend on strength. The major elements of good defensive techniques are combinations of leverage, balance, physical redirection, speed and shock. These principles are explained and illustrated in Chapter VI, Technique Section.

MYTH: Passive escape attempts are the safest and best means of self-defense for a woman.

Passive self-defense is based on the idea a woman should never "hurt" a man or "commit" her behavior because she will increase her risks. Passive self-defense relies heavily on "psychological ploys," the mistaken and unfounded belief that you can always talk your way out of a bad situation. It is based on the dogmatic insistence that nothing else is "safe" nor will work for women.

Passive escape would be a highly desirable option and sometimes is a viable option, except for these major drawbacks. In many cases, passive attempts will not achieve a release from a restraint, or the immediate degree of violence expressed renders this kind of training useless. It is naive to assume passive escape is always a "safe" option. If an attempt to escape is made and is unsuccessful, two major advantages are sacrificed: the element of surprise and an increase of interaction time, which should be **decreased** whenever possible.

This limiting physical coaching is coupled with a thinly disguised prejudice regarding women's degree of commitment and actual ability. Any program that offers this limited approach to all forms of confrontation reveals an instructor who is probably more anxious to infect you with imaginary fears than teach you effective self-defense.

MYTH: If you are ever attacked,

immediately start fighting.

Many people believe that self-defense means you must erupt physically if attacked. This is entirely untrue. Self-defense is learning options; it means that the individual may choose the most appropriate means of resistance based on the situation.

In self-defense we must stress choice because choice is a measure of personal power and confidence. Having "no choice" in any life situation results in despair and hopelessness. The feeling that we have a choice is a measure of psychological health.

Self-defense skills do not exclusively imply physical aggression just as passivity does not exclusively imply willing submission.

MYTH: Women over-react and escalate the degree of violence in an attack situation.

An attack is highly unlikely to follow the "escalation" theory that many proponents of "passive self-defense" or "cooperative self-defense" espouse. In this theory the woman "causes" or "escalates" the degree of violence in the following manner: 1) He gropes her, or presses his body on hers or forcefully kisses her. 2) She responds by aggressively pushing his hand or his body away. 3) He becomes enraged and becomes more physical because she "initiated" the aggression.

This theory promotes damaging male/female mythology and could increase female victimization by encouraging passivity and delayed reaction to physical and sexual harrassment. Reaction or a polite delay is considered "consent" which escalates the situation far more than a firm refusal, either verbal and/or physical. First, the degree of violence in an attack situation is pre-determined by the rapist's needs and motives. The attack style - anger, power, sadistic - depends on his motives. Second, the most common attack style is power rape in which a high degree of violence is unlikely. Third, the opportunity

to commit a high degree of violence must be created and often the rapist must gain the woman's cooperation to achieve this goal. Fourth, this theory encourages women to tolerate social degradation and sexual harassment for fear of "causing" men to erupt in violence. This promotes fear of men and is actually a very insulting concept. It implies all men can be "driven" to rape and violence by a woman who rejects sexual overtures or objects to being handled inappropriately. We need to encourage men and women to respect each other socially and physically instead of discouraging respect and honest communication. The progressive assault is more likely in a known-assailant situation but a delayed aggressive response is what **escalates** this type of assault.

MYTH: A woman would have to maim or kill a man in order to resist successfully.

The most important element of successful resistance is reacting quickly and assertively! **Decreasing interaction time** once you become aware of potential danger is the surest and safest means of resistance. Cooperation and/or attempts to talk the rapist out of assault **increase** interaction time and increase the possibility that you could lose control.

In terms of physical resistance, you do not have to physically overpower an assailant or "beat him up." If you have been physically restrained, you only have to temporarily stun or shock him long enough to free yourself so you can escape. If you recognize a threat soon enough, the assailant won't even be able to restrain you. If you must strike the assailant, you do not have to continue or wait around to see if he has been taught his lesson. Your goal is to **escape** and **report.**

MYTH: Women shouldn't resist because it only enrages the attacker.

The attacker is already "mad" in some sense. Rape is an expression of rage born of powerlessness. A man who rapes hates

21

himself and has feelings of worthlessness. He transfers that hatred to women. This does not mean he is fearless. He is full of fear, especially in the initial approach. This is when he needs cooperation. Resistance is frightening and dissipates the power he is hoping to create by seeing your fear. By resistance I do not mean random struggling and helpless, high pitched screaming. Even so, any type of resistance can surprise the assailant and frighten him away.

Resistance that is forceful, assertive and even righteously angry communicates power even if you are afraid, which you undoubtedly will be. All the warnings telling women not to resist fail to recognize a very important consideration - you and your human needs. This attitude towards women and self-defense coincides with that of social psychologists Sandra and Daryle Bem's comment on female socialization. "It is still the women in our society whose identity is rendered irrelevant by America's socialization practices."[11] How can you be taught anything of value by any practice or person who considers you irrelevant?

Your physiological defense mechanisms are programmed to "fight or flight." This survival instinct is a **human** trait, not a gender trait. Isn't there something to consider besides what if **you make** him mad? What if he **makes you** mad? What if you use the full power of your anger, not necessarily to retaliate but to escape? Also, if you resist immediately and escape, you won't be around when he gets "madder." If you must strike the attacker and stun him with a blow to a vital area, he'll get mad **when he recovers**, but you won't be there. If you knock him down with a well-placed knee to the groin, he'll get madder; but when he gets up to deal with it, you'll be long gone.

Most importantly, don't confuse resistance with retaliation. To resist means to escape and survive even if you **must** cooperate in order to do so. Don't think about resistance in terms of something you must do to the attacker. Resistance is a personal commitment not to cooperate unnecessarily with someone who intends to do you harm. Resistance strategies are explained in detail throughout the Four-Part Study and in Chapter V, Degrees of Threat and Degrees of Resistance.

MYTH: Women are much smaller and weaker than men.

On the average, women are slightly smaller in stature than men. The average American male is barely over five-feet, nine-inches tall. The average American female is five-feet, four-and-a-half-inches tall. In percentages, males are eight percent taller and twenty percent heavier than females. It has recently been discovered that women's strength, relative to lean body mass and after extended weight training, nearly matches the strength of men. Women as the "weaker sex" is a **cultural** preference reinforced by exaggerating trained mannerisms, voice pitch, clothing, hair, make-up and lack of physical development.

Women as "**slightly** weaker" is more accurate and the gap is rapidly closing. The natural disparity of strength and size between men and women is **not** as great as we have been led to believe. The burden of demonstrating the difference by cultivating weakness is the demand of femininity. Women can choose to reject the limits of what we are "allowed" to achieve and express physically. However subtle, these limits have the consistent effect of exaggerating the physical differences between men and women, increasing female vulnerability and "alienating the genders" by **preventing honest interaction**. Without exaggeration, men and women **are** different. The burden of sacrifice should not be a woman's duty.

MYTH: Female aggression is common and accepted in our society.

Female aggression is a cultural taboo in almost every society; male aggression is glorified. These radically different value systems complicate and negatively reinforce the dictates of biological differences.

Our society does not accept female aggression as natural or normal. Healthy aggression in women is suppressed through female socialization practices. One of the most effective methods to suppress healthy aggression is to trivialize female aggression through eroticization, as our culture attempts to trivialize everything women do through eroticization.

Female wrestlers who perform in mud, jello, and whipped cream and "foxy boxing" performers effectively demonstrate how trivial our society considers aggression in women. These are obvious exercises in eroticising female aggression and physical contact. The "bouts" are held in bars with a predominately male audience. The women are made-up and coiffed and prance around before they writhe in the mud, whipped cream or jello or put on the giant gloves and pummel each other. Mud, jello, whipped cream and giant gloves certainly remove the competitive aspect of the "sport." You can see the women "going at it" but it's not "real" competition. This makes it "okay" for women to engage in such activities, especially considering the demeaning aspects of this kind of entertainment.

Eroticizing female aggression by eroticizing several contact sports is a major reason women are afraid of physical contact sports and why instructors have so many conflicts about teaching women contact sports. Avoiding contact with females is actually a written "law" in some martial arts systems. Avoidance of contact learning conspicuously separates students by gender; it is females who are deprived of contact learning.

Deprivation of contact will eventually take its toll on your physical ability. Think of the ways in which it already has.

If an instructor denies a woman's capabilities for healthy aggression and is uncomfortable or excessively concerned with physical contact, he or she cannot effectively teach you.

Watch out for another myth that women are really suppressed, bloodthirsty savages. This has served society very well in suppressing healthy aggression in females. Aggressive females are generally portrayed as deviants. An attitude or act of aggression that would be heroic if done by a male is distorted to psychopathy when a woman does the same act or has such an attitude. In social mythology, nothing good ever comes out of female aggression. Imagine a female in the role of *Karate Kid*, or a female "Rambo." There is no "Karate Girl" making a healthy and necessary social adjustment, no "Ramba" as flaming heroine. (Although in my opinion, no man or woman should attempt to emulate the degree of glorified violence portrayed in *Rambo*.)

Women overcompensate to avoid being labeled "aggressive." This is destructive to a woman's character and counter-productive to her physical and social survival.

MYTH: Violence is increasing because men are enraged by women's freedom and because men have lost respect for women.

I've heard several variations on this theme and as much as I try **not** to be, I am deeply shocked by this attitude. When any authority figure promotes an opinion that violence against women is increasing because of "Women's Lib," I believe it is nothing but a crude, ignorant attempt to scare women back into submission or keep them uninformed and in bondage. On the other hand, it may just be a crude, uninformed, ignorant opinion - regardless of the source.

If you seek education about women's history or "herstory," read current sociological studies and obtain literature from social service agencies that serve women, you will realize that women have **never** been free of the threat of rape and abuse.

I have heard both men and women claim that women learning self-defense will "enrage" men and increase violence. It's strange how logic disappears and irrational fears are imposed on and even **accepted** by women. People rarely claim that education increases ignorance; when you teach people to read, are you increasing illiteracy?

Current popular literature and magazines do little to educate women. In fact, many women's magazines perpetuate myths about women with romance stories and visual images of men and women that maintain the desirability of their respective dominant and submissive roles. Go to a library, especially a college library, and look in the periodicals under "Sex Roles" and "Rape." Look in the card file under "Women's History." After a little personal research, you will never believe the myth that if women would be sweet, nice, nuturing and capitalize on their weakness that we would all live happily ever after. College or women's bookstores are the best places to find books about current studies in sociology, anthropological history and culture and women's issues.

More violence has been done to human beings in an attempt to confirm our social beliefs and enforce gender divisions and differences than would ever be done if we were to accept and affirm the diversity of our human natures.

Results
of the
Four-Part
Survey

Peace if possible, but truth at any rate.
Martin Luther

Chapter 3

Results of the Four-Part Survey

The study completed for this book represents, as far as I know, the only existing information regarding women's subjective realizations prior to an assault; prior apprehension and threat perception; the number of women who had taken self-defense; whether they expressed confidence in self-defense techniques and used them; and certain external circumstances, such as the mode of physical restraint and method of initial contact.

The purpose of the survey was to get closer to the physical and subjective realities of rape and assault from women's personal viewpoints. I placed no limits on "acceptable" subjects. Any woman who wanted to share her experiences was considered a valid subject. The age of the women at the time the incidents occurred ranged from three-years-old to seventy-eight. The majority were in the age group of sixteen to thirty-five. The incidents had happened anywhere from two weeks to twenty years prior to the time the women contacted me. This study also reveals important information about the most common type of rape and assault perpetrated by known assailants.

The four parts of this survey include
- Known-Assailant Rape
- Random or Stranger Attack
- Succesful Resistance
- Assaults

Part 1 Known-Assailant Rape

Known-assailant rape is the most common, least reported, most preventable type of rape. Although I assert that this type of assault is most preventable, a recent study revealed that women are "more likely to be raped when they know their assailant."[1] After personally interviewing many of the women who participated in the survey for this book, I noticed distinct similarities in their accounts which provided some insight as to why women have been less likely to avoid rape if the assailant is known, yet it also provided the reasons why this does not have to be true.

In retrospect, most of these women believed they could have prevented the rape or successfully resisted if they had recognized the degree of threat and responded in time. They realized later that they had been emotionally manipulated and the situation had been manipulated to ensure the assailant's safety and secure time for the attack.

These women expressed a common realization. Almost all of them felt they had over-estimated their attackers' commitment and ability and had under-estimated their own resources and abilities because of ingrained beliefs about rape and resistance. Many self-defense experts promote the idea that a woman cannot and must not defend against any man, regardless of the situation. This attitude is particularly damaging in preventing social rape, which any woman could prevent by initially expressing a healthy degree of assertiveness and **committed** resistance if that fails. The exaggerated risks of resistance are least operative in known-assailant situations.

"Almost all of them felt they had over-estimated their attackers' commitment and ability and had under-estimated their own resources and abilities because of ingrained beliefs about rape and resistance."

In a social rape, if a woman waits for an attacker to "come to his senses," or until all the abuse has occurred in order to determine if the attacker is going to spare her life or bodily integrity, she is physically weakened and psychologically damaged. The attacker increasingly gains control and the victim increasingly loses it. It is more difficult to re-establish control than it is to maintain it.

The known-assailant rape situation has distinct psychological and situational advantages that have, until now, been used by the assailant. These exact elements can be reversed and used by the resistor. Many

social belief systems inadvertently support known-assailant rape. These beliefs facilitate the rapist **if the woman accepts them**. Once the elements of known-assailant rape are exposed, it will be clear why it is the most preventable type of rape and the easiest to defend against.

In the survey, eighty-three women reported an attack by a known assailant. This was the largest of the four groups.

Although it is becoming general knowledge that most rape and assaults are committed by someone the victim knows, very little is known about how and why this happens. An almost automatic assumption about known-assailant rape is that it is a "date rape."[2] Although date rape is a frequent occurrence and probably is reported less frequently than any other known-assailant assault, "date rape" did not represent the majority of known-assailant attacks in this survey.

I believe we are just more comfortable assuming that known-assailant rape is occurring in circumstances with "sexual" connotations such as dating and courtship. This makes it easier to reach an erroneous understanding or a false justification of known-assailant rape.

In this survey, only 16 percent of the women interviewed were on a date when the rape occurred, and the remaining 84 percent were involved in other circumstances.

Known-assailant rape goes far beyond the boundaries of date rape. It can be categorized and identified by more than the obvious fact that the victim knows or has had some prior relationship with the assailant. In my research women reported being raped by bosses, co-workers, personal friends, boyfriends, ex-boyfriends, friends of family or husband's friends, ex-husbands, husbands, fathers, brothers, uncles, step fathers, mothers' boyfriends, classmates, neighbors and church members (including clergy and ministers) from their own churches. Some women were raped by repairmen, home appraisers, landscape and yard workers or other business acquaintances.

The fact that these men were familiar to the victims generally means that some degree of trust or unspoken agreement existed, which I refer to as a "social contract." In every type of social interaction there is an unspoken agreement or social contract. The most basic agreement communicated non-verbally, and sometimes even verbally, is "I won't harm you." or "I'm no threat to you."

Known-assailant rape can be characterized by exploitation of trust and of physical, social and situational advantages. In my survey I specifically asked, "Did you like and trust the person prior to the attack?" Approximately 59 percent of the subjects reported liking and trusting the assailant prior to the attack; approximately 16 percent had not considered the issue, probably because the relationship involved another form of social contract, i.e. , the men were hired help or related to the subjects; 11 percent felt apprehension but ignored it; and 14 percent felt no trust but were required to interact with the assailant for various reasons, i.e., the attacker was a boss, co-worker or family member.

Women in the known-assailant rape group were more likely to panic than in random attacks. I was somewhat surprised by this but it began to make sense to me when I considered the overall information and content of the incidents as they were reported to me.

Women were totally unprepared emotionally or physically to deal with a known-assailant attack. The panic resulted from the unexpected loss of control of a previously controlled social situation. Women who were attacked by strangers often did not feel out of control. They felt that whatever choice they were making, even if it was to not resist, they were at least "saving their own lives."

Victims of a known-assailant rape were exploited and manipulated emotionally and physically, but because of their prior relationship with the attacker, they were hesistant to confront or resist. Their unspoken social contract permitted or required the victims to believe they could talk the assailant out of committing the rape. Emotional shock, confusion, indecision and inability to react resulted in a loss of control for victims of known-assailant rape.

Why is social rape the most common type of rape?

Women are socialized to believe that it is good and natural for them to be passive, weak, naive and compliant. Unfortunately, these behaviors often lead women into trouble and then are used against women as justification for the attack when they are raped or assaulted.

For instance, a woman might be encouraged to dress seductively by magazine articles, advertising, fashion designers or a boyfriend. Seductive clothing might be anything from tight and constrictive clothing to high-heeled shoes, which make it impossible to walk let alone run. If attacked while dressed this way, some will accuse her of bringing the attack on herself. Yet the woman was only dressing the way she had been encouraged, through social rewards, to dress. The sad thing is that most women don't realize they are in a Catch-22 situation. They can risk social ostracism by dressing in coveralls and workboots, but that won't insulate them from attacks either.

"Immediate confrontation and committed resistance is often the only deterrent in a social rape situation."

Supposedly for their own good, women are encouraged not to aggressively confront a man during a rape attempt. This belief is never more damaging or misguided than in a social rape situation. Social rapists rely on the fact that women are reluctant to be confrontive or aggressive. This makes this act almost a sure success leaving no evidence of rape. Immediate confrontation and committed resistance is often the only deterrent in a social rape situation.

This type of rape, and the defenses which can be used effectively to deter it, should always be differentiated from rape in which the resistor has had no prior relationship with the attacker.

It is misguided and ineffective to teach rape prevention without helping women understand that social rape situations, with extremely rare exceptions, have entirely different dynamics than planned or unpremeditated random attacks, planned robbery and rape opportunity, or planned rape and robbery. A known-assailant rape may be premeditated or it may be a sudden decision to attack because the social rapist clearly sees his chance. In social rape, the element of planning rarely matters. The advantages may be manipulated or incidental.

If a social rapist finds himself alone and in a safe situation with any woman, he may suddenly attack or begin a progressive assault that is usually perceived as a sexual advance in the initial stages. The woman mistakenly believes that her verbally expressed "No" will be respected and that a small amount of struggling will convince him she means it. The social rapist needs more than this minor resistance. He must be made aware of the very real possibility of exposure and punishment. This can be accomplished through committed resistance.

Social rape is the result of a continuum of physical and social exploitation of females in our society. Females are socially sacrificed and negated, physically and psychologically bullied, sexually objectified and victimized. Males form strong sexual identities, reinforce social position and exaggerate strength by comparison. By adulthood, most women

no longer recognize bullying behaviors and accept their weakened position as one of life's realities.

Rather than trying to reassert strength and re-establish the weakened aspects of themselves, many women inventively try to find ways to survive without suffering more attacks on their bodies, minds and personal integrity. This has taken tremendous will and imagination; to break these bonds we will need equal will and creativity.

". . . many women inventively try to find ways to survive without suffering more attacks on their bodies, minds and personal integrity. This has taken tremendous will and imagination; to break these bonds we will need equal will and creativity."

Sexual harassment, persecution for sexual activity, gang rape and social rape are extremely common in junior high school and high school. Females are the victims of these social rituals. Males reap the benefits of enhanced status, admiration for sexual prowess, identification with other males and thus perpetuate the illusion of male superiority over females through physical, mental and social cruelty.

In the past several years there has been an increase in overt violence by young males against females in junior high and high school.[3] Social theorists believe this is directly related to the large degree of violence against women depicted in music videos and the eroticization of that violence.

Violence against females used to be a covert activity. Everyone knew of such incidents, but we all looked the other way, especially when gang rapes occurred, or "trains" were "pulled." These acts of aggression were directed at a female who

30

was known to be a "bad girl" (Maybe she was simply self-assertive.) who "got herself into it" or "deserved it." No one questioned why groups of "nice boys" (athletes and the popular crowd) felt gang rapes and trains were acceptable.

As a result of this continuous process of social reinforcement for female sexual persecution, social rape is occurring with great frequency because it is easy to commit and even easier to get away with. The dynamics of social rape have remained largely unexplored and undefined. These dynamics, if understood by the resistor, can be used to her advantage.

There is a very slippery quality to the dynamics of a social rape which explains why it has been so mysterious, easy to get away with and prevalent. Social rapists tread a thin line between socially acceptable and unacceptable behavior. Their victims often don't face the extent of damage that has been done to their self-esteem because they successfully repress these incidents. Repression is usually due to self-blame or fear of blame from others.

A clear understanding that this ambiguity exists makes social rape easier to identify. There are many reasons why social rapists are such successful victimizers who rarely fail in their recreational raping and rarely confront exposure or fear of failure.

Social rapists fit under one of the three main categories of rapists, defined by A. Nicholas Groth, called "power rapists." Groth says a power rapist will use only the amount of force needed to carry out rape. In most cases, this means he is not prepared to commit a high degree of violence and is not prepared and does not intend to maim or kill.

In general, a power rapist who knows his victim and a rapist who attacks strangers accomplish their objectives more by exploiting their victims' fear than by the actual degree of force. Offenders Groth has worked with divide into 60 percent stranger rape and 40 percent acquaintence rape. Groth says to keep in mind that rapists who were incarcerated for raping a stranger have had more offenses off the record than on and many of the unreported or undetected assaults involved victims with whom they were acquainted.

Therefore, the social rapist has most of the characteristics associated with power rapists. He may be more accurately described as an "exploiter" rapist, one who manipulates situational advantages or utilizes any situation in which rape could be carried out.

"A social rapist is well aware that women have been taught not to resist with commitment. This realization is his major psychological advantage."

Because of the high degree of manipulation or coincidental situational advantages involved in social rape, exploiters do not anticipate and rarely have to deal with committed resistance. A social rapist is well aware that women have been taught not to resist with commitment. This realization is his major psychological advantage.

Why is known-assailant rape the least reported type of rape?

A high degree of known-assailant rape is occurring within the primary family unit, in the extended family, or within a network of close friends and neighbors. In addition to the "emotional blackmail" that occurs in these situations, complex relationships and situational variables prevent reporting, not only to the police, but to **anyone**.

The "rules" for women's behavior, emotional blackmail and lack of "evidence" in known-assailant situations make a woman reluctant to report. From the personal accounts of the women in this survey and the reasons given for reporting or not, it appears that a woman is most likely to report when there are the fewest so-called "mitigating" circumstances.

The actual amount of threat, implied threat, force, number of assailants, weapons used and victim intimidation do not seem to influence the rate of reporting as much as the circumstances of the attack. This does not imply guilt. It means only that if a woman had a prior relationship with the assailant(s), or voluntarily engaged in any sort of social contact with him/them, or had a drink or went to a party, she is very likely to blame herself or to feel she will be blamed. Sociologist Diana E. H. Russell writes, "The victim is likely to be blamed for not knowing he was that kind of person." According to current sources, known-assailant rape is least likely to get to court. This was verified by the results in the present survey.

A prior relationship, previous interaction or business relationship generally means that there is some form of "social contract" between the parties. Very few people knowingly interact with another if they are absolutely sure they are in danger.

When women reported feeling apprehension but ignoring it, the reason was not a blatant test of fate; it was because the situation did not logically appear to be dangerous. After this type of attack, there is very little evidence to "logically" prove rape. This is why "acquaintance" rape is rarely reported. There are also personal reasons, especially when family members or close family friends are involved. Rapid, committed resistance would expose these coercive encounters before the attacker had time to carry out the act on the pretense that "We both wanted it." The "polite" forms of resistance will not help you here.

How a psychological scenario known as "power of the situation" prevents successful resistance.

32

A prior or existing relationship, trust, assumed relationship "contracts" and circumstances for which the woman feels responsible, such as being alone in any setting with the attacker, creates a psychological scenario I refer to as "power of the situation." This power is created by the apparent reality and the logic of the situation which makes the reality of rape seem an impossibility. This contributes to the attacker's success by inhibiting and delaying an effective reaction from the resistor.

The circumstances of the situation can relieve the attacker's culpability. After all, she was **there**. This is very flimsy logic; but voluntary interaction, especially being alone with a man, is still misconstrued as an invitation to rape. A woman experiencing incredulous disbelief and shock rarely resists until it is too late. "Too late" means the woman is usually pinned and the rape is in progress, although options always exist for a committed resistor.

"Delayed-threat perception and delayed-effective response are the greatest contributing factors to successful known-assailant rapes."

Social rape is rarely a matter of life and death, but in a more severe situation it is never too late to employ a resistance strategy. **Delayed-threat perception** and **delayed-effective response** are the greatest contributing factors to successful known-assailant rapes.

The problem with uncommitted resistance or verbal attempts to dissuade the attacker is that the aftermath of this type of resistance doesn't look much different than the aftermath of consensual sex. When a women resists by saying no, begging and struggling, but is pinned and raped anyway, there is rarely any "evidence" of rape. There may be a disheveled bed or couch, clothes in disarray and two red-faced people. One is rightfully crying "rape" and the other is righteously claiming "consent."

Sadly, the many men who commit social rapes do not actually view them as "rapes." They feel or claim to feel the woman is "signaling" sexual consent or she wouldn't be there; her presence implies a form of consent. Unfortunately, this illogical rationalization is generally supported by social belief systems.

Delayed resistance or "rational" resistance, i.e., trying to reason or talk the man out of rape, is the most frequent strategy in known-assailant rape. It is rarely effective and lends power to the situation. Verbal protests are weak strategy and easily dismissed by the rapist.

The "power of the situation" is based on these factors:

- Prior relationship and trust factor.

- Blaming the victim tactics. She should have known better, etc.

- The sexually out-of-control male mythology. His "point of no return" was triggered. Often a woman who is raped in a known-assailant situation is not positive she isn't somehow guilty.

- Perceptual ambiguity. The woman is not sure if she is being subjected to a sexual advance, a joke or an assault. By the time she realizes what is happening it is too late to prevent the rape, that is, if she is unprepared at this point to resist physically or use a pain/shock technique.

When I refer to "committed resistance," I don't necessarily mean utilizing incapacitating techniques on the assailant. One of the most effective deterrents to a known-assailant rape is attacking the environment. This is explained more fully later in this chapter.

In many cases a woman will not be prepared to use extreme physical force to prevent a known-assailant rape. She may often like or even love the assailant.

Degree of Force

Most social rape is accomplished with a minimum of force as compared to random attack. Known-assailant rape rarely involves the use of a weapon, and a high degree of violence is unlikely. In this survey, weapons were present in 13 percent of known-assailant attacks, although this is actually a high figure. In the 1984, U.S. Department of Justice, Bureau of Statistics figures, weapons were present in 17.6 percent of all rapes. Weapons are more likely to be present in stranger attacks. The U.S. Justice Department figure was based on 63 percent stranger attacks.

The mode of operation is usually trickery, coercion and exploitation of trust. An additional problem with known-assailant rape is an "apparent" lack of situational advantages for the intended victim. The attacker manipulates a woman into a situation where it is safe for him to attack.

"In a known-assailant rape situation, the assault is often mistaken for a sexual advance in which the woman believes she has a choice."

In a known-assailant rape situation, the assault is often mistaken for a sexual advance in which the woman believes she has a choice. There is often a preliminary struggle in which the woman tries to squirm out of the man's grasp and reason with him. By the time the woman realizes the man is not listening and will not stop, she has been pinned down and is seconds from being raped. In fact, approximately 59 percent of the women in the known-assailant section of the study reported being pinned down with the man's body weight

33

holding them down as the mode of restraint. Some women were attacked suddenly without any obvious warning; however, most of these women were not pinned without some other initial form of hold, grab or restraint.

The reason they did not recognize the initial interaction as an assault attempt has to do with perceptual ambiguity and delayed-threat perception. Women are socialized to tolerate social space intrusion or more physical closeness than men. This makes it difficult for a woman to identify an encroaching male who intends to do harm from a man who may be harmless but does not feel he must observe "social zone" rules with a woman.

Recognize unwanted encroachment as harmful to your perceptual abilities and re-establish distance. If you have assertively refused a sexual overture and the man becomes agitated and continues physically pressuring you, state that you will not cooperate and any further advances will be considered an assault attempt. If this does not stop him, you know that this is an assault attempt - not a sexual overture and you can react accordingly.

"Any display of indecision could be read as encouragement to try harder."

In an unwanted sexual advance, you may be able to firmly refuse without further incident. If you face an unwanted sexual advance from a friend and care for this person's feelings, just be honest with sensitivity and without concessions. This is part of what self-defense for women is all about. Women have to learn to effectively and honestly deal with a man's sexual advances. You can't always indirectly slide out of an advance and continue interacting with the man.

Any display of indecision could be read as encouragement to try harder.

Social and situational advantages contribute to the "code of silence."

The attacker in known-assailant rape can manipulate the situational advantages so that the victim is less likely to report. Women will often be questioned about their demeanor, dress, intentions and whereabouts during a rape trial.

For instance, if a man can gain a woman's trust and then get her to go swimming at a secluded lake, then her intentions can be examined and questioned. In describing the circumstances of known-assailant rape, many women in the study said although they had not considered the possibility that they would be raped, afterwards they felt responsible for not being more cautious. However, the root cause of social rape is not lack of caution or "stupid" decisions on the part of the female.

It is not stupid to want to go to parties or to want to be with other people; it is a human need.

One root cause of social rape is the social assumption that sanctions this act for the male and questions if rape can occur if a woman **voluntarily** interacts with a man.

The other major root cause is a woman's lack of physical, emotional and psychological preparation to defend. She is likely to believe that social rape is precipitated by the victim. She is also likely to be unskilled in threat recognition. This is because she lacks experience with confrontive situations and because she has been socialized to be comfortable with more physical closeness than a male. When a man's "intimate zone" of 18 inches is entered, it is generally considered either a threat or a sexual advance.

For a woman, this either/or distinction is difficult to make. Her intimate zone is violated without invitation in everyday situations. Because this is a common, if unwelcome experience for most women, it contributes to delayed-threat perception. In a social rape situation there is nearly always delayed-threat perception which results in delayed-effective reaction.

In my survey, women reported that the attacker implied or stated that no one would believe the accusation of rape because of the circumstances. These rapists were relying on the social advantage of gender-specific rules for female behavior and the certainty that he could manipulate her guilt.

It is a common, socially accepted belief that men are sexually "out of control" and that women can incite men to rape merely by being in their presence and acting spontaneously or trustingly. All spontaneous female behavior or trust and voluntary contact with males can be distorted and labeled "seductive," or "asking for it." This is why I object to lists of rules for women's behavior to "prevent rape." These lists of rules cannot be followed assiduously by any woman unless she has absolutely no contact with men. She would have to prevent herself from ever trusting a male under any circumstances. For most women this is an impossible and undesirable solution.

These rules and assumptions about acceptable gender-specific behaviors give rapists the advantage of relying on the silence of the victim. This is an important element in social rape. If rapists could not rely on the victim's silence, they would have to suffer at least some consequences after raping a woman.

So far the elements of known-assailant rape have been identified and explained. To briefly summarize, the aspect in the "power of the situation" variables could be all or several of the following elements:

- Violation of trust or "social contract" or prior relationship.

- The dynamics of a social situation, familiar activities and surroundings and gender differences in personal space requirements contribute to delayed-threat perception which in turn results

in delayed-effective reaction.

- Once the threat is identified, resistance is further delayed because the woman is hesitant to harm someone she knows and is likely to believe the assailant can be "reasoned" with.

- The assault is mistaken as a sexual advance in which the woman believes she has a choice.

- The male has social behavioral rules in his favor. A woman has committed a breach of acceptable female behavior merely by "being there" in any setting with one or more males.

- The rapist manipulates the "situational advantages." He arranges to be alone with the woman or takes advantage of being alone with her. After the rape, he manipulates his social advantages, i.e., claiming it was not rape; she could have prevented it; working on her guilt; she "flirted;" and claiming that no one would believe her so she better keep quiet for "her own good."

- After the assault, the degree of force is generally **not apparent**. A considerable amount of force may actually be used to restrain the victim but it is unlikely that she will be beaten or threatened with a weapon. Because of delayed resistance and the circumstances of the interaction, the aftermath of the assault cannot "logically" prove rape through lack of actual evidence.

How to reverse situational and social advantages.

By now you should have a clear picture of what situational and social advantages the rapist manipulates to perpetrate and get away with his crime. A potential victim of rape can turn the tables on an attacker by using the very elements that have previously ensured the success of social rapists to thwart the attack and expose the rapist.

We have discussed why physical resistance is delayed; first there is **delayed-threat perception** which **delays effective action**. Then there is generally reluctance on the part of the woman to overreact or hurt someone that she knows. This is because she is likely to believe that she has a choice and she can talk her way out of a bad situation. Trying to plead with the attacker or calm him down, talk him out of violence and rape has been common advice in the past few years. This has not been proven to be an effective resistance strategy in my research or other recent research. Talking should be a form of trickery, bargaining or commands.

A recent study, *Avoiding Rape: A Study of Victims and Avoiders* by Pauline Bart and prepared for the National Institute of Mental Health, showed the verbal approach to be generally ineffective.

According to Bart's findings,

- The cognitive verbal approach was the most frequently resorted to and was not notably effective . . . In sum, of the five active strategies, (assertive or aggressive statements, pleading, screaming, physical assertion or aggression, or running or fleeing) pleading was the only one associated with a higher-than-sample probability of being raped.

- Interestingly, the least frequently resorted to of the five active strategies, fleeing or trying to flee, showed the most dramatic relationship with rape avoidance.[4]

Pleading is an attempt to convince the assailant of the injustice or inequity in the situation. For example, statements such as, "Please don't do this to me." "I'm married." "I'm a virgin." or begging the assailant not to "violate me," or resorting to claims of illness or disease are verbal pleading strategies shown to be ineffective. In combination with other strategies, a verbal or psychological strategy could only

be suggested as a means to buy time. Verbal strategies alone should not be considered an effective means of self-defense.

The only verbal strategies that can be recommended are assertive statements or "trickery and bargaining." Assertive statements are commands such as, "Don't take one step closer! Don't move! Stop! Don't try it! Don't touch me!" and declarative sentences such as, "One more move will be taken as an assault attempt! I will resist and report to the police and (whomever) if you persist!"

It is important to clarify that the threat of reporting to the police (or others) should only be used in a known-assailant situation. The only time it shouldn't be used as a deterrent to known-assailant rape is if the person is obviously mentally disturbed or psychotic, brandishing a weapon, under chemical influence or all of the above.

Screaming is generally thought to be unsafe unless you are within ear-shot of possible help. However, in a known-assailant situation, screaming is an acknowledgement that an assault is in progress instead of a consensual act of sex.

"The correct Ki-ai or 'Karate yell' is highly effective as a momentary stunner."

I recommend yelling, which can be differentiated from screaming; nevertheless, in a situation where you can attract attention, any noise you can produce is recommended. The correct Ki-ai or "Karate yell" is highly effective as a momentary stunner. If done properly, it should be explosive and shocking enough to create "time and space." It could momentarily stun the assailant and create the opportunity to escape or defend.

Learning to Ki-ai seems to be one of the most difficult aspects of martial arts training. As much as I hate to say this, women are particularly inhibited in this area. However, I don't know a woman who hasn't **yelled** at some time. Women can be very intimidating when angry. So think about the times you've yelled and use that power in a defensive situation.

If you feel you cannot physically defend, try bargaining or trickery. This may be especially useful in the known-assailant situation where the woman is hesitant to hurt the assailant, fears more violence or does not feel prepared to resist physically. Claim you want to do something "first," implying that you are willing to have sex but must go to the bathroom, get a glass of wine, put on a sexy nightgown, model a swim suit, "dance" for him, or any other ploy to distract the assailant and buy time.

Trickery fits in well with the psychological set-up of social-rape situations. The rapist is very likely to be relieved that force is not necessary because the social rapist is rarely prepared to commit a high degree of violence. If social rape required extreme violence, it would not be so easy to get away with. The results of violence leave evidence. The commitment of a violent struggle makes the rationalizations of the social rapist impossible.

Bargaining is a resistance strategy that implies a tradeoff. For example, you're pinned down and the attacker is struggling to pull down your jeans or underwear, and you say, "Just a minute. Let me take all of my clothes off."

Incidentally, social rape often takes place while both parties are clothed. The attacker usually just pulls down his pants and mauls the intended victim, pulls her underwear aside or only manages to pull off her pants or threaten her sufficiently to get her to take them off.

Don't forget. The social rapist's threats are likely to be empty. A social rapist is in a tremendous hurry to impose physical

dominance. He fears time will weaken his position. He is also afraid of anger and resistance. He hits and runs before the realization takes effect and the shock wears off.

"Don't forget. The social rapist's threats are likely to be empty. A social rapist is in a tremendous hurry to impose physical dominance. He fears time will weaken his position. He is also afraid of anger and resistance. He hits and runs before the realization takes effect and the shock wears off."

Because of these factors, asking for time to take your clothes off or suggesting that he at least take his pants off is an an effective bargaining ploy to remove his body weight. You can try to roll away and escape or use a defense while his hands are engaged.

One woman in my survey did exactly this in a known-assailant rape attempt involving two attackers. One was holding her down and the other was trying to pull her jeans off. She was struggling but realized they would eventually succeed. She said, "OK, if we're gonna do this, let's do it **right** and at least get naked." They released her and she bolted for the door and escaped into the street.

Let's assume that the social rape attempt followed a progressively escalating series of events. Forceful verbal commands did not deter the assailant and bargaining and trickery did not work to buy time. You may be engaged in a preliminary struggle at this point, but for personal reasons you may not want to attack the man.

In this case remember one of the most effective resistance strategies for known-assailant rape: **attack the environment.**

37

Let's say it's your own home and you don't want to destroy too much. Then knock off ashtrays, scatter papers, throw plants or, if you have a bookshelf, throw books. During this attempt at resistance, keep yelling and trying to make break for an escape route. Make sure that the degree of force is apparent to ensure that he begins to experience fear of getting caught.

In the rapist's environment, yell loudly, throw all objects previously mentioned, pull down drapes, break lamps and knock over furniture.

In either case, when the attacker is sufficiently stunned or you've physically extricated yourself, run outside yelling all the way. If you're in his neighborhood, it is safe and most embarrassing to yell his name in conjunction with the word "rapist" and other descriptive nouns.

I know you have frequently been told to yell "Fire!" It depends on the situation. If you feel safer or that you are more likely to attract attention by yelling "Fire!" then do so. If you only struggle quietly, the rapist will gain control during and after the assault.

In the face of committed resistance, many men would be totally bewildered and would give up. They don't want this degree of confrontation and are not prepared to kill, maim or seriously injure a woman in order to rape her, especially in a known-assailant situation. A high degree of resistance will blow the rapist's cover, make it easier to report, and break the code of silence on "social rape."

Because it is commonly believed that men have an uncontrollable sex drive and it is a woman's duty to control **her** behavior to avoid inciting men to rape and assault, the social behavioral rules appear heavily weighted in favor of the male. This is only true if a high degree of resistance is not apparent.

The idea is that a man overcome by passion can "take" a woman because "he doesn't know what he's doing." Extreme resistance would jar him out of this so-called "passionate" frenzy and make him absolutely aware of the reality of the situation. You can make the assault attempt obvious by resisting with noise and environmental destruction to show evidence of a struggle.

"You can make the assault attempt obvious by resisting with noise and environmental destruction to show evidence of a struggle."

Even though violence against women is very common, there is a social stigma on men **caught** or exposed in the act. For example, in the prison hierarchy, convicted rapists are lowest in the social strata and are ostracized by the other prisoners. There are apparent inconsistencies in this viewpoint, however. In prison rape, the rapist is not considered homosexual and does not lose stature. In fact the social hierarchy is largely defined by physical dominance, and rapists are considered dominant.

Rape here is called "punking" a man and making a "girl" or "gal boy" out of him. A raped male becomes a surrogate female. The act of penetrating a male is acceptable but to be penetrated is not. Although one might assume that the social ostracism of convicted rapists by other prisoners is a reflection of chivalrous values, it is more likely to be an expression of disgust that they were caught in an act that a "real man" is entitled to perpetrate without punishment.

According to Clinton Duffy, the famous warden of San Quentin, the typical felon will deny that he was a rapist on the "outside" with the declaration that "I'm no rapo."[5] Duffy explained why this is largely untrue.

The opportunity for rape frequently occurs during the course of a robbery.

When an offender is charged with both crimes, a plea bargain is offered and the rape charge is dropped in return for a plea of guilty to robbery. This arrangement has benefits for both the criminal and the system. Burglary carries a one-to-five year sentence and rape can result in twenty years to life. Because of this, the criminal benefits from a plea bargain which automatically drops the rape charge and the system benefits because rape is so difficult to prove. At least the law can get an offender off the street temporarily and hope he will be rehabilitated.

Duffy also wrote, "I have never known of a 'second story' burglar who climbed into the window of a man's apartment."[6] What he is actually saying is that a rapist/burglar is likely to select the residence of a female. In this way he believes that he reduces the chance of resistance if he encounters her during the robbery and he may create the opportunity to rape, or rape may be part of his plan. Regardless of the social strata in prison, which condones male-on-male rape, there is still an immense social stigma and punishment awaiting male-on-female rapists or child molesters caught in the act or convicted of rape.

The rapist's fear of getting caught is **always present** and **always exploitable**. This is why committed resistance is so important. A scene will activate his fears of detection and punishment.

"It is better to be accused of 'over-reacting' than to be raped because you under-reacted."

As you can see, most of the elements of social rape can be used for the resistor's advantage. You must decide on firm guidelines for resistance, not necessarily limiting your lifestyle or your willingness to trust. If a man cannot respect your right to say no, you have a right to create a scene. You can explain it later; he may need the lesson. It is better to be accused of "over-reacting" than to be raped because you under-reacted. Under-reaction is much more of a problem than over-reaction for women. It is important that men understand that any display of sexual force is violent.

Why is social rape the most preventable type of rape?

Known-assailant rape is the most common, least reported, most preventable type of rape. To date it has been easy to commit and easy to get away with. It may seem like a contradiction to state that this type of rape is the most common, yet the easiest to prevent and defend against.

This crime persists because of the code of silence, lack of knowledge about the dynamics of social rape, pervasive social messages and aggressive self-defense programs that teach women not to resist regardless of the circumstances.

There are definitely times when a woman or any defender should not respond with aggression. However, in most known-assailant situations, aggression is the best defense. The irrational fear of physical resistance that is enforced on women is based on the idea that in a confrontation with an "enraged male," his brute strength will win out every time, regardless of relative size, strength or other equalizers, even advanced martial arts training or comprehensive self-defense training.

If every potentially violent encounter occurred in a vacuum with no situational advantages: nearby help, escape routes, environmental obstructions, barriers, and objects; no social inhibitions: fear of detection, exposure during the act, internal moral dictates, fear of punishment; and no human emotional inhibitions: fear of failure, fear of pain, fear of loss as a result of the act; then the assertion that brute strength would win out has partial merit.

39

Still we must assume that a significant size and strength disparity actually exists in each situation, yet in many cases it does not. Many women in my survey reported they were actually much larger than the assailant. Their defeat was psychological, not physical.

Even the strength, or disparity when it exists, may not be sufficient to sabotage a physiological advantage of femaleness. Studies have shown women can endure shock and fatigue better than men. In a rape situation, this could mean evasion and wearing down his endurance. Ashley Montague, author of *The Natural Superiority of Women*, writes at length on this phenomenon. Montague cited Gillespie's study of citizens and soldiers in World War II in which women were found to hold up better emotionally under "siege and heavy bombardment."[7]

If a woman can reverse the shock in a rape situation, she can gain the psychological advantage. These combined situational, social, emotional and psychological advantages **if fully realized** can be advantageous to a female. In a social-rape situation, powerful resistance techniques include reversing the stress bombardment with actions such as environmental destruction and manipulating the attacker's fear of detection and punishment.

Resistance in a known-assailant situation is very likely to be successful. One of the major reasons it has not been, in addition to the previously discussed elements of social rape, is because the common warnings and rules about resistance, which may be somewhat more likely to apply in a random-attack situation, are observed in known-assailant situations. This is a different situation with totally different possibilities.

The following is an explanation of the elements of known-assailant attack that can be used to your advantage.

- The attacker is less likely to use a weapon. In my study approximately 13 percent in the known-assailant category showed a weapon. A knife, which is the most available weapon in any situation, represented 9.6 percent of the weapons in known-assailant assault. A knife is often obtained as an "afterthought." Women interviewed said the assailant cornered them and picked up an object or grabbed a knife off the kitchen counter after the assault was in progress, although use of weapons in known-assailant attack is rare. This is an example of an advantage that can be reversed. Environmental objects are available to the resistor, too.

After reading this book, you can be more inventive in your choice of weapons and draw on a variety of mental, physical and environmental weapons which are always available.

A gun represented a little over two percent of the weapons and a blunt object, a little over one percent. A blunt object is another weapon that is likely to be an after-thought because objects are present in most environments and readily available.

- The attacker is relying on his perceived advantages in a social-rape situation. Shock and stress bombardment can be used to the woman's advantage if none of the attacker's expectations are honored.

- If the attacker is aware that his perceived social advantages and behavioral expectations for females are not operative, he will realize the risk of failure, detection and punishment. A major encouragement for social rape is the lack of fear of failure, detection and punishment. Reverse these realities.

- When a social rapist faces serious, focused and determined resistance, he will become confused, fearful, indecisive and often apologetic or defensive: for example, "I really wasn't going to do anything," or "Calm down. Who'd want to rape a bitch like you anyway."[8]

In the face of absolute resistance a social rapist will usually give up. He is rarely prepared to seriously harm a woman simply because he is known; others may be aware he is with this woman; and detection and conviction is a very real possibility. Social rape is the "easy" crime and indulged in so frequently precisely for this reason. Reverse the fear factor and you will thwart the crime.

Approximately 70 percent of the women in the three categories except Assaults resisted physically. Why wasn't physical resistance more effective in these cases? All of the elements of known-assailant rape contributed to delayed-threat perception and delayed-reaction. The majority of the women in known-assailant rape were pinned down before they realized they were victims of a serious assault. They resisted as a last resort, at a point when they had few advantages left.

This is exactly the problem I'm hoping to teach women to recognize and avoid. A woman must react quickly at the first sign of sexual persistence or unwanted social dominance gestures. Even if you are attracted to the man in question, you must clearly state your feelings about dominance gestures or persistent behaviors that negate your stated wishes. A man who is totally insensitive to your verbal statements and aggressively overrides your non-verbal messages is potentially dangerous. Learn to recognize and confront such insensitivity. You have a right to choose your sexual encounters and interact with men without tolerating molestation.

Now that you are aware of what social rape really is and how it happens, you may be able to perceive the warning signals sooner than the women who participated in this survey. You may be able to believe that a trusted individual **could** carry out a rape. You may not be as likely to try to

"talk him out of it" while he increasingly gains control.

You are aware that you must be firm, even aggressively verbal. If that doesn't work, you don't have to attack the man, you can attack the environment. The rape attempt may not occur in a residence, although known-assailant rape is likely to happen indoors. It could be the inside of a car - honk the horn, or in a park - knock over garbage cans, yell. In any case, if you are forced to fight, you can use techniques from this book after practicing with a partner or instructor or use any of the "Last-Resort Techniques" that apply to the situation.

If you are raped by someone you know, don't internalize the blame and let the matter drop. You should report to the police whether you feel he will be arrested and convicted or not. His name will be on file; repeat incidents may result in arrest.

Known-assailant rape is the most common, least reported, most preventable type of rape. To date it has been easy to commit and easy to get away with. Resist this kind of violation. Make social rape less common. Report to the police or expose the rapist. Remove the distinction of "least reported." Know all the elements of social rape. Know all your options. Share honestly with other women for more factual accounts of social rape.

"You have a right to choose your sexual encounters and interact with men without tolerating molestation."

Breaking the code of silence will contribute to prevention of social rape. Women can make social rape almost impossible to commit and hard to get away with. Honesty and self-defense training for women can nearly eradicate this type of rape.

Part 2 Random or Stranger Attack

The term "random attack" is used here to indicate any rape or assault in which the victim has no prior relationship with the attacker. It is not used to indicate an "unplanned" attack, because that idea is primarily fictional; no attacker rapes without planning or forethought of rape.

The term "random attack" is used interchangeably with the term "stranger attack" because from what I've been able to determine from interviewing victims, the element of "premeditation," or choosing a victim in advance, does not insure success. Even an attacker who chooses a victim in advance must rely on chance for the opportunity to attack successfully.

In addition, a random street attack is premeditated in the rapist's mind. The decision to rape is already made; the selection of the victim is left to opportunity and chance. In either case, chance and opportunity are what make rape possible, not prior selection of a victim.

"Having a personal commitment to your right to live unmolested will project a strong physical presence and a psychic shield effect."

Women can control chance and opportunity through adequate home and car security, awareness and other reasonable precautions. Having a personal commitment to your right to live unmolested will project a strong physical presence and a psychic shield effect.

In this survey, there were sixty-four women in the random-attack group.

Mode of Operation

The "mode of operation" refers to how the attacker chooses to commit the crime of

rape or assault. The number of assailants, presence of a weapon, choice of weapon and method of contact with the victim are aspects of "mode of operation."

A weapon is more likely to be present in a random attack than in the other three groups. A gang attack (two or more attackers) is also more likely to occur.

Although a random attack is likely to occur suddenly, often without discernible warning, in many cases a victim may be tricked or coerced into some kind of interaction with the attacker(s).

To determine if this "trickery" theory had any validity, I asked, "Did you see the attacker before you were approached?" Almost 58 percent of the women answered yes. The next question was, "Did the assailant speak to you, call you or use any come-on or approach to appear friendly?" The answer provides more insight into a random-attack situation. Over 68 percent reported the assailant did make verbal contact with them in some way, usually with a friendly or harmless pretense, before physically attacking them; however, the attacker usually left to re-establish his element of surprise and "sneaked" up on his chosen target.

This is important information for self-defense strategies because it indicates that the rapist attempts to determine if the intended victim is going to be easy to overcome. If a woman acts in a compliant, non-assertive way during the initial contact, then she may be considered a good target. This makes a good case for the "Never talk to strangers" rule, which, for adults, should be modified to "Never talk to anyone if you don't want to be approached."

Women need to overcome the fear of dealing assertively with an unwanted approach. From these findings the unwanted approach could be the preliminary stage of an attack.

"Femininity" as defined by our society

and studied by many social scientists, authors and feminists is almost synonymous with "passivity." A show of "feminine" behavior on the part of a targeted victim may or may not mean that passivity is a dominant aspect of her personality. It may not signal that she would make a "good" victim. It may mean that she is adept in performing the behavioral demands of gender and conforming to gender expectations. I define this state of interaction as "maladaptive femininity behavior." I use this phrase to describe any behavior that signals submission, compliance, passivity and politeness when the situation does not logically warrant or socially demand this behavior.

In the interest of self-defense, your responses and behaviors should be evaluated on the limits of what is socially acceptable **only** when you are **not** at risk of injury or other potential danger. If you are confused by the ambiguity of a situation, as in known-assailant rape and assault situations, choose the safest and most effective response; either leave immediately or assertively confront the assailant to prevent further loss of control.

". . . choose the safest and most effective response; either leave immediately or assertively confront the assailant to prevent further loss of control."

Women are socialized to tolerate much more intrusive behaviors than men. Intrusive behaviors include verbal interruptions, physical "space" violations and "dominance gestures" also referred to as "touching behaviors." Intrusive behavior also refers to the frequency with which women are approached in public by males. This is a socially condoned behavior based on the idea that men are the "aggressors" in a relationship, publicly and privately.

The frequency and social acceptance of intrusive behaviors by males is a factor that sets women up as victims. Many rapes, murders and assaults were preceded by a "polite" or intrusive approach from a stranger. Rapists frequently ask for the time or a match. A simple request is a common approach; the request is generally well within your power to perform. The rapist or mugger may evaluate your nervousness, your physical style of movement as you comply with the request, your speed of compliance or any number of factors to determine whether or not it would be safe to rob or attack you.

It is in your best interest to give some forethought to how you will handle intrusive behaviors, especially by strangers in public. You are not obligated to comply with requests of any kind or even to acknowledge the nature of the approach. If you respond to the nature of the approach when you don't wish to, you've left the situation open-ended and created the possibility for a verbal exchange.

If you respond to a request for a match with "I don't smoke," you are offering information about yourself, thereby immediately establishing a personal contact. The potential attacker could counter with a rambling dissertation about why he smokes, why he wishes he didn't, or elicit further information from you. This could give him time to evaluate you and the situation and determine if it's safe to attack.

Whether or not you choose to respond depends on your evaluation of all situational and social cues.

Prior Perceptions and Reactions to Attack

Quick evaluation of external cues is an important aspect of self-defense, especially when apprehension is experienced and **heeded**. Women in my study expressed the tendency to evaluate such feelings as general anxiety or over-reacting and did not heed these valuable messages. The tendency to be afraid to react because the reaction may be inappropriate has been labeled "ambiguity" by social psychologists. The concept suggests that "any factor that creates ambiguity inhibits effective action."[1]

Ambiguity is present in many situations that develop into an attack. The problem is compounded by gender-behavioral expectations such as the "nice" female role and the socially accepted male aggressor. These two factors dramatically increase women's vulnerability to rape and assault.

In random-attack situations, the majority of the women surveyed reported seeing the attacker before the approach. About half of these women reported feeling apprehension after sighting the attacker; approximately two-thirds reported that they thought apprehension could have saved them if they had heeded it.

It is important to remember that apprehension is always based on some sub-conscious realization. One of the most important rules of self-defense is to **trust yourself.** Heeding your apprehensive feelings is a demonstration of self-trust. Grant yourself this right without fearing you will over-react or "look stupid." In most cases people under-react to dangerous situational cues.

"One of the most important rules of self-defense is to trust yourself. Heeding your apprehensive feelings is a demonstration of self-trust."

These women perceived the assailant's size and strength as intimidating in the majority of the cases in random attacks. However, consider the fact that dominant threatening posturing and behavior has the effect of making the aggressor seem larger.[2] The average size of convicted rapists has been found to be five-feet, eight-inches tall. They and weigh an average of 160 pounds. This is not a formidable size and weight.

One of the most important findings under the heading of "subject reaction to random attack" was the discovery that the majority of women do not panic. My students often state that they **believe they** would "freeze" or totally panic if attacked. It is more likely that the body's physiological survival mechanisms will take over and the person will attempt to fight or flee. Self-preservation is a conscious wish and a subconscious reaction.

The "freezing" reaction is not nearly as common as is generally believed. "Freezing" is often a result of the internalization of the continuous warnings women receive about resistance and the superstitious beliefs designed to convince women they are not capable of sucessful resistance. Their behavior is the result of internalized learned helplessness and not the inevitable reaction of a woman confronted by a man.

The prevalence of this reaction is primarily a media fiction. When this occurs on the screen, it creates tension in the observer, an edge-of-the-seat involvement and moments of stunned inertia, such as the shower scene in Alfred Hitchcock's *Psycho.* Observers initially identify with the victim because they can see the possibility of escape. If there is no possibility to alter the outcome, there is no drama.

Women are the most frequent victims of media violence; they are usually portrayed as physically inept and totally ineffective in resistance. We have all been influenced by all forms of media. To many women, these images may be their only firsthand experience of a woman facing violence or confrontation. Lacking experience and survival skills, it may be difficult for women to realize that the "fight or flight" mechanism is a physiological imperative that can frequently over ride belief systems in the event of danger.

44

This study showed that women are likely to resist physically, even without training or prior thought or conscious decisions. Unfocused self-defense attempts by untrained resistors have thwarted assaults, yet self-defense training heavily weights the odds in the resistor's favor.

"Unfocused self-defense attempts by untrained resistors have thwarted assaults, yet self-defense training heavily weights the odds in the resistor's favor."

Attack Circumstances

Through independent research, I hoped to find out if some of the "myths" about random attack had validity. When advice is dispensed to women about how to "avoid" attacks, we are frequently told to stay out of dark alleys and doorways, don't walk by shrubs or bushes, never park in dark parking lots, look in the backseat of your car before getting in, don't go into "dangerous" parts of town and many other related admonitions. Though the common warnings about random-attack rape and assault have some validity, these warnings are over used and over simplify the complexity of rape and assault situations.

None of the women in the study reported finding an attacker in the back seat of her car. This does **not** mean you shouldn't check the car quickly before entering. More important, you should always lock your car and have the windows rolled up. Even these measures do not guarantee that your vehicle can't be entered. Look around before approaching your car and scan the interior before getting in. A high level of awareness is suggested when you are approaching your car. A parking lot is a likely target area.

The majority of women reported that the attack occurred in a familiar area and they did **not** feel the area was dangerous. A very small number reported that the attacker was concealed by a shrub or in a dark alley. Parking lots were a fairly common place of attack although they were not always **dark** parking lots.

In this section, "attack circumstances" also refer to the initial physical approach and method used to restrain the victim. An assailant is most likely to attack from the rear in every type of assault except known-assailant situations. The type of restraints that were most likely to occur in random-attack situations, in the order of frequency were 1) rear-bear hug, 2) arm or wrist grabs, 3) choke holds and 4) front-bear hugs.

Resistance Strategies

There are five basic types of resistance strategies in two categories, verbal and physical.

Verbal resistance strategies include 1) assertive or aggressive statements, 2) pleading, or attempting to placate the attacker or "trying to talk the rapist out of it," and 3) screaming or yelling (which is my preferred term). Physical resistance includes 4) physical assertion and physical aggression or 5) running.

A recent strategy brought into focus by Pauline Barts' studies of victims and avoiders is trickery and bargaining. (My application of verbal "trickery" in the Last-Resorts Chapter would rarely be used in a random-attack situation unless there is long term interaction and no other option. In cases like these, identifying with the captor can be a valid resistance strategy.)

As a resistance strategy for my study, I wanted to know how many women tried to placate the attacker, figure out his frame of mind, attempt to talk him out of it, or "humanize" themselves to make the rapist see he's violating a human being. Violation is his intent, and in most cases you only confirm his success by these actions. In the random-attack section of the study

45

almost 76 percent tried this strategy. It was obviously not effective.

I think it is an impossible task to expect women to figure out the attacker's frame of mind or the attacker's image of you. These strategies are limited. Claiming venereal disease or some kind of "female problem," pretending to go mad or hysterical, begging and pleading, vomiting on the attacker, urinating, defecating, belching or farting have all been suggested as valid strategies by self-defense "experts."

These types of strategies would increase interaction time with the assailant. They are also related to your compliance and based on the idea that you shouldn't resist. These types of strategies can help the attacker meet his assault requirements, which are 1) time, 2) a safe location, and 3) a passive victim.

Proponents of these strategies discourage initial resistance, which research shows is the most effective defense, and suggest that you do what you're ordered to do, which increasingly jeopardizes your control. Then you try to disgust him or elicit his sympathy, but supposedly you shouldn't antagonize him.

All these suggestions imply that you will be involved in a fairly long term interaction with the attacker, which you should always attempt to avoid. If you are forced into long-term interaction, use **anything** or any ploy you think might help you reduce injury or allow you to escape.

Don't listen to anyone who insists that your only rational option is to systematically sacrifice your advantages in the initial encounter. Self-defense experts rationalize this approach by claiming a random attack occurs as a progressive series of events. In this theory, the degree of violence escalates in the following manner: 1) An attacker gropes or grabs a woman. 2) She responds by aggressively pushing the hand or his body away. 3) He becomes enraged and becomes violent because his victim initiated aggression.

Attacks, especially the random type, rarely progress in this one, two, three manner. An attacker may begin on the verbal level as a means to determine a "good" victim in order to minimize his risks. If he feels he has located the right victim, he may launch an immediate physical assault - not necessarily beginning with simple grabs but with punches and blows.

Attackers, both those who are known to victims and those who are strangers, always try to preserve the element of surprise. Their fears are great and they can be defeated by resistance which wastes time and could attract attention which is dangerous to them. This is why all attackers attempt to "control" against resistance.

A random attacker generally chooses the location and plans the escape route. When he locates a victim and unless the area is totally secluded, he threatens the victim to gain enough control so that she will help him meet his assault requirements. One requirement is her cooperation so that she will accompany him to a secure place to carry out the attack. A random attacker generally chooses an area that is likely to have a high traffic rate at a time when it is relatively deserted such as late at night in an apartment complex, recreational area, parking lot or parking garage. The random attacker also controls for resistance by verbal testing and proximity testing, i.e., he tries to get close to a potential victim to determine her degree of awareness or if she will be relatively compliant.

"A random attack may often be a progressive series of events but this is different than the escalation theory in which the victim 'causes' the degree of violence by resistance."

A random attack may often be a progressive series of events but this is

46

different than the escalation theory in which the victim "causes" the degree of violence by resistance. An attacker follows a progressive series of events to protect himself. He **escalates** the degree of force as he gains courage and control through the success of each action. In "safe" situations, a victimizer may immediately attack to frighten and subdue the victim.

In either case, the best possible strategy is to **decrease interaction time**. In general, the sooner a woman becomes assertive or aggressive the better are her chances of escape.

The majority of the women surveyed reported "resistance" in random attack but it is important to clarify that women untrained in self-defense will generally "struggle" which is an involuntary, unfocused, energy-wasting activity. Almost 90 percent of the subjects in the random-attack section of the study did not have prior self-defense training. If the attacker has carefully controlled for safety and his chances of detection are minimal, the victim's unfocused struggle may reduce her chances of escape because she wastes her energy, loses control and may panic.

Struggle **can work** and has worked because of several variables such as the element of surprise when the assailant is not expecting resistance and because the women reacted immediately. Any type of resistance can be effective with a power rapist or a known assailant whose goal is sexual conquest because he is counting on using minimal force or only the amount necessary to carry out the rape.

Immediate resistance, even unfocused struggling and screaming, is more than he is bargaining for. He expects that his commands, threats, forceful restraint or grabbing will accomplish dominance.

This is a rapist's mental script: Man commands; woman obeys. Or man applies physical force; woman meekly submits.

Blow his mind with righteous anger. A

rapist must dominate a victim mentally as well as physically. He can't mentally dominate or control a woman who is not already psychologically defeated by fear and socialized myths about resistance and her supposed limitations.

"Blow his mind with righteous anger."

An important basic disagreement with the idea of struggle as a resistance strategy is the fact that it is an **unfocused**, energy-depleting attempt at defense. If it does not work in the beginning of the attack, the resistor loses the element of surprise and depletes the initial charge of adrenalin. This results in fatigue and a decreased ability to resist or escape.

Self-defense is **not** strength against strength. It should incorporate awareness, inventiveness, trickery, bargaining, buying time, creating escape openings or **focused** techniques to primary vital areas: eyes, throat, groin, knees; or to secondary vital areas: temples, solar plexus, spine, instep, shins, etc..

A strike to a vital area does not have to incapacitate. If there is a possibility for escape, you only need to **buy time**. If there is no possible avenue of escape, you may have to wait until you can safely react and revert to techniques from the last chapter, Last-Resort Techniques.

In terms of "cooperating with the attacker to avoid injury and survive the attack," I asked random-attacked women if they left the scene with the attacker and approximately 69 percent said they did. The follow-up question was, "If you left the scene with the attacker, were you injured later?" It was fairly significant that 38 percent did report being injured after complying with an attacker's demands. Leaving the "target area" **with the attacker is never** suggested if there are any other options. In leaving with the attacker, a victim is helping the attacker meet his assault requirements.

Consider this. Why is the attacker concerned about leaving the area?

It's because he feels insecure and cannot attack safely there. A target area is often a high traffic area. An attacker can't wait at the end of a dark alley for victims because very few would pass his way.

In the survey, women who left the target area with the attacker were taken to a vehicle (15.9 percent), a house or apartment (9.1 percent), a nearby secluded area (34.1 percent) or a far more secluded area (40.9 percent).

If the attacker is anxious to leave an area and you cannot escape the attacker immediately, use trickery. Remember, the attacker is in a hurry to accomplish his first objective, which is physical control. Make him believe he can meet this objective but **resist leaving the area** by claiming to want to comply right there. Act as though you are just as anxious as he is to have sex. Make up an excuse such as time: "We won't have time to do it if we don't do it right here." Then add a reason.

This is effective because you are not resisting him or the idea of his raping you. You are simply resisting leaving the area. This can buy you time and increase the chances of detection and interference in a high traffic area. In some cases, the attacker will flee because he can't safely drag a woman down the street. In other cases, the attacker may decide to carry out the rape right there. This is the time to use a physical last-resort technique, several of which are described in the last chapter.

In most cases, compliance does not guarantee protection for the victim. In fact, cooperation with a violent attacker can facilitate brutal murders and attacks that could not have been carried out if the victim had not helped the attacker meet his assault requirements. If the victim did not believe passivity would placate the attacker, she most certainly would not assist the attacker

or comply in any way.

The victim is usually so consumed by her own fear she rarely thinks about the fact that the attacker is taking a tremendous risk and has numerous fears to deal with, especially in the beginning stages of the attack. The attacker is afraid of detection and subsequent punishment. He fears physical harm. He fears the unexpected and committed resistance.

". . . the attacker is taking a tremendous risk and has numerous fears to deal with, especially in the beginning stages of the attack. The attacker is afraid of detection and subsequent punishment. He fears physical harm. He fears the unexpected and committed resistance."

Type of Rape

A. Nicholas Groth in *Men Who Rape: The Psychology of the Offender*, identifies three major categories or "attack styles" for rape.

1) **Anger rape** is characterized by physical brutality or "blitz attack." The attacker is discharging feelings of pent-up anger and rage.

2) **Power rape** is where the offender's goal is sexual conquest. He uses only the amount of force necessary to accomplish this objective.

3) **Sadistic rape** is a sexual transformation of anger and power so that aggression itself becomes eroticized.[3]

Anger rape is characterized by a "blitz attack." In some of the cases reported for this study, rape was not even a factor. A blitz attack is a sudden, brutal assault with the motive of discharging anger and frustration.

Power rape is characterized by methods of intimidation, primarily verbal threats and sometimes threats with weapons, to gain physical control in order to accomplish rape.

Groth states that power rape offenders entertain "obsessional thoughts and masturbatory fantasies about sexual conquest and rape."[4]

Rapists often have a mental or fantasy script in which everything must go a certain way for them to achieve any kind of satisfaction. Rapists have reported losing interest in carrying out an attack when the intended victim does not react according to the script. The script usually involves a female paralyzed with fear or succumbing sexually to the rapist.

"Rapists have reported losing interest in carrying out an attack when the intended victim does not react according to the script."

Recognition and awareness of this script could facilitate several effective defenses. If a woman is unable to resist immediately because of situational factors: i.e., weapons, sudden brutal attack, no immediate escape routes, being surprised at home while asleep, she could play into the script which would elicit the fantasy in which he is in control. In this way the element of surprise is preserved because the assailant is confident that she is no threat to him. When he is convinced he is safe, she can reinstitute the element of surprise and re-direct the dynamics of the assault situation to unbalance the attacker.

The issue in rape is the exercise of illusory power. If the rapist believes that he has the power and control, he has accomplished his goal. If resistance is immediate and effective, he never gains control. If resistance is delayed but the resistor is only going along until she can safely react, she must be convincingly non-threatening in order get and keep him off guard so the element of surprise can be reinstituted.

Rapists usually are convicted of crimes perpetrated on a random victim. However, as Groth says, these rapists have more offenses off the record than on and most of them have raped acquaintances ranging from casual to very close; i.e. common-law wife. Because women do not report social rape enough, men are rarely convicted or sent to prison for it, even though the experiences and consequences may be devastating for the victim. Because of this reality, Groth's rape categories more likely define random-attack rapists and situations.

It is important to note that the majority of rapists, both known assailants and random attackers, are power rapists. Any type of rape is emotionally and psychologically damaging, but as far as physical injury is concerned, this is least likely to happen on an extreme level in power-rape situations.

Groth says that a "characteristic fantasy scenario" of a power rapist may go like this.

". . . the victim initially resists her assailant, he overpowers her . . . in spite of herself, the victim becomes sexually aroused and receptive to his embrace."[5]

According to Groth, a power rapist

". . . does not feel reassured by either his own performance or his victim's response to the assault, and therefore, he must go out and find another victim, this time 'The right one!' His offenses become repetitive and compulsive, and he may commit a whole series of rapes over a relatively short period of time."[6]

Known-assailant power rapists will use threats, which are generally empty, and force; but they are mostly exploitive using situational advantages and the element of surprise. Groth clarifies the fantasy script of a power rapist which shows his vulnerability to trickery if escape in the initial encounter is impossible.

"Frequently the power rapist denies that the sexual encounter was forcible. He needs to believe the victim wanted and enjoyed it. Following the assault, he may insist on buying the victim a drink or dinner and express a wish to see her again."[7]

Sadistic rape is often the domain of the potential or actual serial murderer. According to experts of a number of disciplines, symbolic rebirth is the purpose of sadistic, serial murderers. The killer is reenacting his childhood pain and powerlessness usually at the hands of physically and emotionally abusive parents, or reenacting other instances of abuse by significant others.

In the August, 1984 issue of *Life* magazine, there is a comprehensive article called "An American Tragedy" by Brad Darrach and Dr. Joel Norris. The writers reported, "In every case the killer reenacted in his crime the disastrous experiences of his childhood with the roles reversed."[8] This reenactment accomplished "symbolic revenge" and reclaimed power and lost identity caused by suffering.

The interpretation of this act is further explained in the article, " . . . the killer made sure that he saw in his victim's eyes the same helpless terror that he himself had felt as a child. If he had screamed and pleaded for mercy, he tried to make his victim do the same. If he had felt castrated, he mutilated the private parts."

A "blitz" attack or a sadistic rape is likely to be the beginning act of a budding serial murderer. Famous rapists and rape murderers have reported beginning with relatively harmless acts such as "peeping tom" behaviors, exposing themselves and stealing articles of women's clothing, then graduating to high degrees of violence.

The violent acts were initially practiced on the weakest and most vulnerable victims the attacker could find, such as old women and very young girls. Convicted sadistic rapists and serial murderers Winston Mosely, Albert De Salvo and Ted Bundy all reported practicing or experimenting with various degrees of violence and assault then escalating the violence as they gained courage from success.[9]

After the Assault

According to the four-part study, women were most likely to report a stranger attack. This result was also found in Diana E. H. Russell's study. Over 50 percent reported that "significant others" among friends, family or authority figures like police and/or hospital personnel held them accountable or "blamed" them in some way for the occurrence of the attack.

"'Blaming the victim' is a reaction a person must be prepared to face. Accepting the blame is an entirely different matter."

"Blaming the victim" is a reaction a person must be prepared to face. **Accepting** the blame is an entirely different matter. Facing the injustice of blame may be difficult and painful but accepting the blame confers devastating consequences on quality of life and self-esteem. Women who did not accept the blame, regardless of the pressures to do so, regained psychological strength and often built increased self-esteem by aggressive coping mechanisms which promoted self-knowledge, awareness and social conciousness. Many of these women became active in the community, volunteering at rape crisis centers, finding women's groups and taking self-defense courses.

The interpretation of violence against women and using their fear as a form of social control may be an accurate definition of society's intent; however, today, "keeping women in their place" through fear may not be served. Yesterday's victim is today's survivor. For many women these experiences inspire a relentless new pursuit of the social forces that perpetuate violence rather than forcing women deeper into helplessness through fear.

The majority of women in this study experienced adverse psychological damage after the attack. Psychological damage includes reports of increased fear, mistrust of men in general, a decline in relationships and relationship quality, sexual dysfunction, insomnia and generalized anxiety.

One-fourth of the women in the random-attack section reported feeling, in retrospect, that they could have fought the attacker off physically. One-third of the women took a self-defense course after the attack. Over 50 percent reported they would have used physical self-defense techniques if they had known them.

In conclusion, many women revealed in many different ways that they had been defeated more by their own belief systems and femininity training than by the attacker. They realized their defeat happened prior to the attack. This realization contributed to their personal growth and internal revolution.

Part 3 Successful Resistance

Forty-three women in the survey reported "successful resistance." Successful resistance was essentially defined by each woman. If she resisted and escaped, even with injuries, but felt the outcome was preferable to her perceived outcome had she **not** resisted, then by her own definition she was a successful resistor.

The issue of physical resistance is an area fraught with fear, doubts and misconceptions about men, women and rape. Often the goal of many self-defense programs has been to encourage women to submit to rape to prevent serious injury. Women have been encouraged to tolerate groping, fondling and dominance touching so men won't be antagonized. In either case, women are presented with a choice based on theories proven to be erroneous: either submit to sexual abuse, or resist and risk beating or death.

In effect, these self-defense programs pretend to teach women to choose the lesser of two evils. What this seemingly logical approach fails to acknowledge is that compliance and submission do not ensure that the victim will not be harmed, raped or killed. They simply ensure that the attacker has chosen a good victim.

This approach fails dangerously to prevent rape/murder in which the victimizer nearly always elicits the victim's "trained" cooperation. It fails miserably in preventing rape by promoting fear of death and mutilation, which is a remote possibility. This fear is directly related to successful raping.

This type of thinking ignores a major point. Rape, even without outward physical injury, is extremely painful emotionally and psychologically. These wounds linger long after physical injuries heal. Remember that resistance is an intense commitment not to cooperate **unnecessarily** with someone who intends to harm you. This attitude cannot possibly increase your risks.

From the results of the survey, recent studies of resistance and the case histories of serial murderers and rapists, there is nothing to indicate that women's "over-reaction to attacks" or to intrusive groping behaviors result in rape and serious injury which otherwise would not have occurred. The decision to rape already exists in a rapist's mind, yet every man is not a rapist. Though rape is often planned by the individual rapist or a group of rapists, in many cases the selection of the victim is left to chance. In other cases, a rapist decides on a particular victim; however, the opportunity to trap his victim relies heavily on chance. The degree of violence and the attack style is a function of the rapist's motives - not the actions or reactions of his chosen victim. His opportunity to express a high degree of violence must be created by controlling situational factors and manipulating psychological factors.

Recent research has shown that the common social theories of rape and the dangers of resistance are largely erroneous.

There is **no** evidence that resistance results in death and mutilation that would not have otherwise occurred in a rape or assault situation. There **is** evidence that an immediate physical response is successful in terminating a rape or assault attempt.

The pathological insistence that the woman is responsible for the degree of violence in an assault situation and for precipitating behaviors that result in rape or assault is matched only by the persistent denial of responsibility for the degree of violence and shifting of the blame by convicted rapists. Warden of San Quentin Clinton Duffy explained that two-thirds of convicted rapists he knew denied guilt or claimed "she was asking for it" or they were "too drunk to remember."[1]

Because these rationalizations support society's dominant notions about rape and men and women, they are accepted as valid, if not excusable grounds for rape. As a result of often well-meaning but misguided assumptions about the dynamics of rape and resistance, women are instructed to conform to the round-eyed fear philosophy which is "Don't resist!" or "You'll really make him mad." The other, slightly more refined version of this theory is "Don't escalate" the degree of violence. Very few women need to be warned about over-reacting. Under-reacting is a much more widespread problem.

A man who is **not** a rapist will **not** be driven to rape by a woman who is verbally aggressive or physically assertive in dealing with an unwanted sexual advance. It is highly unlikely that a woman will become "inappropriately" aggressive at the slightest provocation.

Unless really pushed, a woman is likely to be polite to a fault. Studies have shown that women are more sensitive to social cues than men; they are skillful in correctly evaluating situations. Instead of self-defense instructors actively teaching women not to trust their superior ability to read social cues, these abilities should be stressed.

Greater sensitivity to social cues is reinforced by female socialization practices so there is still contention on how this appears and why. Nancy Henley, author of *Body Politics: Power, Sex and Non-Verbal Communication* says, "Greater social sensitivity itself may well be the special gift or burden of subordinates."[2] I feel women should capitalize on this ability and consider it a gift. It could serve as an equalizer and a survival advantage, physically and socially.

The only "proof" for the reason women are warned not to resist or to become aggressive in a confrontive situation comes from accounts given by rapists. I find it strange that rape is the only crime in which the criminals' rambling, self-serving, rationalizing accounts are blindly accepted.

"To prevent rape, women are expected to conform to the demands and expectations of the rapists. To prevent crimes against property, we're never told that if robbers encounter obstacles, they will only get angry and increase their efforts."

To prevent rape, women are expected to conform to the demands and expectations of the rapists. To prevent crimes against property, we're never told that if robbers encounter obstacles, they will only get angry and increase their efforts. Security measures, such as locked doors, are well-known deterrents in crimes against property.

The theory of "loss aversion" states that the fear of loss or failure is dominant over expectations of gain. The degree of difficulty in committing any crime creates fear of failure, detection, punishment and loss. Many will find disagreement with this because I'm comparing man-against-environment with man-against-woman. Yet according to psychologists, the process of decision-making is generally influenced more by fear of losses than expectation of gains.

I intend to see that violence against women will become extremely difficult to commit and get away with on a societal as well as individual level. If rapists are thwarted and exposed on every level, we can create a more intense fear of loss rather than the expectation of easy gain, which is the common experience of rapists to date.

"If rapists are thwarted and exposed on every level, we can create a more intense fear of loss rather than the expectation of easy gain, which is the common experience of rapists to date."

There is rarely socially sanctioned, open admiration expressed for an occasional or career rapist after his exposure and prosecution; although there is notoriety, fame and an obsessive interest in the details of such crimes and the offender. Rapists, primarily those offenders who have been caught, are held in contempt by other prisoners. In order for a convicted rapist to protect himself from retaliation by prison inmates and preserve an internal sense of rightness, he must distort the facts and/or deny them.

Often to support the theory that women must not and should not resist, interviews with rapists have been filmed and shown to audiences of women attempting to learn self-defense or in general media presentations. Some of these rapists openly admit "losing interest" when a woman resisted. Other rapists in these interviews often state that if a women resisted, they would beat her into submission. (This, of course, assumes that they could effectively control resistance, which will be far less likely as more facts are discovered and exposed.)

Imagine if convicted burglars smugly asserted that the public would be better off to stop using home security. Who would accept this as a reliable method to prevent further crime? It only makes sense that convicted rapists, who are still dominated by their desire to control women and express power through rape, have a motive for discouraging resistance.

The "escalation" theory or the "resistance will make him mad" theory is not based on any real facts or research. It is based only on the greatly exaggerated strength disparity between men and women and ignores all the other variables: situational - time and place; environmental - barriers and escape routes; and human factors - fear of failure, loss, detection and punishment.

When a disparity does **truly** exist, it is largely because men cultivate strength and physical fitness while women have not always done this as a matter of course. Men in our culture are expected to cultivate body strength and are rewarded for it by the definition of enhanced masculinity. Women are encouraged to cultivate weakness and are rewarded for it by the idea that it is a natural aspect of femininity.

Society is now in a transitional phase and is beginning to accept and encourage female strength. However, we can't allow society to set limits for women's strength, nor trust that once women begin to build strength they will remain positively "redefined" by society. Consider this:

53

why must women be subject to continous redefinition anyway?

The social tendency to blame the victim is one explanation as to why rape often goes unpunished and why victims are reluctant to report. An additional complication is society's well-defined guidelines for **females** to prevent getting raped; yet there are few controls or responsibilities to discourage men from raping.

Mode and Circumstances of Attack

A weapon was present in about one-third of the cases. Gang attacks with two or more attackers represented approximately 14 percent. These percentages were not radically different than the other groups in which resistance was not successful. Successful resistors were attacked in a familiar area or their own home with almost the same frequency as assault victims. In many cases these women reported using a familiar environment to their advantage, even though they were caught off guard in a "safe" situation. Successful resistors quickly recovered from the initial shock and realized that familiarity with the surroundings was a definite advantage.

Resistor's Reaction to Attack

Successful resistors were more likely to be able to recall the angle of approach and attack, although they were 10 percent less likely to have seen the attacker before he approached in a stranger-assault situation. Of the successful resistors assaulted by strangers who **did** see the attackers before they approached, a higher number felt apprehension prior to the attack than in random-attack situations in which the assault was completed.

Successful resistors reported less panic as a reaction to the attack than the other groups, which is probably a demonstration of their prior preparation or experience, either physical or mental. Forty percent of successful resistors had prior self-defense

training, which was the highest degree of such preparation reported in this survey.

This group was **more likely to use physical resistance** and **less likely to attempt to talk** the attacker out of raping or assaulting them. This outcome corresponds with Bart's study of victims and avoiders in which pleading was correlated with a higher incidence of completed rape than the other strategies.

Successful resistors suffered the fewest "extreme consequences," which were defined as a high degree of physical injury, termination of an important relationship, being fired from a job or changing a residence as a result of the attack. The aftereffects of successful resistance are healthier psychologically than victimization. The ability to control outcomes is a powerful component of self-esteem.

"The aftereffects of successful resistance are healthier psychologically than victimization. The ability to control outcomes is a powerful component of self-esteem."

Successful resistors faced more weapons than the known-assailant rape or assault group, although fewer than with stranger rape. The number of gang attacks in successful resistance stories is comparable to the other three groups. According to McIntyre's 1981 research, a weapon decreases but does not eliminate the possibility of escape. From the results of this survey, the presence of multiple attackers does not eliminate the possibility of escape either.

A higher level of awareness at the time of the attack seemed to be the major difference between successful resistors and the other three groups of known-assailant rape, stranger rape and assault. Successful resistors were more likely to recall the angle of approach and attack. They were less likely to panic and they were more likely to physically resist **immediately** and not attempt to talk first, even though they faced similar circumstances and attack methods as the other groups.

A 1976 study by the Queens Bench Foundation identified another difference in successful resistors. Victims were primarily concerned with survival and death; those who escaped victimization considered methods of resistance and were concerned with thwarting an attack. This finding surfaced again in Pauline Barts' research. It is essential to stress that the probability of death in a rape or assault situation is extremely low. Susan Brownmiller speculatively calculated the reported incidences of rape and rape/murder multiplied by the unreported incidences of rape and found the occurrence of murder in conjunction with rape would be less than two percent.

Current research has estimated that anywhere from 3.5 to 10 percent of rape is reported. This means the actual incidents of rape/murder, calculated with the actual number of rapes, would be infinitesimal. (U.S. Census Bureau, FBI, National Opinion Research Center)

In my study, successful resistors were more likely to have had prior self-defense training than the other groups. The prior self-defense training may be directly related to the subject's reaction to the attack. A woman who has taken a physical defense course is likely to be aware that increased knowledge, physical defenses and realistic preparation are not factors that increase the probability of violence or increased injury in the event of an attack.

There is definitely a strangely twisted, superstitious application of "logic" applied right across the board for women's self-defense. Successful resistors applied **real** logic and faced the facts; an event cannot be prevented by denying the possibility that it might occur, and negative outcomes cannot be reversed by failing to prepare.

After the Attack

Successful resistors were most likely to take a self-defense course after the attack. It appears women were less likely to engage in denial and more likely to confront their fears. They were more likely to believe in the effectiveness of physical self-defense which is also a demonstration of faith in themselves and their own physical integrity and ability.

Women who reported adverse psychological effects, defined as increased fear, anxiety, insomnia, decline in quality of relationships, mistrust of men in general, and sexual dysfunctions, were comparable to the other groups. It appears that emotional trauma after an attack was evaluated as highly adverse even if the escape was successful, even though these subjects were not as likely to be judged negatively by "significant others."

Successful resistors were more likely to report the attack than known-assailant rape victims or assault victims. Indirectly, this may indicate that the subject feels more credible, which demonstrates a better post attack self-image than was found in the other groups.

"... however, from this data, it appears that the prejudicial belief that rape victims caused the rape or wanted to be raped is still prevalent."

The number of successful resistors who reported being blamed for the attack was significantly lower than random rapes and known-assailant rapes. The number of women blamed for the attack was lowest in assaults. It is interesting to note that the women in these two groups **were not raped** and therefore were less likely to be blamed. Social attitudes towards rape **have** changed and "rape mythology" is slowly being exposed; however, from this data, it appears that the prejudicial belief that rape victims **caused** the rape or **wanted** to be raped is still prevalent.

Max Lerner, a prominent social psychologist, defines a theory related to the above mentioned phenomenon of "blaming the victim." Lerner's "just world" theory states, ". . . Most people tend to believe that justice triumphs in the world and that people get the rewards and punishments they deserve."[3]

If a woman has been raped, she is more likely to be blamed. If she has been badly beaten but not raped, she is less likely to be held responsible. Apparently society finds it difficult to believe a woman would "provoke" a random assault, yet this is still commonly believed about rape. The women who **were** blamed in assaults were likely to have been assaulted by someone to whom they were related or with whom they were involved.

"Although women frequently are warned not to resist, society demands evidence that a woman resisted in order to absolve her of blame or to arrest and convict the attacker."

A woman who was successful in resisting demonstrated by her escape that she did not **want** to be raped. Although women frequently are warned **not** to resist, society demands evidence that a woman resisted in order to absolve her of blame or to arrest and convict the attacker. In 1975, the rape law that demanded corroboration of resistance was dropped in forty states. Yet injuries still demonstrate proof of forcible rape and an unwilling victim. Many women are not aware of legal changes or even if they are, they feel more confident and are more likely to report if they can show evidence of resistance or injuries.

In one successful resistance case, a woman was subjected to a knife attack by a man who lived in the neighborhood. She had previous martial arts training and was prepared to use situational advantages. The assailant entered her residence through an unlocked door and pulled a knife on her. She quickly stepped behind a table to put something between the assailant and herself. Then she shoved the table into the attacker, pinning his arms briefly and used this opportunity to run. She called the police and they arrived to question her.

After recounting the incident, one of the police officers told her she would have difficulty proving the attack took place. His exact words as quoted to me were, "It would have been better if he had cut you." This example is not meant to negatively reflect on police officers but to indicate society's beliefs and the requirements of the law in some states.

Women are warned not to resist and are socialized not to be capable of effective resistance. This creates a double bind. After the fact, an incident is not considered rape unless the woman can prove she resisted. In other cases, even though the law no longer demands such proof, an assault or rape is not considered valid if the woman shows no evidence of injury.

The "just world" theory fits in well with the finding of decreased blame in success stories. Psychologically, it is much more difficult to deal with a victim than with a "winner." We must search for the reasons the person was victimized and as a result negative inferences must be made about the victim or the victim's behavior. "Winners" are much easier to deal with because they do not frighten us in the way that a victim does. A "winner" was able to control the outcome of a situation in the way we need to believe we can control the outcome of events in our own lives.

In *Men On Rape* by Timothy Beneke, two lawyers clearly demonstrate belief in the "just world," in "blaming the victim" theories and in the idea that society has well-defined guidelines for women to prevent "getting themselves" raped. One deputy D.A. said, "If a woman goes to a singles' bar and she only **wants** to go so far, she better have some collaboration as far as I'm concerned before she says so-and-so raped me. . . When you get into your social settings and dating situations, your outrage is diminished by the preparation and the situation in which the woman has voluntarily placed herself."[4]

This statement basically condones "open season" on females who are voluntarily interacting with men and especially those who are foolish enough to trust **any** man. A woman engaging in voluntary social interaction with men in any situation is **not** asking to be raped, she is merely exercising social freedom and fulfilling her human need for social interaction. It will take time to change these social prejudices. In the meantime, develop a firm sense of what you believe and act accordingly. Do what successful resistors did; fight, flee, use trickery or bargaining. They were able to resist in time because they were sure of themselves, their intentions and their rights. No matter **where** you are, if someone physically restrains, abuses or attacks you, resist and escape as soon as possible.

"A woman engaging in voluntary social interaction with men in any situation is not asking to be raped, she is merely exercising social freedom and fulfilling her human need for social interaction."

Another lawyer said, "If I could get my client off by appealing to the jury's sexism, I probably would."[5] Exploitation of sexism and social belief systems help provide "emotional loopholes" by subjectively affecting the prejudices and morals of the judge and jury. The victim's defense can be penetrated and destroyed,

especially since **she** may be influenced by these belief systems.

These social and internalized beliefs and morals are often the major reason women fail to report rape. Women expect to be blamed for rape; they expect to have their actions and intentions questioned and their characters derogated.

"If you are afraid to attack the rapist physically, attack the environment."

As previously mentioned, successful resistors were more likely to report. This may be because they **demonstrated** unwillingness and so felt more confident that they would be believed. If a rape victim or successful resistor is unruffled or uninjured, **she** will arouse suspicion during reporting. Several women in my survey reported the police said things like "Why aren't you hysterical?" and "You don't **look** like a woman who's just been raped." If you are afraid to attack the rapist physically, attack the environment. At least you can "prove" you resisted without increasing your chances of injury if that is how you perceive the situation.

Successful resistors reported a high degree of "psychological damage" yet this is an entirely subjective question (as were many of the survey questions). Several other outcomes reported by successful resistors suggested that these women recovered faster and had a healthier outlook after resisting successfully than women who did not. Engaging in coping behaviors and demonstrating coping skills is a healthy attitude and outcome. Even though this group reported a high degree of psychological damage, their coping skills became apparent with the high number who stated they would **not** panic if a similar situation occurred again. Less than 20 percent of successful resistors said they believe they would panic if a similar situation occurred now. After the initial emotional and physical shock, successful resistors got angry. This is far healthier than withdrawing in fear and making negative judgments about yourself. These women knew the attack was unwarranted and did not blame themselves as much as women who were raped did.

Prior to the attack, the successful resistors reported perceiving a threat sooner, demonstrated a higher degree of awareness and had prior physical self-defense training. During the attack, successful resistors reported panicking less frequently and resisting **immediately** and **physically** by fleeing or fighting and yelling. Reacting quickly is the key to successful resistance. The idea of "reacting quickly" does not always mean reacting physically. It means thinking fast and determining whether or not immediate physical resistance is safe. Successful resistors faced weapons and multiple attackers, and in some cases their reaction was **not to react**. They retained mental control and therefore created the opportunity to escape or defend.

After the attack, successful resistors were less likely to be blamed by "significant others" and authority figures, although they were likely to report to the police.

Women who were successful resistors used another coping strategy with the highest degree of frequency: they were more likely to take self-defense courses after the attack.

"Some women vehemently stated they would 'fight to the death' if they were ever attacked again. It is important to note that no woman who reported successful resistance expressed regret for her actions."

I did not specifically ask women if they regretted their reaction whether they choose resistance or submission. However, without prompting, many women I interviewed who were raped or assaulted, voluntarily stated they wished they would have resisted because later evaluation revealed many viable options and possibilities. Some women vehemently stated they would "fight to the death" if they were ever attacked again. It is important to note that **no** woman who reported successful resistance expressed regret for her actions.

Part 4 Assaults

"Assault" was defined in this survey as a violent physical attack apparently without the motive to commit sexual violence. The attackers were both known assailants and strangers. Assaults comprised the smallest of all four groups with a total of nineteen subjects.

Mode of Operation

The women in the assault group reported attack from behind in almost 89 percent of the cases. The attacker approached from the side in 11 percent of the cases. In both the angle of approach and low number of subjects who saw the attacker before he approached, there were fewer situational advantages present in random-assault situations than in the other groups. Another decrease in situational advantages was in the number of assailants who spoke to the victim prior to attacking. In the assault group, only about 22 percent of the attackers tested or targeted the victim verbally before attacking.

In assault data, the subjects were attacked in a familiar area approximately 89 percent of the time. The women reported that the assault occurred in their own home 50 percent of the time. Both of these figures are higher than the other groups.

Attack in the home or familiar area can be an advantage if there is negotiating time.

In assaults, the attack generally occurs without warning so the home or familiar area could be a disadvantage because the person is off-guard or lulled by the apparent security of the environment.

A weapon was present in a low number of cases at approximately 16 percent. Gang attacks were lowest of all groups at 10.5 percent. Many of the survey questions did not apply in assault situations for several reasons. In a sudden assault, many subjects could not recall specific information such as mode of restraint. This is because an assault is likely to be a "blitz attack." In these cases the suddenness and brutality of the attacks were sufficient to confuse and subdue the victim. The "element of surprise" is real, yet it can be neutralized by awareness: preparedness, knowledge of options, inexpensive security "tricks" and the body's natural wisdom of "correct response."

Victim Reaction to Assault

In a sudden brutal attack there is rarely time for negotiating or any interaction attempts. In the assault group approximately 22 percent of the women reported trying to outsmart the attacker and figure out his "frame of mind." Thirty-seven percent reported cooperating with the attacker in the belief they would not be harmed further. Of those who cooperated, 40 percent said they did not feel cooperation saved them from further harm.

"All of the women who reported feeling apprehension said that apprehension could have saved them if they had heeded it."

A smaller number in this group reported seeing the attacker before they were approached than the other three groups, yet of those who did, 50 percent reported feeling apprehension. A high degree of apprehension was experienced by the women in this group in the cases where the attacker was seen before he approached. All of the women who reported feeling apprehension said that apprehension could have saved them if they had heeded it.

This was the highest reported "apprehension would have saved if heeded" response of all groups. It may be the attackers in other groups were far more subtle in the attack and approach. The attackers who were observed by the victim before attack in the assault group may have exhibited more bizarre and recognizable antisocial behavior immediately before attacking. I think we have all been witness to antisocial public behavior and felt apprehension but not taken any steps to prepare to defend or escape.

Ambiguity Prevents Reaction

In American society, we tolerate public displays of violent, antisocial behavior. People roam the streets in every large city shouting obscenities and exhibiting bizarre behaviors. Social psychologists have found that any factor that creates ambiguity inhibits effective action. Ambiguity could be created in a pre-assault or rape situation precisely because we have witnessed antisocial behavior in the past and did not become the target of the individual displaying the behavior. People do not like to "overreact" or show fear if it is **not clear** that it is "appropriate" to do so.

Although some of the attackers exhibited violent, antisocial behavior before attacking, the others sneaked up on the victim giving no prior warning.

Resistance Strategies

Fewer resistance strategies were used by this group. This may be related to the sudden attack style. In an assault situation, I have several suggestions based on the accounts of the women in my study and the current research on effective resistance. Running is the number one option. Most of the women were so shocked they only cowered under the blows. The assailant was not mollified by submission, in some cases the attacker became more vicious. If the initial encounter is punches and blows and you remain conscious after the first blow (only one woman in the entire study reported unconciousness at the first blow), and you are not being restrained, you must run immediately and make as much noise as possible or try an "incapacitating" technique. My definition of incapacitation is any blow that will buy 10 seconds to several minutes. If you are covering while trying to protect yourself from blows, try to grab, pull and twist the attacker's testicles. If you are in close, jam a knee lift as hard as you can, even several times, into his groin. You may also be able to do several instep stomps to slow him down while you escape. If you can put a few feet between you, use the knee stomp kick. If you have anything in your hands (purse, packages, grocery bag), shove it upwards into his face. As he lurches backwards, knee lift his groin.

"The first suggestion in a random- or known-assailant assault that begins with blows is to run and make noise, the second is to attempt to slow him down with pain or temporary incapacitation, then run and make noise."

The first suggestion in a random- or known-assailant assault that begins with blows is to run and make noise, the second is to attempt to slow him down with pain or temporary incapacitation, then run and make noise.

The Nature of Assault

Violent attacks on women, without additional motive such as robbery or rape, are a social problem related to gender socialization. Today's society is in the midst of a social transition; the clearly defined male and female roles no longer apply to the general population. Although women have always been subjected to physical violence, I have recently noticed a consistent resurgence of an old justification which I call the "surrogate victim theory." Current research has shown that rapists are likely to have been victims of child abuse. Serial murderers are recounting abusive childhoods. This is a contributing factor, but it surely cannot be the only cause. Women are equally at the mercy of abusive parents, yet no female murderer fits the profile of a "recreational" killer or rapist. The "surrogate victim" theory is a veiled warning, a slap on the wrist to warn women that they are responsible for socially deviant males. They either raised them, married them or somehow incited their rage. Men who commit these assaults and murders, almost without fail, recount some incident of "abuse" by a woman. The wife or girlfriend walked out on them, or their mother or aunt abused them emotionally or physically. Rape is viewed, at least by some, as a goal-oriented crime. Random savagery is harder to understand, so we search for "reasons" and end up blaming the victim directly, or indirectly by blaming someone who resembles the victim, primarily because of gender. This is the basis of the "surrogate victim" theory.

"The 'surrogate victim' theory is a veiled warning, a slap on the wrist to warn women that they are responsible for socially deviant males. They either raised them, married them or somehow incited their rage."

Women who were victims of a random assault reported a common subjective reaction that often prevented them from running or physically defending. Their first reaction was that the assailant had mistaken them for someone else. These women often attempted verbally or non-verbally to make the assailant "see" he had the wrong woman. You must realize that an immense amount of damage can be done in a few moments of blows delivered by an enraged attacker. Don't waste one precious second trying to communicate anything to such an attacker.

"These women often attempted verbally or non-verbally to make the assailant 'see' he had the wrong woman. You must realize that an immense amount of damage can be done in a few moments of blows delivered by an enraged attacker. Don't waste one precious second trying to communicate anything to such an attacker."

Options are in this order: 1) Escape immediately; 2) Create distance and strike a vital area to slow him down; 3) Stay in close and strike a vital area, then escape; and 4) If possible, incapacitate the attacker, then escape. These rules apply in a known-assailant assault or a random assault. An immediate physical reaction is often the only option for a sudden physical assault. A physical reaction does not mean retaliation. It means either running or, if necessary, creating time by inflicting momentary pain and shock on the attacker, and then running.

In sum, the major difference in the assault group was the sudden attack style. In a "blitz attack" there are often few prior warnings such as a verbal approach or the visual advantage of seeing the attacker before the approach. A high degree of apprehension was reported by women who **did** see the attacker before he approached; however, situational ambiguity prevented the women from reacting in time to escape.

Attack Deterrents

I have met brave women who are exploring the outer edge of human possibility, with no history to guide them, and with a courage to make themselves vulnerable that I find moving beyond words.
Gloria Steinem

Chapter IV

Attack Deterrents

Guidelines for **avoiding** rape take up a large portion of various women's self-defense publications, pamphlets, presentations and seminars. These voluminous lists of rules serve several purposes. They make the reader or the participant feel as if she can control events by performing compulsive rituals.

The process of compulsively using "avoidance" as a defense against any type of perceived negative event is one symptom of neurosis. Neurotic defenses stem from general difficulty in coping with life's problems and feelings of inadequacy. This describes the general attitudes of any instructor who stresses avoidance rules.

Such an instructor perceives women as inadequate and unable to cope in more effective ways. A woman who is susceptible to these beliefs is usually suffering from low self-esteem and a generalized belief that she deserves punishment if she breaks a social rule such as going out alone at night.

Each time a violent crime occurs, an avoidance specialist examines all the details determined to discover how the victim brought the attack on her/or himself. A person who is a strong believer in avoidance rules is also a skillful victim blamer.

Psychologists say avoidance would be a good tactic if it worked. Unfortunately, avoidance is based on the idea that you control and change your activities without addressing the need for altering your own attitudes and without preparing to cope on a more effective level with the actual problem you are attempting to avoid.

The quote in the first chapter, "Men do not rape their equals," is a basic focal point in my efforts to communicate the values of self-defense to women. This statement could be misinterpreted as being dangerously close to blaming the victim or stating that women are unequal and are therefore victim material. The point the statement is actually trying to make is that through socialization, men and women are taught certain behaviors in accordance with their respective genders. Women are taught socially subordinate behaviors and are rewarded for them. Males learn through **their** socialization to expect subordinate behavior from women and most are shocked, insulted or even outraged when women fail to behave as sex roles dictate.

To react as an honest person without conforming to sex role expectations is not a simple matter of knowing how social interaction works. Many factors are involved, a few of which I'll cover briefly, which inhibit women and prevent them from exercising all their social options. Social interaction factors or dynamics pressure women into playing subordinate roles. These types of inhibitors were explained in one study by Mark Snyder and William B. Swann entitled "Behavioral Confirmation in Social Interaction: From Social Perception to Social Reality." The researchers state, "A perceiver's actions, although based upon initially erroneous beliefs about a target individual, may channel social interaction in ways that cause the behavior of the target to confirm the perceiver's beliefs."[1]

There are other factors in social control and influence. One factor is obedience by forceful verbal demand in which persons, even those lacking authority, can induce submission from others. In one study of obedience and social influence by researchers M.E. Shanab and K.A. Yahya, it was revealed that " . . . the most direct technique that one person can use to modify the behavior of another is that of simply ordering him or her to obey."[2]

Powerful and effective communication is created by actions; it is not determined by gender.

The idea of a "self-fulfilling prophecy" is that social labeling and categorization can produce expected behaviors or alter an individual's self image. In *The Psychology of Being Human,* authors Elton B. McNiel and Zick Rubin use the following example. "If a man is labeled 'schizophrenic,' it is likely that he will develop the behaviors associated with schizophrenic cases - even if he did not have them at first. Being told he is schizophrenic causes the individual to perceive himself as such, while his therapist and family may unconsciously treat him in such a way that brings out their expectations."[3]

Personally held beliefs can also influence the outcome of events or social interaction. These factors can work against a person who is making an effort to change his or her behavior. However, if you are aware of these interaction determinants, you can at least know **why** you might fail at times.

High- and low-status communications should be identified so that women can communicate effectively as equals rather than subordinates. A subordinate position is a function of many variables and is appropriate in certain situations. Subordinate behavior should not be assumed as a characteristic of females nor should it be expected of them.

The best example of situational, subordinate demand behavior is the ranking system in the military where firm rules determine the behavior of subordinates to their superior officers. These rules are built essentially on the same foundation as all subordinate behavior. In some circumstances, these modes of communication are appropriate, as in situations involving students and teachers or parents and children; but certainly women should not be automatically relegated to the role of subordinate due entirely to their gender.

These specific examples of dominant and subordinate behaviors occur during everyday social interaction and exist between employers and employees, husbands and wives, siblings, peer groups, and so on. As you look over this list, try to identify situations in which you have found yourself displaying the subordinate behaviors.

Was it really necessary for you to demonstrate lower status than the person you were with? Was it an automatic learned behavior? Were you pressured by social expectations?

High- and Low-Status Communications

Speech

1. Non-reciprocal terms of formal title

- Low-status speaker is addressed informally.

- High-status speaker is addressed by titles (Doctor, Professor) and pronouns (Mr., Mrs., Ms., Sir).

If you feel uncomfortable with non-reciprocal usage, insist on being addressed formally as Ms. or Mrs., even if you have no other title. Every adult, regardless of social status, has a right to be addressed as he or she wishes.

2. Imposed silence or speech demand

- Silence is imposed on low-status communicators. They are also under demand to respond when spoken to by superiors.

- Dominant communicators exercise freer choice including interrupting, verbal bullying and contradicting.

Numerous studies have shown that in mixed groups, men talk more, interrupt women frequently, override women's attempts to speak, and extinguish topics introduced by women by a brief silence and then immediately changing the subject. Why is there a social myth that women talk more than men? Probably because it is unusual for women to succeed in mixed gender conversations, so when they get together, their need to communicate is intensified and concentrated.

3. Speech style

- Subordinate speakers are hesitant and self-disparaging, full of qualifying phrases such as, "I'm not too sure about this, but . . "

- Dominant speakers use declarative sentences and are firm and assertive in their delivery.

The subordinate-speaking style shows social insecurity.

Touch

- Social subordinates do not use touch frequently as a method of communication, and especially not with social superiors. For example, a person would be more likely to touch a child than his or hersupervisor or employer.

- High status people are less likely to be touched, except by their peers, and use touch more freely with subordinates. For example, men touch women more frequently than women touch men; older people touch younger people more frequently.

- Dominance as a **personality trait** is also related to more frequent use of touch as a method of communication. This personality trait can be developed through increased self-esteem because touching can be a true means of communicating caring and closeness. Touch is not always intended as a way to show social dominance. It may be simply a means of personal communication.

Demeanor

- High-status communicators are relaxed and informal in their demeanor. They retain more flexibility in their mode of dress. Even though they are relaxed, they generally stand tall and move assertively with better over-all posture.

- Restricted movement and tension is characteristic of lower status communicators. Tense postures are indicative of submissive attitudes. A low-status communicator is always "on guard" not to offend anyone by casual attitudes and attempting to look as if he or she is alert and ready to take orders.

- Women move in more restricted ways than men and hold their bodies in tenser postures. They are also more careful of how they dress. Women do not generally sit or stand in "undignified" positions, which are common male postures and generally more comfortable, or lounge around without regard to how they look. Women have been taught to deliberately arrange their bodies in the most appealing postures.

Personal Space

- Dominant communicators make use of more personal space which makes them hard to approach casually. However, they approach subordinates closely. They use more flamboyant gestures because their personal space "bubble" is larger.

- Submissive communicators take up less physical space and even shrink that space in the presence of dominant communicators. They are crowded more easily, their personal space is more easily invaded, and when approached by a dominant communicator, submissive communicators move or get out of the way.

- Although I promote assertive communication on every level, there may be one slight inconsistency. I suggest that women **create space** and **maintain distance** as a method of self-defense. In some cases, this may seem like subordinate communication, but it is actually dominant communication. If you are maintaining greater personal space and create distance when you feel it's necessary **before** you are forced to give up space or move when approached, **you are in control** of

space and the power space implies.

Many aspects of communication which signal social dominance or subordination are not covered in this brief outline. More aspects, which will be covered in a little more detail later, are specific problems of male/female interaction reflected in demeanor, conversational patterns, eye contact behaviors, personal space and restrictive clothing.

Social Self-Defense

Now that some of the elements of high- and low-status communications have been introduced, we can examine some of the related issues in depth. Nancy Henley, author of *Body Politics: Sex, Power and Non-Verbal Communication,* presents an important consideration: non-verbal communication is a mechanism, not a cause of prejudice. Henley states that unless prejudice is eliminated at its roots, retraining women to be non-verbally assertive will result in their being negatively evaluated as "castrating bitches."[4] I've always said that worse things could happen to you than being called a bitch, although Henley's point is well-taken.

It is important to stress that any behavior whether submissive, seductive, assertive, even aggressively angry is appropriate in some contexts but not in others. The term "castrating bitch" implies that women are required to stay carefully within the boundaries of sexually appealing behavior. This behavior will not be effective for many situations. A woman will lose ground in business or all forms of negotiation if she attempts to conform to standards of sexually appealing behavior.

If a "castrating bitch" can get the job done, she may have to resort to behaviors that may inspire this label or get a man to do the job for her, which is an undesirable, socially unproductive solution. When female assertion is commonly seen, supported and not sabotaged, it will be respected because assertive behavior is effective. Nothing inspires respect like effectiveness.

Behaviors and reactions should be **situationally appropriate**; this is the key to effective social interaction.

The popular contention that women communicate weakness and inadequacy by their non-verbal behavior and become victims also concerns Ms. Henley. Concentrating on non-verbal behaviors or asserting that women should change these behaviors dangerously borders on "blaming the victim" and "victim analysis." "Victim analysis" is an obsessive concern with the presumed defects and personality problems of the victimized.

Although I focus on non-verbal behavior as a means to change non-verbal messages and to project more power, I do not claim nor secretly believe that women's behaviors are the cause of violence or the source of social inequality. I contend that women are socialized to exaggerate vulnerability and weakness through their non-verbal and verbal behaviors. These behaviors make them appear to be easy targets for victimization.

Changing these behaviors will not eradicate male rage nor the foundations of a society that breeds this rage. It will, however, make women feel more in control and improve communication. It will also eradicate submissive signals in that individual, thereby decreasing the possibility that she will be targeted as a "victim type."

Women are not the only easy targets for victimization. Any vulnerable target is game when forced subordination and domination are equated with eroticism. This is why child molestation is so common. The best hope to prevent such violence is the latest development in child abuse prevention.

Today's children are taught that their bodies are their own and no one has the right to touch them. This will make sexual abuse and violence increasingly less attractive and more difficult to commit

because the ability to commit violence is countered by belief in the ability to resist and refuse with force. Children are being taught from the start that they have physical rights and they are supported by society in exercising those rights. That belief itself lends power to refusal.

Today's woman is living in the midst of this social transition. Few of us were encouraged to be physically or verbally assertive. One of the best answers to the problem of the negative evaluation of "bitch" for a woman's assertive behavior is found in Toni Scalia's book, *Bitches and Abdicators*. Her solution is to positively redefine the meaning of "bitch." I propose examination of non-verbal behaviors and assertiveness because a woman must develop a personal foundation to express free choice and independence. This foundation is built on small successes which lead to larger personal and social gains.

Seemingly small changes such as non-verbal and verbal assertiveness contribute to numerous small successes in the way a woman influences others and reflects her effectiveness and self image. On a personal level this makes a big difference.

"Today's woman is the role model for the next generation. Perhaps today's small changes will lead to tomorrow's social revolution."

Today's woman is the role model for the next generation. Perhaps today's small changes will lead to tomorrow's social revolution. Sex role socialization is the root cause of social and economic inequality of females and of most violent behavior in males.

Certain behaviors are consistently encouraged, rewarded and attributed to women. The "reasons" women are not influential and are not taken seriously are

69

inherent in the definitions of femininity. A leader or self-motivated individual cannot avoid assertive behavior nor always defer to others' opinions or authority. One must pursue answers through research and seek solutions and information. Knowledge is power. Power influences and power is communicated by firm assurance - not by contrived behaviors.

Henley makes another essential point in reference to non-verbal behavior. " . . . Such behavior, when it exists, is not simply emitted by one participant. Rather, it is cued by others' behavior, in an interactive process. Moreover, this cueing process accomplishes more than simple discrimination. . . It is an education and affirmation process for both parties."[5] This is an example of the self-fulfilling prophecy and the social-confirmation process mentioned earlier. You may try to express yourself and be subjected to intense taming campaigns from other communicators, males as well as females, who are threatened by this kind of honesty or who resent a woman who has the "gall" to act as if she were not a subordinate but rather the social equal of anyone she meets.

Many women are afraid to express social equality and they aren't even aware of it. It is painful but true that women who aren't ready to be socially equal will assist males in taming those women who do act assertively, thus earning themselves subordinate "brownie points" with men.

It is very important to remember that there will be social obstacles to breaking out of the defined, yet ambiguous role cast for you as a woman.

"It is very important to remember that there will be social obstacles to breaking out of the defined, yet ambiguous role cast for you as a woman."

Many women project a powerful non-

verbal presence. They do not wear confining clothing nor display constant submissive postures or behaviors. Yet, in interaction with others, roles are cast which will place a woman in subordinate positions. This may be a largely unconscious process, yet it reflects the deepest beliefs of a group. As women interact with others and are humored, ignored, interrupted and negated, they begin to feel invisible and inconsequential. In fact, this feeling is reinforced by the group's behavior. Even when a woman appears to participate in group conversations and interaction, this is often an illusion. As I have said, studies of conversational styles have shown that males interrupt females more often than they interrupt other males and more often than females interrupt either males or females.

Many researchers on social interaction define power as something created in an interaction, not as an attribute of an individual. Mary Brown Parley in an article in *Psychology Today* magazine, writes, "The person who interrupts is creating and exercising power by violating the other's right to speak."[6]

Topics that failed or succeeded is another important aspect of conversational politics covered in Parley's article and was demonstrated by Fishman's study. The topics men introduced succeeded 96 percent of the time and topics introduced by women succeeded only 36 percent of the time. Over-all, women introduced more topics, 62 percent, and put more effort into keeping the conversation going even though their topics were dropped or ignored. Women asked nearly three times the number of questions that men did. This was both a strategy to keep the conversation going and a method to increase their chances of success in introducing topics. It was found that men "killed" topics introduced by women through a minimal response or silence after she finished speaking.[7] A woman may appear to be as verbally involved as a man in a conversation but may suffer repeated

70

failures and rejection.

These behaviors serve as "cues" that place women in subordinate positions where they have very little control over the direction of the interaction or of the topics discussed. This feeling of lack of control and social negation may serve to reinforce what she has continuously experienced in social interaction. In order to continue with the interaction, a woman must take the conversational leads provided by men and jump into the female role of asking questions in order to remain involved. So here we are again: nodding, looking interested, drawing the male out and bolstering up his ego again. No wonder submissive posturing is right around the corner.

A woman may not even be "emitting" submissive social cues, but she is in danger of being misread for a number of reasons. For one, men are not as sensitive to non-verbal cues as women are. In addition, because women are usually smaller, or make every attempt to look smaller, they are more likely to be encroached on by both sexes. Because women appear less threatening, a person is unlikely to give much thought before entering their "intimate zone," especially if that person is male.

Women have another problem with non-verbal behavior. Threatening non-verbal signals or simply signals that say "I'm not approachable right now" will be read differently when performed by a woman than a man. Men thrust their chests out to display aggression; a woman who does this may be thought to be putting on a sexual display. Men spread their legs both standing and sitting; this is considered "sexually aggressive" non-verbal behavior when a woman does it.

With all the inconsistencies and drawbacks of non-verbal behaviors, a woman must seriously consider these behaviors in order to communicate more effectively. All behaviors should be situationally appropropriate. "Courting" signals which are performed by males and

females alike should be reserved for these situations alone. A woman is not under obligation to court the world, even though she has been socialized to do this.

"A woman is not under obligation to court the world, even though she has been socialized to do this."

A woman must make a concerted effort to alter certain non-verbal behaviors that signal helplessness, such as rounded, slumped shoulders, especially when the shoulders invert towards the chest. Another submissive signal is "pigeon toeing;" that is observed as a courtship signal that both men and women perform and which also happens when a woman feels threatened. When you stand or sit, keep your feet from rotating in unless you are in a "courtship" situation and not alone or at risk.

Submissive Posturing and Space Requirements

Non-verbal communication and behavior have received superficial attention in the last few years with the advent of the "body language" fad. "Body language" hardly describes the pervasive implications of non-verbal communication.

Non-verbal communication involves posturing and movements, physical space requirements, allowed proximity, touching behaviors and eye contact. It is not an unusual reaction to become uncomfortable when touching behaviors and other forms of non-verbal communication are discussed because people prefer to believe touching behaviors are totally a function of personal preference. Research has shown, however, that these behaviors go beyond interpersonal preferences; there is a social power structure that controls space, touch, eye contact and styles of movement.

Non-verbal behaviors are extremely important to examine in your quest for your

71

right of physical and social freedom - the **bottom line** of self-defense for women. If our non-verbal behavior is radically different from our internal beliefs and our verbal assertations, we will be continally misread and forever frustrated in our attempts to communicate effectively.

"Non-verbal behaviors are extremely important to examine in your quest for your right of physical and social freedom - the bottom line of self-defense for women."

Women have been trained in submissive posturing. Look at fashion models and observe the one major similarity. The aura of vulnerability is sold as skillfully as the product represented. Strong female imagery is generally tempered by some demonstration of vulnerability. These trained displays of vulnerability preserve the concept of femininity. These exact behaviors are also used to justify violence against a woman. Nancy Henley wrote, "Females in our society are trained to be physically weak, naive and passive, and rewarded for seductive walk and clothing but then blamed for these behaviors when men attack them."[8]

What are examples of submissive posturing? When a woman hunches her shoulders forward, it communicates the message that "I'm harmless." Incidentally, this is the most employed model posture of all. Models rarely square their shoulders or throw them back. They may arch their backs and twist their torsos to accentuate breasts and hips but they rarely look solid and unafraid. Intertwining the hands and crossing the feet communicate insecurity. Add downcast eyes to any submissive posture for the overall effect of helplessness.

Women are anatomically constructed to move differently than men. The actual differences though are not nearly as dramatic as the trained exaggerations of female movement. The same rule applies in non-verbal behavior as in any modification or exaggeration of female behavior. If the behavior involves a survival skill or a display of competency, it is minimized. If the behavior involves demonstration of a sexual difference, it is exaggerated.

Women are expected to display submissive behaviors and postures yet avoid acting openly seductive in most situations. The double bind is that by our sexual standards, submissive behavior from a woman **is** seductive.

A woman is told to cover her body to "prevent" violence yet is encouraged to display it. Men are not expected to cover their bodies nor are they punished or rewarded for revealing them. A male torso will not stop traffic or incite "justifiable" violence. Henley asserted, "Men are often much more openly seductive but they do not risk being attacked, beaten and killed by women because of their sexuality."[9]

Males claim a larger personal space than women do. The amount of physical space utilized is a protective device and it signals power. Males can feel free to sprawl out and claim all the space within reach of their arms and legs. Women rarely exhibit such behavior and are likely to develop the habit of maintaining a closed posture with legs together, arms folded and hands clasped to prevent intrusion. Unfortunately, this habit will not prevent physical encroachment from an aggressive intruder; it will communicate the intended message only to someone who is sensitive to non-verbal cues and would probably respect your physical space anyway.

A closed posture communicates the message that "I am not confident nor comfortable, and I need to protect myself." This is the perfect non-verbal communication to maintain the predominantly socialized illusion of male/female sex roles. Males, who can move freely and claim more personal space, have a social and

72

survival advantage. Women draw in, taking less space then they could rightfully occupy. This makes their territory easy to encroach upon and makes them more approachable.

Women are particularly easy to get close to because social proximity rules are not so carefully observed in relation to women as they are in relation to men.

Most males feel free to approach and touch women in almost any situation. I have found that women and men are very threatened when issues of touching and closeness are referred to as political ploys or power plays. People will defensively say that when a male co-worker places an arm around their shoulders, he is being "protective." Dominant gestures of all types are viewed as courteous gestures, such as leading a woman through a door or guiding her around corners.

"Non-verbal equity is good even when you are not feeling manipulated. It is a return of gestures that shows you care for and accept the other person."

We have all experienced ambivalence about these gestures. We enjoy being touched in some situations and are made uncomfortable by touching that seems intrusive and unwarranted in other situations. It is difficult to assume a defense against an ambivalent issue. This is why I teach non-verbal equity as a means of dealing with the problem of women being subjected to power ploys through touching behaviors. Non-verbal equity is good even when you are **not** feeling manipulated. It is a return of gestures that shows you care for and accept the other person. Non-verbal equity is explained fully in the chapter "Degrees of Threat/Degrees of Resistance: Application of Strategy."

Although touching remains a sensitive subject, research has shown that the social power structure determines who does the touching in any interaction. If you are having difficulty conceptualizing this idea, then imagine this situation.

A professor leans over a student's desk, places an arm across the student's shoulder and begins a discussion. Then reverse the situation. A student approaches a professor's desk, leans over him or her, places an arm around the professor's shoulders and begins a discussion. The latter behavior is obviously inappropriate. It would be a transgression against a power structure for a student to behave in this manner towards a professor.

When women touch men, it is almost always interpreted sexually. The exact same behavior demonstrated by a man could be explained as a fatherly or protective gesture. If a woman were to approach her boss or co-worker and throw an arm across his shoulders or lead him around corners, it would be interpreted as a sexual advance or an irritating intrusion. However, one of the principles of non-verbal equity is assertively, politely and persistently returning unwanted "protective" gestures which are actually **dominance** gestures.

The trick is combining assertive persistence with politeness. Non-verbal equity must usually be conservatively applied; stroking or unwanted hugging and squeezing gestures should not be returned. These should be dealt with by **assertive removal**. Firmly place your hand on the offending hand and quietly remove it, usually in conjunction with brief assertive eye contact.

Non-verbal behavior is one of the more subtle aspects of self-defense for women. It has been simplified to "body language" and misconstrued as "seductive" behavior. Knowledge about non-verbal behavior has been abused in recent magazine articles and gossip pulps which encourage women to perform submissive behaviors to attract men. Non-verbal behaviors have been used against women to again blame the victim.

My students expressed continual frustration in dealing with men who encroach on them physically and territorially. I've been asked what techniques can be used; what reaction is justified. These women did not have much success with verbally asking men not to touch them in intrusive ways. The men's reactions ranged from genuine surprise and hurt feelings to "What are ya, one of those women's libbers?"

In a healthy context, touching behaviors are the most desirable and communicative of all human behaviors. When a woman is intensely uncomfortable about touching and encroaching behaviors, something is wrong.

"In a healthy context, touching behaviors are the most desirable and communicative of all human behaviors. When a woman is intensely uncomfortable about touching and encroaching behaviors, something is wrong."

How do you deal with this problem? What are your non-verbal behaviors? Do you consistently take up less space than you physically need? Do you keep your arms and legs crossed, your briefcase or purse under your chair, behind your feet or in your lap? Notice that men claim space all around them. A person must ask for permission to sit near them. When you do not want anyone encroaching on you, claim the space around you. I know that dresses and skirts can be restricting but you can stretch your arms out comfortably and wear pants to move freely.

Watch your posture carefully. Do not carry your shoulders down and forward in the "model" posture. Study magazines and look for the message in the model's posture. Usually several are communicated. Often the apparent message is carefree gaiety; the underlying message is "the right kind of man could capture me." Sometimes the apparent theme is a strong, dominant woman; the underlying message is "I'm only protecting myself until someone stronger comes along."

Claiming your space and territorial protection involves using as much space as you physically need. You can protect your space by arranging items or furniture to make you physically less accessible when you need this ploy. Looking at your environment without giving submissive facial cues will re-claim your basic right to see the world. Protect your space by claiming your right to move freely. Use as much space as you need and look at your environment.

These behaviors will help you deal with daily intrusions from "harmless" sources. When these behaviors are employed for protection in situations that may not be harmless, you will find they contribute heavily to "avoidance." A thousand do's and don't's will not prevent an unwanted approach from a victimizer skilled in reading submissive cues. You could go by all the rules for women's behavior to "avoid assault" but, if you are mincing along in restraining clothing with your eyes downcast and shoulders hunching forward trying to be acceptably feminine yet as unobtrusive as possible, someday even in broad daylight in the middle of a crowd, a victimizer is likely to spot your anxiety and discomfort and decide on you as a target of repressed rage or power fantasies.

Be observant of your own non-verbal behaviors and the behavior of others. Look for the messages in the media images of women. Be honest with yourself and project yourself honestly. You have nothing to lose but social powerlessness and your vulnerability to attack.

A Balancing Act

A burglar or rapist seeking entrance to a residence or car generally takes the path of least resistance. The same principle is often applied in an assault or mugging. A victimizer seeks a likely victim. This choice is based on more than the commonly believed characteristics of the "victim type." To prevent giving off "victim signals," the usual advice about projecting an air of confidence is not adequate. In addition to the low-status behavior previously mentioned, a potential victim is also identified by an **unbalanced style of movement.**

"You have nothing to lose but social powerlessness and your vulnerability to attack."

Muggers use a general set of criteria for choosing an easy mark. Betsy Grayson, a professor of marketing and communications at Hofstra University, did a study involving fifty-three inmates at the Rahway State Prison in New Jersey. Inmates viewed subjects who were not aware they were being filmed and rated them on a scale of one to ten in "muggability" and "assaultability."[10]

Frequent advice to prevent becoming a victim is to "walk quickly away from potential attackers with your eyes fixed confidently forward."[11] These factors did **not** prove significant in Professor Grayson's investigation. This is probably because a person who is not aware of high- and low-status communications may physically express his or her interpretation of a confident stride ineffectively. He or she may make quick, jerky movements which communicate fear and nervousness. In response to advice to keep the eyes fixed confidently forward, he or she may affect the glazed expression of someone who is preoccupied rather than aware and confident.

Professor Grayson's study did point to five specific kinds of movement made by potential victims.

1) Unusually long strides relative to overall body size.

2) Victims tended to lift their feet in non-rhythmic weight shifting.

3) Victims moved unilaterally with the leg and arm of the same side moving forward or back at the same time. Non-victims moved arms contralaterally; the right arm would move forward when right leg was coming back.

4) Non-victims' walk was characterized as "postural" because their movements seemed to originate from an organized center of their bodies.

5) Victims moved "gesturally" as the motion of an arm or leg seems separate from the motion of the body as a whole.

In general, the difference between victim and non-victim as stated by Professor Grayson "seems to revolve around a wholeness or consistency of movement."[12]

The common advice to stride confidently is good but incomplete. To practice a "non-victim" walk, make sure you stride contralaterally and center your weight. Practice in the martial arts stances will help you understand the concept of centering your weight and balance. Perfecting balance through stances may be one of the reasons why martial arts practitioners report fewer public approaches and confrontations after studying than before.[13] Watch people around you. You will see that many people are not centered and appear physically unbalanced. Evaluate how this makes them appear more vulnerable; then evaluate your own strengths and weaknesses.

75

Checking Out the Environment

Avoidance rules for women usually list compulsive "looking behaviors" that make a primary sensory experience an exercise in paranoia. Women are told to look under the car before getting in, to look in the back seat of the car to see if someone is hiding there, to scan a dark parking lot before going to their car. These are all good suggestions but the negative implications of these looking behaviors are deplorably limiting.

Remember one of the major rules in drivers education courses? **Get The Big Picture.** This was to remind you to continuously scan your entire field of vision to keep you alert and aware of what is happening or what could possibly happen. When people learn to drive, they are often frightened at first. As a result, they tightly clutch the wheel and fix their eyes rigidly on the road directly in front of them and steer straight ahead. This is hazardous because by the time another vehicle or pedestrian enters your peripheral vision, it's too late to safely alter your course.

How does this relate to women and self-defense? It is a good example of how women steer their bodies through life limiting their scope of vision. As a result of the learned practice of limiting vision, it is difficult to convince women that looking at their environment means more than that they are furtively checking for rapists. Why is this such a problem? Because women are covertly socialized not to look at their larger environment. Women have learned that the risk of meeting men's eyes is the ultimate danger. Women get in the habit of watching the ground to avoid "signaling" an interest in the men around them. This becomes a habit even when no one is around.

It also becomes a practice rooted in blinding fear. A woman going to her car or to her door at night is often in a panic to proceed as quickly and inconspicuously as possible. It's almost as if women believe that if they don't look, they won't be seen; or if they don't look around and "signal" their anxiety, they won't give a potential attacker ideas. Furtive looking behaviors transmit fear; asserting your constant right to view the environment is not a fearful signal.

"Furtive looking behaviors transmit fear; asserting your constant right to view the environment is not a fearful signal."

Timothy Beneke described women's limited visual behaviors in an article published in *Mother Jones* magazine called "Male Rage - Men Talk About Rape." He describes the different experiences of a married couple who live in Manhattan, both artists and sensitive to the visual world. Beneke said, "When they walk separately in the city, he has more freedom to look than she does. She must control her eye movement lest she inadvertently meet the glare of some importunate man. What, who and how she sees is restricted by the threat of rape."[14]

Limiting the scope of your vision is ultimately more dangerous than meeting a man's eyes by chance. You should practice variations of looking at your environment until you feel comfortable. Your eyes are one of your most important assets in avoiding danger. Eye contact is an important non-verbal behavior, yet women are taught to fear eye contact. No one has to teach a woman she can't look men directly in the eyes. The lesson is communicated non-verbally; the experience speaks for itself. Direct eye contact from a woman to a man is considered an invitation to approach. Women live with the fear that they can't casually view the world; chance eye contact implies a commitment.

When other non-verbal behaviors that signal submission are altered, you can make assertive eye contact without fear of being misread. As with any human behavior, this is not always predictable, yet the practice of strenuously trying to avoid meeting men's eyes does not ensure safety either.

The most unfortunate consequence of training women to avoid eye contact for fear of giving off mistaken "sexual signals" is that women stop looking at their world. Unless a woman is in a "safe" situation, she rarely freely looks at her environment. One of the first rules of awareness is to scan your environment to be aware of what is going on around you. This should not be a furtively performed act of paranoia; it is an absolute necessity and an expression of freedom.

I have struggled with this problem for many years and have experimented with it on every level. I carefully avoided any eye contact with males but then I found that this behavior signaled submission. When I accidently met a man's eyes and then quickly looked away, he knew he had located a "trained female," a woman hoping to avoid confrontation who could be easily moved in on.

Then I tried the direct stare and when a man caught my eye I stared directly back. This got mixed reactions. Often a man would stop in his tracks and follow me, shocked by a direct gaze from a woman. He perceived it as a challenge or a direct invitation. It also brought out another approach. The more timid man who never would have turned on his heel and followed me would smile nervously, say "Hi" and attempt to strike up a conversation. The direct stare brought more unwanted attention from both the merely annoying and the directly confrontive types than the submissive-downcast-eyes ploy.

Then I began watching other women and looking directly at them. I found a strange response. Women would furtively glance at me and grimace quickly. This knee-jerk response was supposed to pass as a smile but it also communicated

submission. It stated the message of all acceptable female behaviors: "I'm no threat to you."

In *Body Politics,* Henley cites numerous studies which show women are socially trained and expected to smile more than men. Henley says, "The smile is a woman's badge of appeasement . . ."[15]

Then I monitored my behavior again when looking at my environment and accidentally catching a man's eyes. I found that if I didn't glance away with lightning speed when someone's eyes meet mine but gazed briefly and assertively without altering my facial expression, I was not harassed, followed or misinterpreted. This also gave me a chance to size up a situation or a person. Men gaze at each other long enough to see the other and sometimes to acknowledge each other's presence.

Men briefly lock eyes and nod quickly or tuck their chins and drop their eyes slightly. This seems to be a version of tipping a hat as a greeting. It is a respectful acknowledgement of the presence of another person. When a woman acknowledges the presence of a man or woman in this way, it is likely to be understood. Instead, women often smile deferentially practically every time others look at them, which is a display of submissiveness.

" . . . exercising the social freedom to be yourself in public is not demonstrating social subordination or fear."

I do not smile deferentially, but I do return genuine, friendly smiles from strangers and often I am simply happy and smile or even laugh to myself in public. I am not going to suggest that you limit or confine genuine happiness or give any advice. I can only communicate my experience with this; it seems that exercising the social freedom to be yourself in public is not demonstrating social subordination or fear. I have not had any negative repercussions from smiling or laughing when I feel like it. On the other hand, I often exercise caution with non-verbal and verbal communication in public. I never compromise my safety or limit my vision by avoiding eye contact as women are taught to do. I neither drop my gaze immediately when I meet someone's eyes nor do I rudely stare.

Allow yourself some experimentation with eye contact and facial expression. If you give them a chance, it may make the difference between moving freely and seeing your surroundings or scurrying around like a hunted animal. Practice assertive looking behaviors and you will soon use your eyes naturally again. It is not human nature to go around with downcast eyes. This is a learned behavior and it is not healthy for you psychologically.

Beauty and Bondage

Although artistic and aesthetic expression through clothing, hair and make-up are thought to be a privilege of femaleness, they can also become a means of social persecution and physical bondage. Women today are relatively free to dress beautifully in clothing that is also functional. I say "relatively" free because of the limited availability of attractive and functional clothing. Women's clothing is usually flimsily constructed with few pockets. It is also subject to seasonal fashion whims. One year you can find a certain garment and then it may disappear from the market for five years. Men can always find functional garments with predictable availability.

Women are constantly subjected to pressures to wear "bondage fashions" or "return to romantic fashions." You can count on periodic exploitation of a "return to femininity." This approach usually features clown-like ruffled creations to promote the illusion of childish vulnerability.

Bondage fashion never really disappears. Currently, old merry widow corsets and the "bulletproof" bras of the fifties are now being worn as outer garments. This is supposed to flaunt convention instead of guiltily accepting it. The eroticism of female bondage motivates the sale of such clothing. I reject the notion that bondage lingerie or clothing is "sexy." It merely reinforces the idea that women are the playthings of men.

I believe that only the privilege of expression through clothing should be accepted. The freedom to use color and fabric creatively should not be confined to fashion dictates that keep women appearing as safely submissive slaves to beauty, blindly following the latest new twist on the old ideal.

The worst form of bondage is footwear that hinders women's walking. I wear heels, but only heels that are possible to walk in.

"The worst form of bondage is footwear that hinders women's walking."

You've heard this one before: "Wear sensible shoes." Well, a compromise must be reached since few women are willing to wear loafers with their evening clothes. Cybil Shepherd wore bright orange Reeboks (flexible athletic shoes) to the Emmy Awards with a long black gown. Shepherd said, "I've always been told high heels are sexy, but I don't need them to look sexy. The only way I'd be comfortable in high heels is to wear them in bed."[16]

This is really hilarious. It clearly makes a statement beyond.the concept of beauty or "sexiness" or comfort. Shepard also said, "My mother always said that you have to suffer to be beautiful. Well, there's a certain point in a woman's life when she must choose between her feet and her shoes."[17]

78

First of all, why should female suffering create beauty? Second, why would crippling shoes be "sexy?" Third, wearing high-heeled shoes in bed would create discomfort for a bed partner as the heels would gouge, stab and poke another soft, nude body. If a woman wore high heels in bed because it unleashed her true sexuality but created discomfort for her partner, we would have dispensed with this concept a long time ago.

High-heeled shoes that prevent mobility and cause pain perform the same function as the Chinese custom of foot binding, which existed for 800 years. Susan Brownmiller in her latest book, *Femininity,* describes the painful process of foot binding in detail and explains that crushed, deformed, non-functional feet were romanticized and eroticized. Brownmiller says, "Making love to the lotus foot, an elaborate art of manipulation, postures and poses, was a dominant theme in Chinese pornography for 800 years while the custom of foot binding flourished."[18]

Almost all of the physical alterations women have been socially induced or required to make on their bodies have sacrificed a functional capacity. Certainly walking is one of the most basic. In reference to foot binding, Brownmiller writes, "It imposed an ingenious handicap upon a routine, functional act and reduced the female's competence to deal with the world around her."[19]

The point of all physical alterations, even those that handicap a woman, is to increase femininity or make her more sexually attractive to **men** by **current cultural standards**. Brownmiller makes another important point. "The truth is, men have barely tampered with their bodies at all, historically, to make themselves more appealing to women."[20] Their muscular development may be the major exception, but this **increases** a person's ability to survive rather than being a survival handicap as are women's attempts to increase sexual attractiveness.

Women's shoes, even low heels, are not constructed for running or rough terrain. The only sensible shoes that would not inhibit you in an escape attempt would be good running shoes. In Grayson's study on "muggability," she isolated a "victim-type step," which is lifting the foot off the ground instead of a heel-to-toe stride that characterized non-victims. Grayson found that women wearing high heel shoes tend to make the typical "victim-type steps."[21]

Women's clothing and footwear may frequently be a reason an attacker targets a certain women, even if she is prepared to fight. I am not saying "provocative" or "revealing" clothing attracts rapists. I am saying that restrictive clothing, such as high-heeled shoes, may make women move in ways that transmit submissive cues.

It is unfortunate that fashion for women is still a form of physical bondage, inhibiting mobility and transmitting submissive signals when the woman may feel anything but submissive. After walking a few blocks in high heels, you usually feel like spitting nails.

> **"It is unfortunate that fashion for women is still a form of physical bondage, inhibiting mobility and transmitting submissive signals when the woman may feel anything but submissive."**

Many women carry dress shoes in a shoe bag and wear tennis shoes to walk. It is not hard to understand why a woman would not want to wear Hush Puppies or tennis shoes with a dress suit, but the idea of carrying indoor or dress shoes to your destination and then putting them on makes sense. I frequently see women lumbering around on high heels, their bodies pitched forward and obviously in pain with each step. It is easy to see why this would set them up as victims. The lack of mobility and preoccupation with physical discomfort are apparent. In a more general sense, I could see how this contrasts with the over-all appearance of non-victims who "function comfortably within the context of their own bodies."[22]

Many women will find the suggestion of carrying shoes in a bag or leaving a pair in the office a bothersome option to increase safety. If you cannot imagine walking out of the office in tennis shoes, then at least keep a pair in the trunk of your car or the back seat. Changing shoes several times a day may not be your preference; you may not have to walk very far in heels and don't think it's worth your while. But what if your car broke down in a deserted area or you had to use a phone in a dangerous part of town? You should have some extra running shoes in your vehicle for emergencies.

Determine Your Own Location, Pay Your Own Way

Women face a higher risk of rape by an acquaintance than a stranger, so it is important to take a firm stand on physical control in your social dealings with others. In addition, many attacks by relative strangers involved some form of social contract; and, in many cases, the women was approached and became a likely target because she looked as if she needed a ride or some kind of assistance. This is often true but I think assertiveness should prevail here also.

"... you choose whom you will approach for help."

When you need assistance, don't wait untill someone notices, **you** choose whom you will approach for help. A person cannot always be in control of events. It can happen that you are stranded and without any money. It would be better to panhandle than to accept a ride offered by a stranger. In panhandling, you choose whom you will approach. You may be

offered a ride but it is best not to take the chance. In most cases all you need is phone change or bus fare.

You can ask women for assistance. If approached by a woman, keep in mind that both women and children have been used to lure victims. Henry Lee Lucus, confessed mass murderer of 360 victims, used his niece and nephew to lure victims. In my survey, a woman reported accepting a ride in a supermarket parking lot when her car broke down. She was approached by a woman. She was abducted and gang raped. The woman had been an accomplice. Use caution when approached by a woman in such a situation.

Several other women in my study accepted offers of assistance and were reassured by the presence of children. In these cases, this did not prove to be a deterrent to rape and violence because the children were used to attract victims or initially assuage the victim's fears. A woman or any person who appears distraught will stand out in a crowd. This is an especially encouraging signal for a victimizer. If a victimizer can gain the distraught person's confidence, her need can be exploited. If a person is not willing or unable to give you a quarter to make a phone call, you should be suspicious of any alternate offer.

In some cases in which help is offered, your judgment may be sufficient to indicate that the person means well; but if you have any doubts, heed them. If persons offering help appear argumentative, insistent or appear anxious, do not accept. Brush them off by rushing in the direction of another person or car saying you've found a friend or you see your ride.

If a car stops while you are on a deserted road and the occupants look suspicious or you get "bad" feelings, tell them that a trucker already called assistance on a C.B. for you. The major point to remember is that you choose whom you will approach when you need assistance. Don't look distraught and wait for someone to choose you.

There is more to determining your own location than not accepting rides or assistance from strangers. As previously mentioned, rape and violence are not confined to stranger against stranger. It is increasingly being found that most rapists are exploiters; and social situations, especially the premise of "dating" and most male/female interaction, provide ample opportunities to exercise the calculated opportunity to rape.

"In the initial stages of a relationship or new friendship, you should make your own arrangements for transportation."

In the initial stages of a relationship or new friendship, you should make your own arrangements for transportation. Many "dates" have turned unpleasant, ended in unwanted groping sessions or resulted in rape because the premise of "dating" is that a woman surrenders herself into the care (and at the mercy) of a man.

It is a romantic expectation that women surrender all control and responsibility to go on a "date." You are actually in a man's custody for a designated time. This is ridiculous, unnecessary and puts a woman at risk. This does not mean that you can never trust a man to pick you up or allow him to pay for an evening or outing. It means that **you** decide and **you** make the rules.

"You can meet and get acquainted without giving up control and independent decision making."

Social expectations need not dictate your behavior. In the first encounter or the first few, you should reserve and exercise

the option to provide your own transportation. You can meet and get acquainted without giving up control and independent decision making. If you do not get along, you are not dependent on this person.

I also strongly think that you should always be prepared to pay for your share of the check or entertainment.

Women often resist paying their own way because some men prefer to pay or have been conditioned to believe this is the correct behavior. In a committed relationship or an ongoing relationship, an understanding about finances can be reached. In the initial stages, regardless of assumptions about finances or his preferences, you should insist on paying your own way. If necessary, arrange for less expensive entertainment.

In doing this, several important things are evident. You are not allowing a man to pay for your company and you are not surrendering your independence. You are showing that you are spending time with this man because you want to, not because you expect expensive entertainment. Keep in mind that you can discuss finances later if the relationship progresses. If you like the man enough to spend a day or an evening with him, it naturally follows that you should be willing to pay your way. If you were going to spend time with a female friend, you'd expect to pay half or take turns.

Personal assumption of financial responsibility is a gesture of respect. Respect given is respect earned. Male/female social encounters will not be dictated by expectations based on unspoken trade-offs implied by temporary custody and monetary provisions that are the usual premise of "dating." Your decisions will be independent and not based on need.

If a man is insulted by this behavior, assure him that it is a compliment that you choose to be with him, not depend on him. His response could reveal a lot about him.

If he is extremely controlling or has ulterior motives in "providing," he will not be willing to see you as an equal. It is in your best interest to find out how a man reacts to this situation. You may find out things it could otherwise take months to know if you allowed romantic illusions and expectations to control events.

How to Outwit a Mugger

Physical and sexual assault are not the only potentially dangerous situations a woman is likely to encounter in life. Robbery of a home or business could become a violent crime if you are present. Anytime you are confronted by a car thief, a mugger or burglar - especially if a weapon is shown, **decrease the interaction time**. Immediately give them the goods they ask for without argument. Any criminal knows that chances of success are better if he moves fast. Don't make him hang around for any reason. The longer you interact with him, the greater your chances of being harmed.

If you surprise a burglar in your home, **give him an out**. Immediately say something like, "Oh. You're the repairman. Have you checked the water pipe outside?" as you back away towards the door. Don't make him panic or back him into a corner.

In a situation where you are dealing with a mugger, first determine your advantages. If you are in a brightly lighted parking lot near other people and a lone mugger is pulling on your purse, you may be able to use any number of physical techniques shown in this book.

One of the women in my study reported this success story when a man attempted to mug her. She was living on an Army base with her husband and was recovering from a cesarean section. She had not left the house for weeks. She had to cash the family's payroll check so she found a friend to watch the baby. After cashing the check, she went to her car. As she reached the cement underpass to the parking lot, a

man grabbed her and started wrestling her for her purse.

Guess what? She'd completed an Army-sponsored self-defense course about six months previously. She used a knee kick and a heel-palm strike to the base of his nose. He fell down, blood spurting from his nose, screaming, "You hurt me, bitch." She had broken his nose and dislocated his knee. He was thrown in the brig and she escaped unharmed. This woman told me she wasn't about to give up her purse and all the money she had in the world to pay bills.

Although this is a successful resistance story, it **is** also an example of the fact that a woman will think in terms of the purse and its contents instead of herself. This does **not** only apply to women. Many people will defend property as though it were as valuable as their physical well-being.

I do not advocate defense of property unless the situation is heavily weighted to your advantage. I advise my students not to carry a purse. Many women feel this is nearly impossible. If you must keep credit cards, pictures and important papers with you in a purse, then keep it locked in the trunk of your car or under the seat.

"Don't carry irreplaceable snapshots or papers. A purse is not a safe-deposit box."

A large, bulky purse can increase the risk of attracting a violent criminal. If you have to carry a bag, carry a small handbag that can be clutched in one hand and wear clothing with pockets. A wallet-type hand clutch can be used to execute a heel-palm-like strike to the base of an attacker's nose. Your change will probably shower all over, which is distracting. Make sure, however, that it is the attacker whose attention is diverted, not yours! A briefcase can be a fairly good body shield or weapon if it has hard edges. Don't carry irreplaceable snapshots or papers. A purse is not a safe-deposit box. When a quick escape is needed, a purse is physically restricting and always a consideration. You will lose time looking for your purse. A purse also makes a woman forget what is important; **her** safety, **her** person is all that is worth fighting for. A woman clutching a purse sometimes forgets to defend herself; instead, she defends her purse.

A purse could be used to fend off blows, especially to the face; a purse can be thrown or dumped out to distract a mugger; a purse can be jammed in the attacker's face. In fact, a purse must **never** be defended. When all the advantages are in your favor - time, place, proximity to others, safety, training and confidence- you may feel justified, even obligated, in defending your right to live without harassment. But a purse or its contents is never worth permanent damage or loss of life.

A large, bulky purse makes you a target for mugging and carries an important message to a would-be mugger; you are insecure. A woman clutching a purse has got to have something important in it. She must be unorganized and unprepared, afraid of unforeseen events. She will also concentrate on hanging on to her purse if attacked and forget her bodily weapons.

If you intend to carry a gun, a purse is not the place for it. A woman with a gun in her purse will forget the immediate options as they present themselves and concentrate on getting the gun. This could end up in a fatal struggle with the possibility that the attacker will gain control of the weapon.

"If you carry a weapon, you are ensuring a weapon will be present in one hundred percent of the possible confrontations where you are involved."

This is a good opportunity to explain my theory of weapons. According to recent figures released by the U.S. Department of Justice, a weapon is present in under twenty percent of assaults. If you carry a weapon, you are ensuring a weapon will be present in **one hundred percent** of the possible confrontations where you are involved.

Before your mouth hits the floor and you reiterate the hackneyed saying, "If guns are outlawed only outlaws will have guns" consider these points.

- Almost all random attacks are "sneak" attacks or surprise attacks.

- Known-assailant attacks are "confidence rapes." This means the resistor is usually comfortable; the rapist has gained her confidence; she is unlikely to carry a weapon in this situation nor have it handy.

- If you do carry a weapon, you will immediately think of the gun and of getting to it, forgetting your first concerns - **decreasing interaction time** and **escaping**. Furthermore, most women who carry guns keep them in their purses, which are not always within reach.

- It is difficult to conceal a gun under your clothes on your body, which is the most accessible place.

- Jerking a purse off a woman's arm is the goal of a mugger. A woman who carries a gun in that purse is likely to resist **because** of the gun. Her hands, which are weapons in their own right, will be occupied and her energy directed toward maintaining control of the gun rather than saving herself.

- If the gun is not on her person, where is it and what good is it? Can you get to it before the attacker does and without his knowledge?

If you cannot escape or defend safely, throw your entire purse or wallet as far from you as you can. If you allow a group of muggers to surround you and you hand them your purse, your compliance and proximity may arouse other ideas. Many times a robbery or mugging has resulted in rape and physical assault. If you throw your purse, the mugger will go after it and may take the time to rifle through it. While he's doing that, you can be long gone.

Many women will immediately reject this idea because they are considering the contents of their purses. This is why you should not use your purse as a safe deposit box. In any case, it is a trade-off. You may loose your purse, but you may escape unharmed and report the incident.

If you were carrying keys, credit cards or your license and identification, the mugger knows your address and can get into your home. You should stay with friends or family until you can change the locks on your residence and attend to security measures you may have neglected. Keep all credit card numbers in a file so you can report them missing immediately.

If you persist in carrying a purse, at least remove valuables and items of sentimental value. Do not carry all your credit cards or identification and keep your car keys on a separate key chain. Your house keys should be locked in your glove compartment. That way you will not be tempted to drop a bulky set of keys in your purse when leaving a grocery store, place of business or in any situation. Your car keys should be in your hand. Then if your purse is snatched, you will have your house key and other keys in a safe place so you can get to them. Keep change in your glove compartment to call the police and a supportive friend, husband or boyfriend.

It may not be easy to give up your purse; you may feel outraged. Just remember, it is a small price to pay to preserve your personal safety. Some wounds will never heal, but any material item can be replaced. Many people become enraged over petty material things. In doing so they have lowered themselves to the level of a petty thief. When something

much more precious is lost in the struggle to maintain control over any item, people realize how little material things matter.

A thought to remember in a material crisis - have faith, almost anything can be replaced. Nothing is more important than your life and the safety of your loved ones. Finally, never risk your life unnecessarily.

Home Security

Adequate home security is of primary importance. Two major arguments exist on the home security issue. One is money and the other is that locks are for your friends because a committed burglar can outwit any system.

In answer to both issues, an expensive system beyond locks is not essential to protect yourself. The most important consideration is to keep a criminal outside while you are inside or to impede entry while you escape or call for help. While most of us would prefer to protect our homes from burglary, home security need not be an all-or-nothing project. Eighty percent of attempted burglaries take place most commonly during the day when no one is home. Actually to secure a residence from burglary may be both an extensive and expensive project; to take steps to keep an intruder out while you are in is much simpler and cheaper.

"The most important consideration is to keep a criminal outside while you are inside or to impede entry while you escape or call for help."

Sliding windows and doors can be secured with "jimmy bars." All you need for a jimmy bar is an old broomstick, a dowel rod available at any hardware store or some other scrap of metal or wood cut to fit your sliding door or window.

Another inexpensive method to secure

windows is eyebolts or nails. Drill an angled hole through the top frame of the window and insert an eyebolt. The window can't be opened until the eyebolt is removed. This method can also be used on sliding windows or doors. Drill holes in the window or door frame and its runners and insert a bolt or nail. This will prevent lifting the door or the window out of its frame.

You often hear "dead bolt" locks are best to secure doors. You may be thinking about installation and cost. In addition, a key lock can be cut or picked. A good keylock deadbolt is a deterrent, but time, cover and darkness may give the intruder time to break the lock. You can buy a sliding deadbolt or auxiliary rim-mounted lock with dead bolt to install on the inside of your door. You do not have to change the existing key lock. A sliding deadbolt should be installed on your bedroom door also. Should an intruder enter the house or apartment, you will have forewarning if he attempts to enter your bedroom at night when you are asleep.

You should have a phone extension in your room to call for help. An intruder has no way of knowing if you are alone, so you can even loudly say, "Butch. Wake up. I think there's somebody in the house."

I often hear the complaint that people like to sleep with their bedroom windows open. I would never condone this practice without protection. There are several ways to secure windows. Ornamental iron grillwork makes it safe to leave a window completely open for full ventilation. I know that iron grillwork throughout a house is not safe because of fire danger; it is also expensive.

However, in your bedroom you could put iron grillwork on the one window you like to leave open. You can buy standard sizes for most windows at many home improvement stores. You can also use the "pin trick" for partial ventilation. Just secure the windows you like to leave open.

Women who live in apartments often do not want to invest the time, effort and money in security. I have also heard the argument that the manager won't allow modifications or additions. Remember, Connie Francis was raped in her rented room and sued the innkeepers of a Westbury, New York hotel for failing to provide adequate security.

If you live in an apartment with a flimsy "kick down" door or a bevel door lock that can be opened with a credit card, you should ask your manager to provide better security. A heavy wood or metal door with a wide angle viewer should be installed to protect you **and** the owners. If you did all of the above mentioned security measures, except iron grillwork, you would not have to invest more than fifty dollars and three hours. None of these measures would be noticeable or damaging to the premises. The only modification the manager may not allow is the iron grillwork.

If you are in a ground floor apartment, you should utilize a jimmy bar and keep your windows closed and locked when you are gone. With most windows you could use the "pin trick." Make a set of holes with the windows partially opened for ventilation. In this way you can be forewarned should an intruder start "jimmying" the window. I know that it is not fair that you must lock yourself in at night. I also know that many of the women in my study admitted that the attacker entered through an unlocked door or window.

". . . a rapist will take the path of least resistance and look for unlocked doors or windows. Remember this and take steps to preserve your home safety."

According to the U.S. Justice Department, in approximately 57 percent of home burglaries, the robber simply walked in. Before an experienced robber enters a home by force, he will always try the doors or windows. In over 50 percent of the cases, this method is successful. According to the reports of women in my study, a rapist will take the path of least resistance and look for unlocked doors or windows. Remember this and take steps to preserve your home safety.

Car Security

Keeping your car doors locked is as important as your home security. Car doors can be fairly easily "picked" with the coat hanger method, but this takes time and is much more dangerous than calmly trying doors or reaching through open windows to unlock doors, then climbing in to wait for the owner. Even though you lock your car doors, always scan the interior of the car before getting in.

A variation of "trying car doors" was recounted by one of my students. She was going home late at night and stopped at a red light on a deserted street. A man calmly and methodically began trying to open her doors. When she recovered from the shock, she sped away. He attempted easy entry first, but he may have tried other methods if he had time. I can't stress this too much. When you are traveling, **always** keep your doors locked, especially the passenger and back seat doors. If an opportunistic rapist or mugger happens to see you sitting at a stop light or sign or in a parking lot and quickly enters your car, you are in a bad position. You are sitting down and off guard because you are in your own vehicle and probably had felt secure.

If you are within the vicinity of environmental escape routes or in traffic - even if facing a weapon, I suggest you immediately jam the car in park, snatch the keys out of the ignition - or leave them- and jump out. Don't give the criminal time to get his bearings and gain control. If you don't face a weapon or you're in traffic, you could flip on the hazard lights often located on the steering column or continuously honk the horn. If you are

abducted and forced to drive, act distraught and confused. Drive erratically and violate traffic signals and lights, especially on busy streets. You may get lucky and get stopped by police.

An important element of car security is maintenance. It's a good practice to utilize the full service pumps often and have the attendant check tire pressure, water level in the battery cells and inspect cables and posts. Attendants will also check hoses, belts, radiator, oil and brake fluid, transmission fluid and power steering fluid. For a more complete explanation about car maintenance, send for *Every Woman's Car Care Handbook,* The Firestone Tire and Rubber Company, 1220 Firestone Parkway, Akron, Ohio 44317.

You should keep several emergency items in the trunk of your car. As I said before, always keep an old pair of running shoes or tennis shoes in case you are stranded and must walk a distance to a phone.

Essential items are wooden blocks. In case of a flat tire, you can place these behind the wheel of your car to prevent it from rolling and slipping off the jack when you change the tire. You should also have a tire jack, an owner's manual, a spare tire, a flashlight and roadside flares. To be really prepared, Firestone suggests a fire extinguisher, battery jumper cables, a standard screw driver, a Phillips screwdriver, a crescent wrench, pliers with insulated handles and rags and old gloves. Actually, most people have unused tools and tool boxes in their garages. Locate these tools and put them in your car.

If you are stranded in a deserted area, turn on your hazard lights and stay in your car until highway patrol is alerted. Most truckers who see a distressed motorist will radio your location to the highway patrol. It is unnecessary and often hazardous for them to stop, so don't imagine you're being overlooked when truckers don't stop. When truckers go by, flash your headlights to make sure they see you.

If truckers or other motorists stop, remain in your car and tell them the highway patrol has been alerted by citizens band radio even if this is not true. Then ask the motorist or trucker to follow up and call the highway patrol a second time. This is just a tricky little ploy to make sure you're protected from your protector. If you are not in a deserted area, chances are that the highway patrol will discover you within twenty minutes. If you do a lot of traveling, a citizens band radio for your vehicle is a good investment.

Another device that could be used as a self-defense tool is the Car Finder.© It is intended for people who frequently forget where they've parked their car. It consists of a small key-chain transmitter and a receiver in your car. When you push the button on the transmitter, it signals your car's receiver to flash the car's lights and honk the horn. This could be extremely valuable in an attack situation, even one in which the assailant is already in the vehicle. It could even be effective in another high risk situation besides a parking lot. Assailants often attack women near their front doors. They may wait until a woman turns her back to unlock the door to enter or may try to catch her as she is coming out the door and locking it. In both cases, the key-chain would be in your hand. Depressing the button on the transmitter could create an unexpected disturbance. The assailant may not even be aware that you created it. You could set this up as a signal to your neighbors that you are in trouble and they should call the police.

The Car Finder© is distributed by Design Tech International, Inc. 941-B 25th Street N.W., Washington, D.C., 20037. The price is $99.95. If you work a night shift or travel frequently, this could be an important investment in your security.

Another useful device normally used to prevent car theft is the Knight Hawk.™ You plug the cord from the unit into your cigarette lighter and turn the ignition key to "accessories." You then have 60 seconds to leave the car. When you return, you have 15 seconds to turn the alarm off after you re-enter. If an assailant did assault you and force you into your car, **not** turning off the alarm in 15 seconds would trigger it. It would create extreme confusion in your assailant because you wouldn't have done anything at all. The alarm continues for two minutes even if the assailant realizes what is happening and pulls the plug. The alarm is a "deafening" 80 decibels with flashing red lights. The assailant might think he attacked a police woman.

The Night Hawk™ is available through Exeters Catalog, 3303 Harbor Blvd., Suite B-5, Costa Mesa, CA, 92626, for $79.00

Improving locks and securing doors

Most ordinary door locks offer very little protection. Any intruder who knows what he is doing can usually enter the house easily using a small screwdriver or even a credit card. Door locks that will provide more protection and slow down a burglar are usually the deadbolt type. They have a heavy bolt that thrusts securely into the door frame and cannot be pried back easily.

1A. Double tubular deadbolt locks generally require a key to open them from both sides. This is a good lock for a door that has a window in it. The burglar can break the glass but he would be unable to reach inside to open the door. The bad feature of this type of lock is that you must keep a key handy when you are inside in order to open the door. Other deadbolt locks are available that can be opened without a key from the inside.

1B. Surface-mounted cylinder deadbolt locks can be easily attached to any door. The kind in which the bolt comes down through holes in the strike are virtually jimmy-proof.

1C. An inexpensive way to secure a door that is opposite a wall is to cut a 2"x4" to fit the space. You can cover the ends with felt or rubber. To provide more protection, you could put a metal angle on one end to fit under the door.

1D. If the door has no wall opposite but one nearby at right angles, a 2"x4" cut with a 45° angle on both ends can be wedged against the door and the wall.

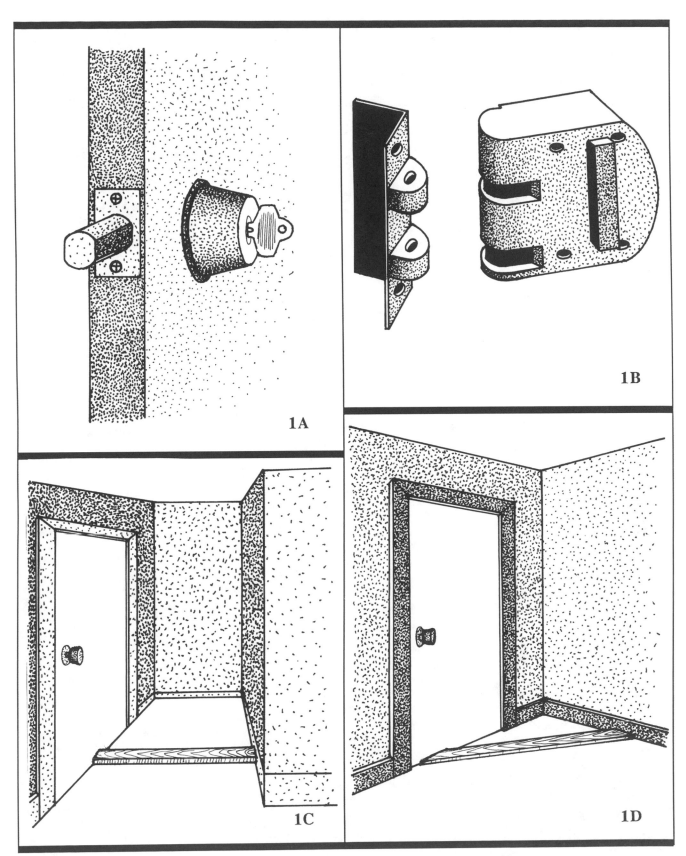

1A

1B

1C

1D

Fear or Freedom by Susan Smith ©1986

Sliding glass doors or windows

Sliding glass doors provide easy entry unless they are secured in some manner.

2A. The cheapest and simplest way is to place a length of wood or metal in the track making it impossible to slide the door or window open.

2B. Anti-slide blocks or bolts can also be installed on the doors.

2C. To prevent lifting the door or window out of the track, drill two 1/4" holes in the slide track at the top at either end and screw a 1/4" by 1 1/4" sheet metal screw partly into each hole, leaving half the screw protruding. Adjust the screws so that they just clear the top door frame when sliding the door.

2D. Another way to secure the sliding door or window is to drill a hole on a downward angle through the inside door frame and part way through the door. Insert a nail or metal eyebolt in the hole. You can remove the pin to open the door but the burglar can't.

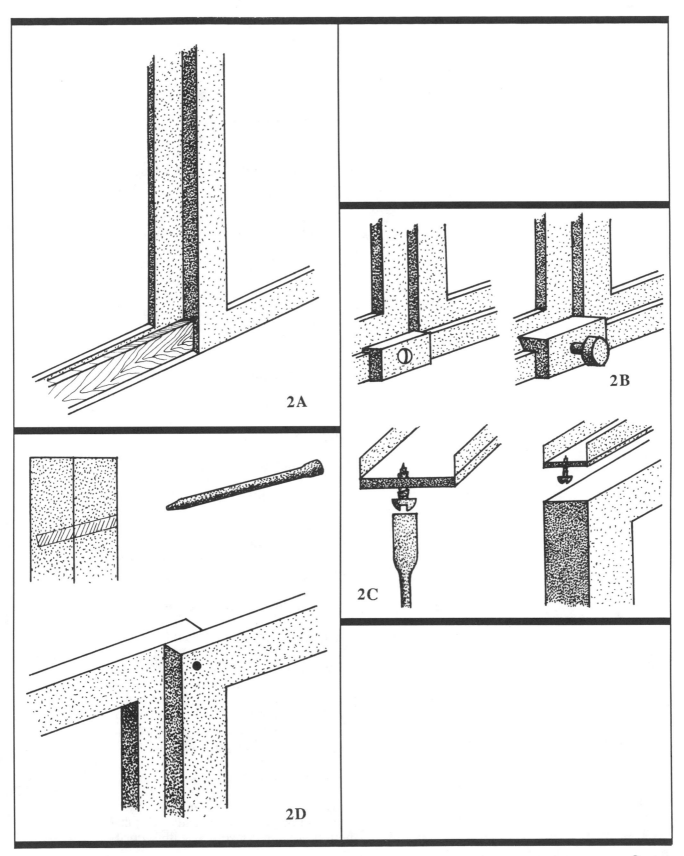

2A

2B

2C

2D

Double hung windows

3A. The same pin fastener method that can be used for sliding doors and windows can also be used for double hung windows.

3B. Drill the angled holes on both sides through the top frame of the lower window partially into the frame of the upper window. When you insert a sturdy nail or eyebolt in the hole, the window can't be opened until you remove the pin. A second set of holes can be drilled with the window partly open to allow ventilation without inviting intruders.

3C. It is possible to buy special key locks for windows at a hardware store, but you must also keep a key handy to unlock tham.

Grillwork

Ground level windows can be secured with ornamental grillwork; however, a person would not be able to escape through the window should there be a fire. Some city ordinances require that bedroom windows open from the inside for emergency exits. Grillwork should not be used in homes with small children.

Casement and crank windows

3D. It is easy to secure this type of window by drilling a hole through the latch frame and handle. A pin inserted through the hole will lock the window. A small padlock can be used in place of the pin to lock the latch, but again the problem of finding the key in an emergency might suggest this is not a good alternative.

Louvered windows

Louvered windows offer **no** security. They can be pried open easily. Replace them if you are concerned with security.

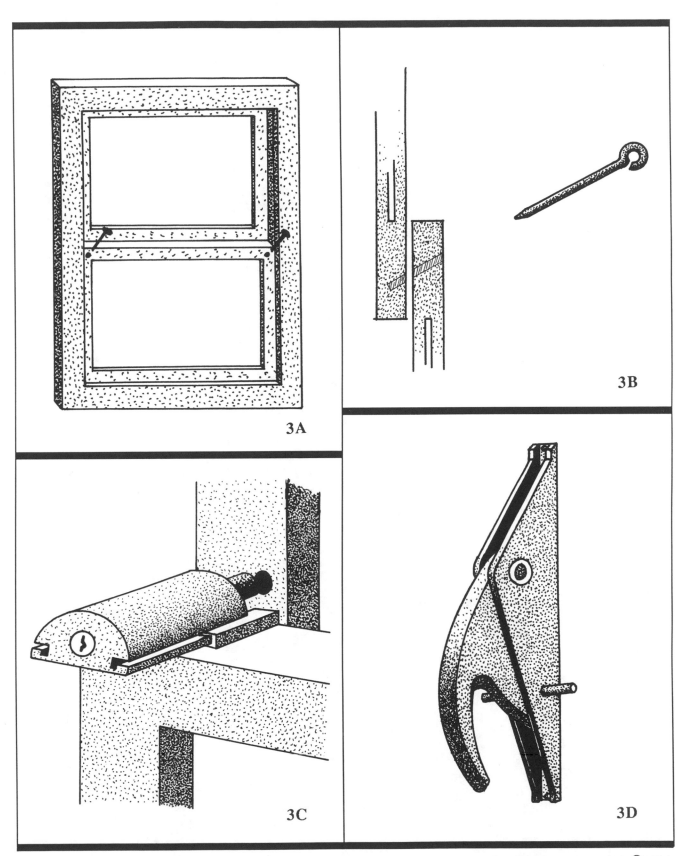

3A

3B

3C

3D

Fear or Freedom by Susan Smith ©1986

Garage doors and storage sheds

Standard locks on garage doors are easily pried open. If you have an attached garage on your house, you should consider securing the garage door with stronger locks.

4A. Cane bolts and hasps with padlocks are good alternatives.

4B. Secure both insides of the garage door to prevent an intruder from getting one side open and crawling through. A good lock on the door leading from the garage into the house is also a good idea. Often, that door is the least protected.

Hasps and padlocks

If you are going to use padlocks to lock your garage, storage shed or whatever, don't buy an inexpensive lock. Cheap locks can be easily pried open or cut with bolt cutters.

4C. A good padlock has a double locking or hardened steel shackle with a healthy diameter, a five-pin tumbler and a key-retaining feature that prevents removal of the key when the lock is unlocked. A good hasp is made of strong steel and is designed to lock over any screws that could be removed.

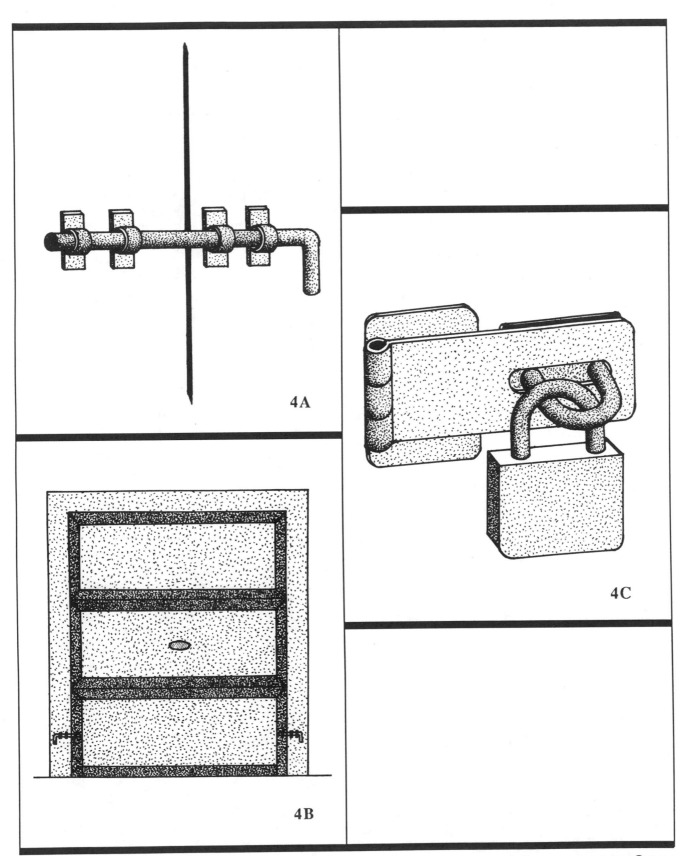

4A

4B

4C

Outside your home

5A. Ideally, if your home were surrounded by a six-foot fence locked with a strong hasp and padlock, it would keep all but the most determined burglar out. This is not always possible or desirable but even if only part of your yard is fenced in, it may prevent some burglaries. A burglar likes a clear path of escape. Fences slow him down.

5B. A sturdy or thorny hedge can serve the same purpose.

Lighting

5C. You can make sure that all your entry ways are well lit and that the lights are located high and out of reach. You could install inexpensive timers or electric photo cells to turn the lights on automatically at a preset time.

Landscaping

It is a good idea to keep shrubs and bushes around your doors and windows trimmed so that intruders can't conceal themselves while they are trying to get into your home.

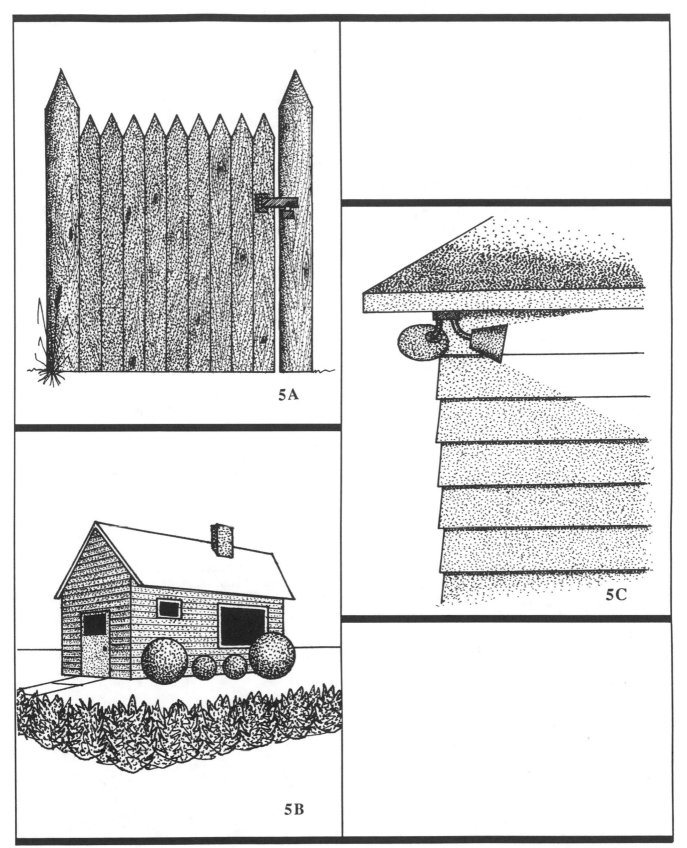

5A

5B

5C

When you go out

These tips may keep a burglar or intruder out of your home. Leave a light on. The bathroom light is best. The intruder will be less certain the house is unoccupied if he rings the doorbell and no one comes to the door. Leave a radio or TV playing. Secure your doors and windows. Lock the garage door even if you leave for just a few minutes. Lock up your tools accessible from outside or in your storage shed. The burglar could use them to get into the house. Don't leave ladders lying around. Does anyone have to remind you not to leave a house key under the mat or in the mailbox? If you must keep a key somewhere outside, be more creative. Those are always the first places an intruder will look. A note left on the door **advertises** where you are and how long you will be gone.

What if the intruder comes when you are away?

If you come home and believe someone has broken into the house, **do not enter!** The intruder may still be inside. Go to a neighbor's home or public phone and call the police. When they come, resist the impulse to close doors or windows or otherwise "tidy" up until they have finished their investigation. Assist the investigating officers as much as possible. You will probably feel as if you have been violated because someone has been in your home and perhaps stolen some of your treasured things. Consider yourself lucky you weren't personally violated. Unfortunately, the intruder could come back. Be willing to testify if a suspect is apprehended.

Alarm systems

You may want to install one of the many alarm systems on the market. If you are thinking of an alarm system, you should choose one that meets your individual needs. Shop around; ask questions.

Some types of alarms are perimeter alarms and include conventional wired alarms, radio frequency alarms, light pulse alarms and house current carrier alarms. Perimeter alarms have sensors attached to windows or entry ways. When the entry way is jimmied or forced, the alarm is activated. They act as early detection devices before the burglar enters the home.

Other types of alarms are not activated until the intruder is inside the home. These include pressure mats under carpeting activated by footsteps, ultrasonic/microwave alarms activated by interruption of the silent soundwaves and light-beam spans or electronic eyes in entryways.

A good type of alarm is one that scares off the intruder with lights and noise. Beware of expensive complicated systems that need expensive maintenance. There should be a delayed action "on-off" switch with the controls inside the house.

One of the best alarm systems is a barking watchdog!

Cautions with the telephone

Phony telephone surveys and fake wrong numbers may be ploys used by intruders to "case" your home. Tell your children and babysitters never to give any information to strangers over the phone. Be cautious revealing information yourself. Never let strangers into your home to use the telephone. If you feel you must help them, offer to call for them while they wait outside. Be careful of "inspectors" or bogus utility people. Ask for valid identification before letting any stranger into your home.

What if the intruder comes when you are home?

If you should see an intruder **before** he has broken in, make noise, turn on lights and make him aware he has been seen or heard. Try to scare him away. If you see you are not scaring him away, **get out of the house! Run!** Get to a safe place. If you can't get out, lock yourself in a room that has a good lock. Telephone the police immediately for help. If there is no phone in the room, open a window and yell for help.

Degrees of
Threat and
Resistance

A reform is a correction of abuse; a revolution is a transfer of power.
Bulwer-Lytton

Chapter V

Degrees of Threat/Degrees of Resistance

Application of Strategies

One of the most common martial arts sayings is, "Your best defense is not to fight." This idea confuses beginners and students who believe that the result of self-defense training is physical invincibility, and the goal is to physically defeat an opponent or attacker. This erroneous assumption may be why women tend to avoid self-defense training, and why they rarely join martial arts schools or progress to the higher levels of belt rank systems.

If the goal of training is physical defeat of an opponent, few believe this is even within the realm of possibility for females defending against males.

The issue of social survival and physical defense is not an issue of women against men, it is simply a matter of physical and mental integrity and the recognition of the need for choice and effectiveness in human affairs. The promotion and encouragement of choice and effectiveness is the only truly civilized social option.

Martial arts is said to be a "male dominated" sport, yet this is not an exclusive or historical fact. Several styles were developed by women or women played major roles in their development. Wing Chun and Five Pattern Hung Kuen are two examples in which women were style originators and master instructors as well as practitioners. Throughout history in every phase of society, women have been **there** making significant but largely unrecognized contributions. "Male domination" is an illusion which requires women's cooperation in order to exist.

Instructors and students alike are often tricked by the **apparent** reality of martial arts systems. The misguided view of the martial arts as a means to learn violence misses the central concept of the martial arts, which is to learn the way of non-violence. Masters have known, without the aid of psychology as we know it, that internal powerlessness is the foundation of violent behavior, fearfulness attracts external negative events and feeds internal negativity. This perpetuates a cycle of fear which creates and dominates the offender as well as the victim.

103

Martial arts systems and philosophies are as complex as they are diverse, yet all have one thing in common: all the systems teach ritualized aggression. This learning process is not intended to result in an increased expression of violence just because the ability is developed. It should serve as a means to prevent violence because violent behavior, not defensive behavior, is the **last resort** in the vast range of behaviors learned through ritualized aggression.

The powerful self-assurance that can be realized through the processes and stages of martial arts and other types of self-defense training should eradicate the need to prove one's fearlessness or to defeat others. If violent behavior is fully understood as an expression of the peak of powerlessness, one who knows the techniques of self-defense and believes in his or her own capability will not be eager to fight to prove anything, nor would he or she be easily provoked.

It should be understood that when one must draw on the innate and learned capacity for violence in defense of self or others, it is still a last resort - but a justifiable one. I do not believe a person should submit to violence or create or provoke violence. The way of peace lies exactly in the middle of these extremes.

This chapter presents threat and confrontation in an orderly fashion. Understanding and reacting **appropriately** to the initial stages of aggression, when or if there are warning signals, is a means to prevent further action by exerting control through communication techniques which stop short of actual violence. Once violence is in motion, it is not neat and orderly; in fact, once true violence is expressed, it is totally chaotic. Beginners should be taught the progressive steps of confrontation and assault deterrence, yet they must remain aware that assault can begin on any level so they will not be left defenseless in a sudden violent attack.

Always remember that your best defense is not to fight. However, without a firm basis for this belief and the knowledge that you **can**, it may be difficult to convincingly back out of a confrontation. It may look more like "chickening out," which gives the aggressor confidence. You learn options to passive victimization so that you can defend when you must; yet when you choose not to, your decision is based on the powerful knowledge that you can. This option is much more convincing and effective than backing out of a fight because you've already been defeated by your past beliefs.

I am not promoting exaggerated bravado, but I do encourage you to believe you **do** have a chance in a fight for survival, and you do have a choice of weapons: physical, psychological and environmental. If you believe in your power to defend yourself, then you have defeated your greatest enemy: your own fear. When you are not paralyzed by fear, all your decisions and choices will be more powerful.

"If you believe in your power to defend yourself, then you have defeated your greatest enemy: your own fear."

I teach the **options** to victimization at every level of confrontation because knowledge of choices lends power to decisions.

If a woman must choose a method of passive resistance, at least she may make her decision from a position of psychological power. Compliance or passivity is then no longer the inevitable outcome of lack of choice. It becomes a survival strategy because it is a calculated effort to survive or to reduce injury. In this way, a resistor remains in the mental mode of control, considering resistance options and the possibility of escape.

Several of the previously cited studies found that rape avoiders were more likely to be thinking of ways to escape, while victims were more likely to be controlled by fear of death and mutilation. Avoiders retained mental mobility and control; victims felt trapped. To have choices, whether exercised or not, is an important aspect of psychological health. To teach choice should be a goal of self-defense instructors.

There are many disagreements among self-defense experts and individuals about how to decrease the risk of violence or injury, yet there is one prevailing concept. All attempts are to decrease risk regardless of the chosen means, whether it is "turning the other cheek" or carrying a loaded gun. In any case, risk is an element that exists for every choice and every action or non-action.

It is unfortunate that the prevailing idea of decreasing risk for women in self-defense situations involves teaching them to limit their resistance strategies to those of passive escape attempts, verbal ploys or last-minute defenses.

Passive escape is rarely a viable option because of the types of attacks and restraints used on women. The most common methods attackers use are chokes, bear hugs, wrist grabs, hair grabs, blows and tackling, which end up as restraint by bodyweight. These restraints and attack methods are nearly impossible to break or to escape passively.

Recent studies have shown that verbal ploys are the least effective means of resistance. In fact, as we have seen, pleading has been correlated with being raped.

Finally, last-minute defenses: that is 1) waiting until all the damage has been done, or 2) systematically sacrificing your advantages **before** using physical resistance or until there is no other option but a last-resort, pain-shock technique, could be an unnecessary and psychologically damaging measure.

Based on the unfounded concept of decreasing risk, the idea of initial uncommitted resistance is dangerous to the goal of preventing rape and violence on the immediate level as well as on a larger scale. Without training, a woman who reacts immediately has a fifty/fifty chance of escaping an assault attempt, unharmed physically and, hopefully, psychologically.

One of the favorite rationalizations for confining and limiting women's self-defense programs to so-called safe options is that "a little knowledge is dangerous." The idea that knowledge of physical self-defense concepts is dangerous to women is superstitious, prejudiced and somewhat bizarre. Knowledge itself is never dangerous, although **misused** knowledge may be dangerous. Yet why should such knowledge be so strenuously withheld from women? Why would it be assumed that they would misuse it? I have seen instructors show significantly less fear of conveying combat and defense knowledge to classes of children than to classes of adult women.

Another fact exists. All violence and death techniques which are humanly, mechanically and chemically possible are already exposed, though often unrealistically, through all forms of media. I believe socially conscious instructors would want to tread through this territory and remove as many obstacles as possible for their students to arm them with as many rational, logical and effective options as possible. One cannot impart the wisdom to use knowledge wisely, yet one cannot encourage wisdom when controlling, limiting or withholding knowledge.

Aside from the rational, logical and learned options of self-defense, there is a totally irrational element to successful resistance. The most important rule of self-defense is to **trust yourself** and your ability to read social and situational cues and believe in your right to life.

> **"The most important rule of self-defense is to trust yourself and your ability to read social and situational cues and believe in your right to life."**

This "irrational element" is almost beyond explanation and is totally open to your own interpretation. Many people feel protected by unseen forces that cannot be defined absolutely by anyone, often even by the person who feels, experiences or believes in such forces. Remain open to this power and believe in your right to live unmolested with basic integrity and dignity.

Self-defense training and the knowledge of options increases a person's ability to make intelligent decisions and to believe in his or her own innate abilities. A person can train in martial arts forever, but unless that person believes in him- or herself, the training will be worthless as a means of self-protection.

Self-defense training means a woman can learn escape or defense possibilities at every level of assault. In addition to increasing the possibility of escape at **any** level, this would assist her in coping with **any** attack outcome! Knowing you are prepared and understand all options, even if you were unable to use them, will certainly alleviate the common problem of self-blame through lack of preparation. Self-blamers have a much harder time recovering emotional and mental control of their lives after an assault.

Teaching decreased risk by passive escape attempts or verbal ploys is only a one dimensional consideration. The belief that a woman cannot effectively resist is based on a theory of **strength versus weakness.** This is only **one** aspect of a confrontation which only takes into account the apparent physical realities of the attacker and the victim. In addition to tangible factors, there are also what might be called "supernatural" means of protection and psychic communications which are particularly intense in high-risk situations - if you remain open to these forces. These elements are usually suppressed or avoided because they could alienate many people with diverse philosophic ideologies or create a conflict because this concept could be construed as almost religious. Divine intervention and protection by God or higher powers can be an experience or a religious belief. I don't care where you get your divine energy or what you label the channel, it is a valid aspect of self-defense. Public schools and formal educational systems must avoid what cannot be explained or proved because what cannot be explained confounds the most orderly and logical of methods, theories and techniques. The idea of "psychic self-defense" and reacting to threats without **always** confining the reactions to logic appears to negate systems, techniques and training. The truth of logical and irrational self-defense lies between the extremes. Your maximum effectiveness draws on training and knowledge yet remains open to self-trust and trusting the power that confirms the worth and rightness of your existence by the very fact that you exist.

Beside considering your options in self-defense methods, you need to consider other variables in attack situations. These are

- **The location of the assault**

  In most cases it is in a familiar area. This means that you may be off-guard because of the apparent familiarity and security of your environment. Remember this and make a conscious effort to be more aware. Familiarity with the environment should be an advantage.

- **Condition of the assailant**

  In a random attack, the assailant generally must wait for a safe time to attack a chosen victim or wait until a chance victim crosses his path. He may have spent a fair amount of time in fear and anticipation which causes over-

106

stimulation of his nervous system by repeated bursts of adrenalin. This could mean the attacker's energy is depleted. Any assailant will be nervous, even an experienced rapist. In the first few seconds of the assault, his fears and doubts about his ability to gain control, carry out the crime and escape safely are at a peak. Many women in my study said the attacker was noticibly nervous. Exploit the attacker's fear of failure and detection.

- **The mode of attack**

In the mode of attack, consider the degree of threat including the intensity of the attack and presence of weapons. The latest figures released by the U.S. Department of Justice showed weapons present in only 17.6 percent of rape victimizations. Verbal threats should be taken seriously and you should defend accordingly, but do not cooperate when no other type of threat is present.

- **The floor plan**

What are the escape routes? In a home or residence, all you need to do is get to any available exit and escape. If you can get out of a door, run out screaming "Fire!" If you can escape from a window or scream "Fire!" from a window, exploit these possibilities. In many cases, windows cannot be opened. I suggest breaking a window if you can't open it, especially in an apartment building or where neighbors are close by. The noise will attract the attention of anyone nearby and this type of disturbance will scare the attacker. If you are stranded in an unfamiliar area, business or residential, make a quick mental map of strategic areas. Are there any fire or burglar alarms on the route? In a life-threatening situation, you may have to activate alarms. Locate the phones, well-lighted areas, convenience stores or block homes. Know these strategic locations in your familiar traveling areas.

- **If the time is right or safe for the attacker**

The only time an attacker is safe is when he has silently and quickly abducted a victim to a secluded, uninhabited area or taken a lone victim by surprise in her own home. Even an attack on a deserted street late at night is risky for the attacker. When is noise most noticable? When there are no other distracting noises.

Degrees of Threat

Non-Verbal and Verbal Equity

The following progression of degrees of threat is from low to high. Keep in mind a confrontation is not necessarily progressive, it could begin on any one of these levels. Assault situations can incorporate several of these steps in practically any combination, and in some cases (though rarely), nearly all of these events occur.

1) **Non-Verbal**

   - Staring

   - Glaring

   - Territorial encroachment

   - Following

   - Chasing

2) **Verbal**

   - "Polite" approach

   - Come-ons or coercion

   - Verbal abuse

   - Threats

3) **Non-Verbal Physical**

   - Inappropriate, unwelcome touching behaviors

107

- Groping or sexual advances

- Simple limb restraint - Example: grabbing wrists, hands or arms.

- Compound restraints - Example: bear hugs or chokes.

- Restraint by body weight

- Slapping, punching, kicking

- Presence of weapons

- Multiple attackers

Degrees of Response

Non-Verbal and Verbal Equity

In a threatening situation, the "ideal" pattern of progression for response is 1) verbal assertion; 2) verbal aggression; 3) physical assertion; and 4) physical aggression. However, attackers rarely observe the rules of progressive assault as is so often assumed by instructors of self-defense, especially women's self-defense. As I've stressed before and in some cases, the behavior of a potentially violent person can be calculating because he is attempting to reduce or eliminate risk. In other cases, violent behavior is chaotic and the range of behaviors can span all possibilities. Emotions can change rapidly as well. Therefore, it is dangerous to teach and promote these progressive resistance theories exclusively because it leaves women unprepared for the reality of a rape or an assault which doesn't follow the pattern.

"... it is dangerous to teach and promote these progressive resistance theories exclusively because it leaves women unprepared for the reality of a rape or an assault which doesn't follow the pattern."

The degree of response and degree of resistance should generally be consistent with the degree of threat. Yet teaching women exclusively to observe the behavioral rules of progressive assault is naive and unrealistic. I must stress again that this progression is based on confrontation **ideals**, just as martial arts systems are based on combat ideals. Combat or confrontation ideals are based on the idea that there will be a progressive confrontation or forewarning and challenge preceding a violent encounter.

It is incomprehensible to most men that an attacker would sneak up on a woman; based on the strength-versus-weakness theory, he wouldn't have to. However, strength alone would ensure a successful attack only when there are no situational or psychological factors weighing in the woman's favor, which is almost never the case.

Another important concept is **encroachment deterrents**.

Anytime you need to protect your physical space or prevent unwanted approaches, deterrents to intrusion can be applied. If you do not want someone to sit next to you, make the space near you less accessible. For instance, when you ride the bus, sit in the aisle seat and place your belongings in the window seat.

As an encroachment deterrent, maintain your mobility and choose a sitting or standing area in which you can't be cornered. It is a common practice to seat a woman between two males. Men will often attempt to control the seating arrangement. There is nothing undesirable about social situations in which you are seated between men - with one exception - if you don't feel comfortable, don't comply with these attempts or expectations.

Often in restaurants the maitre d' chooses the woman's chair by pulling it out. Practice asserting yourself by choosing your own chair so you can eat your dinner from a vantage point which you find comfortable and secure. The maitre d' is demonstrating politeness by pulling out your chair; he can do it just as well after you decide where you would like to sit. It is not his place to choose your seating position, particularly since a maitre d' tends to defer to males and is likely to treat women in a dinner party as subordinates.

You might also find someone attempting to control your physical position prior to entering a vehicle with other men and women. Men will often go to great lengths to avoid sitting next to each other when a woman enters the scene. You are not there to relieve their imaginary abhorrence for male-on-male contact. While in many situations it is not undesirable to be flanked by males in a car; in others, you may feel more comfortable if you sit by the door, even if you must sit in the back seat. Don't consistently relinquish the outside position if you feel uncomfortable doing it. This can happen in any situation. If you feel uncomfortable about it, do not allow this physical manipulation.

Assertive Verbal Acknowledgment

Assertive verbal behavior is another communication technique to ward off violence and should be **situationally** applied for maximum effectiveness. It is often assumed that aggressive verbal exchanges or responses escalate violent situations. This may be true in some situations, but it is not true in others. I believe assertive verbal acknowledgment is less a defense technique than it is a method to build confidence. Inner strength must be built on a foundation of self-esteem. Women do not have to respond to social verbal abuse; yet if they do not respond because they don't believe they have the right nor the ability to carry it off, they will lose respect for themselves.

I have often heard and read that women should not respond to verbal aggravation and abuse because words can't hurt you

and a response is an "over-reaction." Ideally, when the foundation of self-esteem is firm, words cannot hurt you. Yet a person who has respect for other human beings and has the ability to make an impact to better our society would feel the responsibility to do so **whenever possible**. This is why I promote assertive verbal acknowledgment to the social verbal abuse women are subjected to in this society. I differentiate between safe and dangerous situations in which to do this, however, and I do not believe a woman should be easily provoked or actively look for social slights. I simply think this type of social persecutor, the verbal abuser, should suffer some repercussions, and the embarrassing and humiliating effects of this behavior should be redirected toward him.

". . . this type of social persecutor, the verbal abuser, should suffer some repercussions, and the embarrassing and humiliating effects of this behavior should be redirected toward him."

The assumption that women overreact to degrees of threat is erroneous. It is probably based on observations of verbally-aggressive women made by people who have an ingrained prejudice towards this type of behavior from women. Studies show that women are far less likely to even **speak**, much less be unnecessarily aggressive in their speech.

Women are verbally adept and have often been reduced to aggravated verbal aggression as their only means of self-assertion. This is readily cited as an assault escalator when a woman is observed being crude or confrontive. This is often an outpouring of suppressed aggression from being the target of years of verbal abuse that men freely engage in. In high school both males and females engage in verbal abuse, usually in groups. For adult women in this society, the abuse never stops. I believe this is because there are no punishments or negative repercussions for this behavior.

This type of social harassment should be addressed in most cases which I term "safe situations." A generally safe situation is when you are harassed in a public place in the proximity of others. This is usually where this type of harassment takes place anyway because demeaning a woman in the presence of others seems to be part of the thrill.

Use controlled, calm statements when a man makes kissing noises and other vulgar noises or remarks. Look directly at him and say, "That's immature and rude." or "Don't direct that kind of behavior at me." For some real kicks, look at the offender threateningly, then quickly glance over your shoulder and say, "Rocky, some creep is bothering me!" I have done this in supermarkets, on the street, and in shopping malls. I make my statement and continue on my way.

Don't worry about insulting such a person or hurting his feelings; he obviously didn't care if he hurt yours. It may seem contradictory to the principles of integrity that I promote for women and self-defense to use an imaginary man as a threat technique or a ploy to avoid social harasssment. However, this is the only threat some men understand. If they had any degree of respect for themselves, they would not need to embarrass and harass women (or men, for that matter). If such persons with self-esteem problems were not afraid of other men, they would verbally harass them also. I don't consider this ploy as hiding behind an imaginary male authority figure. I consider re-directing the threat factor a method of exploiting the fear of an assailant in order to reverse the threat.

I find it ridiculous that even middle-aged men make crude noises and gestures and expect women to be the polite, passive recipients. Men who do this sort of thing are immaturely exercising their assumed

social dominance. They usually do it in "safe" public situations because they assume women will not make a fuss and cause themselves even more embarrassment.

How do you determine whether it is safe to respond?

If you're in a public place such as a supermarket, shopping mall or library, you can be fairly sure you can successfully reverse an attempt at social dominance.

If you are on a deserted street and a lone male or a group makes rude noises or remarks, he/they may be looking for an excuse to attack. In such a situation, do **not** respond verbally. Instead, move assertively and **create distance** immediately. If you believe you are at risk in such a situation that begins with verbal abuse, or if you even suspect danger for any reason, remember this strategy: distance or distraction creates a delay. Delay increases the time you need to escape; attracting attention can cause the attacker to flee or allow **you** time to plan your next move if you're temporarily trapped.

We have covered degrees of threat, the "ideal" progression of response and encroachment deterrents, the concepts of non-verbal equity and verbal and non-verbal assertive acknowledgement. Now we will corelate the degrees of threat with the degrees of resistance.

Degrees of Resistance

Non-Verbal and Verbal

Non-Verbal

- Staring - Assertive acknowledgment; maintain distance.

- Glaring - Assertive acknowledgment; maintain distance.

- Territorial encroachment - Assertive

acknowledgment, reestablish distance.

- Following - Assertive acknowledgment; maintain distance.

- Chasing - Run. Yell. Utilize environmental advantages: barriers, alarms, all possibilities to make noise, attract attention, confront.

Verbal

- "Polite" approach - Reestablish distance; polite but assertive refusal or conversation depending on your judgment.

- Come-ons or coercion - Reestablish distance; assertive refusal; non-verbal assertive acknowledgment.

- Verbal abuse - Non-verbal assertive acknowledgment. No verbal response is often the best deterrent to halt continued interaction. Maintain distance.

- Threats - Reactions range from all degrees of verbal and non-verbal reactions. Attempts to escape or physical defense depend on the situation and your perception of the assailant's ability to carry out the threat.

Non-Verbal Physical

- Inappropriate, unwelcome touching behaviors - Non-verbal equity means to assertively remove hands or touching in exactly in the same ways to make an instant impression or non-verbal statement, also to reestablish distance.

- Groping, sexual advances - Assertive removal and assertive verbal assertion; reestablish distance. Leave immediately if these measures do not put a stop to unwanted attention.

- "Simple" limb restraint: wrists, hands, arm, shoulders - Ideal progression:

verbal assertion; verbal aggression; physical assertion. Restraint-escape techniques. Escape.

- Compound restraint: restraint of limbs and body in possible combination with chokes or arm twists - Physical aggression techniques; pain-shock by primary or secondary target strike to facilitate release from restraint. Escape - Run. Yell. Utilize environmental objects, obstructions or barriers.

- Restraint by body weight - Verbal trickery or bargaining to get assailant to remove his body weight; i.e., "Let's both take our clothes off." Last-resort techniques: testicle twist; eye gouge; biting down on nerve center of upper lip to escape. Run and yell but use physical resistance and environmental destruction if you must.

- Slapping, punching, kicking - Physical aggression techniques: Run. Yell. Utilize all situational and environmental advantages or use psychological last-resort technique. Temporarily submit to create opportunity to utilize physical last-resort technique(s).

- Presence of weapons - Compliance as a survival strategy; trickery and bargaining; last-resort techniques when opportunity is created or presented. Utilize all situational and environmental advantages. Escape.

- Multiple attackers - Utilize existing environmental advantages. Determine the "leader" and concentrate on "taking him out." (This idea, along with psychological and physical defenses, is explained more fully in the Last-Resort Techniques chapter).

Application of Strategy

The preceding degrees of resistance corresponded to degrees of threat. The decision to respond equitably and the probability of success are based on

111

situational, environmental and psychological factors. First of all, what does an attacker need to carry out a successful rape or assault? The attacker needs time, a relatively safe place to carry out the assault and a victim who is sufficiently under his control.

Let's explore situational and environmental advantages that are needed for his successful attack.

Time - Always a Factor

A random assailant or stranger needs to procure a victim quickly or must take steps to ensure enough time and a safe location. In many cases, stranger attackers plan their crimes and choose a victim in advance. In other cases, the decision to rape is made in advance; the selection of the victim is left to chance. The attacker who leaves his selection of the victim to chance will frequent a high traffic area, parking lot, recreational area, college campus or shopping center during a relatively safe time. From seven p.m. to midnight is the highest risk time frame for a rape to occur.

A known assailant needs to commit the crime as fast as possible before any delay causes a loss of control. Situational and social ambiguity confuse the victim's threat perception and delay committed resistance. A rapist who knows his victim through any sort of relationship is well aware of situational and social ambiguities. This is why speed is essential because if the victim is not really aware a rape is about to occur, she will not react effectively until the rape is already well underway.

Place - Sometimes a Factor

Unless a rape is accompanied by a successful abduction, the place may not be ideal to avoid detection. A known assailant usually commits his crime in a residence or car. He has usually manipulated the victim into a safe attack area, however this does not generally mean out of range of detection.

Physical Control - Always a Factor When Determining the Probability of a Successful Resistance

A random attacker must gain enough control to silence and subdue the victim if the attack takes place in or near a public area. An attacker in an apartment building, residence or car is still within range of possible detection.

Martial arts defense systems are generally based on combat **ideals** which involve open challenge and facing the opponent to fight. I have received **very few** reports of rape and assault which were an open, progressive challenge. Known-assailant rape doesn't involve open challenge either. This type of assault may be progressive, but what escalates known-assailant rape is not a high degree of resistance on the woman's part. It is **delayed-threat perception** and **delayed-effective response**. An open challenge sometimes occurs in spouse abuse and known-assailant assault, though this usually involves family members or male/female teenage and adolescent confrontation.

". . . a rapist or violent assaulter does not intend to do battle with a woman; he intends to control and dominate or express anger and frustration."

In general, a rapist or violent assaulter does not intend to do battle with a woman; he intends to control and dominate or express anger and frustration. The prospect of losing control in an attack attempt on a woman is frightening to the attacker. Remember, the attacker must accomplish his goal rapidly to ensure safety. Committed resistance takes time, energy and could attract attention. With every passing second, the attacker loses control and power.

The first few seconds of an assault are

the most crucial. This is when the attacker's doubts and fears are at a peak; he is unsure if he will be able to gain control at a **minimum of risk** to him.

In many cases, he needs to get the victim to a safer location than the target area. Remember an unknown, random attacker is likely to target a victim in a high traffic area, college campus, street, apartment complex, recreational areas, etc.

If a woman follows the progressive theory of assault, she may be at more risk because the attacker is likely to gain control as the length of interaction increases. She may have no intention of cooperating with the attacker but is attempting "to avoid escalating" the violence by observing the rules of progressive assault. Instead of warding off violence, she may be inadvertently helping the attacker meet his assault requirements.

Response to Preliminary Threat or Social Intrusion

I promote a policy of **non-verbal equity** and **verbal and non-verbal assertive acknowledgment** for a large number of preliminary threat situations.

Assertive acknowledgment is simple and powerful.

"Assertive acknowledgment is simple and powerful."

When you are subjected to direct or indirect threatening, non-verbal behaviors, you acknowledge your awareness of the other person's behavior without signaling your willingness for more interaction or your inability to thwart further interaction.

Many women have told me that they "ignore" all non-verbal behavior which makes them uncomfortable. Although this may be effective when you're dealing with non-threatening individuals, it is a submissive signal otherwise. An exception

is when verbal abuse by groups or individuals is already in progress. Verbal abuse is an attempt to establish an exchange or to arouse an aggressive reaction. By not participating, you are not complying with the expectation.

Other non-verbal behaviors are committed with the hope of arousing expected behaviors. When a man stares openly at your body, you are supposed to glance quickly away or study the ground. This is the expected response. It serves his purpose of eliciting a submissive reaction and asserting non-verbal social dominance. If you look back briefly and assertively, square your shoulders and stand solidly, you have reversed the situation by indicating your unwillingness to be a passive recipient of unwanted attention. If you return the gaze and don't correct submissive facial or physical cues, you may experience what women are trying to avoid by "ignoring" these behaviors. The individual will see it as a signal to approach.

Practice non-verbal assertive acknowledgment in "safe" situations until you can carry it off efficiently, comfortably and convincingly.

Non-verbal equity is a method of resistance in the early stages of a threatening situation, providing that there is a progressively escalating series of events. It is also a valid response to socially intrusive behaviors.

Women are often subjected to intrusive unwanted touching behaviors such as "shepherding." That's when a non-intimate contact steers you around corners by possessively poking his fingers in your back or "herding" you by grabbing your upper arm or palming your back. In most instances, this is unnecessary and irritating. It non-verbally implies that you can't figure out how to navigate a corner or walk through the threshold of a door.

You may feel helpless to put a stop to this behavior without insulting the

113

perpetrator. In that case, you can apply the non-verbal equity method. Simply return such well-meaning but irritatingly possessive gestures in kind. You will make a non-verbal statement that is understood instantly although often sub-consciously. It may take persistence but you will get through.

Remember, "shepherding" behaviors are almost exclusively reserved for blind people, small children, elderly people and women. In the case of children, these behaviors are needed to direct and control; in the case of the elderly or blind, they are needed to direct or to steady someone; but why are they needed for normal adult women?

In some cases these may be courtship behaviors. With an intimate contact, you must decide whether you enjoy these gestures.

Non-verbal equity has another application in response to the beginning stages of a threatening situation. When you are groped or grabbed, **assertively remove the offender's hand.** Place your hand firmly on his and remove it with determination, not sudden brushing or throwing. Assertive removal with assertive eye contact is a powerful deterrent to further action. You've made your wishes known without overreacting.

Assertive removal is not escalation or an infuriating invitation to more aggression. It is a clear communication that does not humiliate the offender in public, such as at a party, in the office or in a crowd, bus or subway, as verbal resistance might. You have not aroused a need for retaliation, increased your risk, or signaled fear or compliance. You have re-established your physical space requirements.

Psychological Factors

Your internal psychological commitment and preparation are the most important factors that determine the probability of successful resistance. This is

114

true with every confrontation besides the external factors and the attacker's needs, such as the necessary time, place and physical requirements.

In information available to the general public, the psychological factors and needs of the resistor as an important determinant in the outcome of an attack situation have been largely ignored.

Psychological factors have usually been explored from the **rapist's** point of view. Women are told to try to "psych" out the attacker and give him the ego enhancement he needs. This viewpoint totally ignores the human needs of a woman and fails to evaluate the attack situation from her point of view. I do not rely heavily on the usual advice of "figuring out the attacker's state of mind" and "appealing to his ego." This is an extremely complex suggestion for most attack situations, particularly a random-stranger attack when the element of surprise and speed of the attack eliminate the supposed social interactions of trying to figure out and give the attacker what he wants.

When the attacker has successfully manipulated **his** time, place and safety requirements, it is unlikely that **you** will have the time or the inclination to appeal to his ego. Seriously now; once you've been jumped, grabbed, struck or dragged through the dirt, how are you going to convincingly "appeal to his ego?"

In a known-assailant situation, this suggestion is a form of trickery to create time and distance, to escape or defend. You indicate compliance and willingness in order to get free of his body weight, the most common known-assailant restraint. Actually there are other restraints or grabs preceding the body-weight restraint, but a woman is unlikely to perceive these gestures as threatening with someone she knows. Women so consistently tolerate personal space violation that an actual threat is rarely perceived or is hard to differentiate from a sexual advance.

When you determine the probability of successful resistance, don't try to remedy a lifetime of unmet ego needs that the attacker has brought with him to the assault. Rather, consider these factors: 1) what might the attacker have to lose and 2) what is **he** afraid of? These factors have been ignored in the common rape and resistance mythology. They are not mentioned in women's self-defense programs and consequently, they are rarely considered by women themselves.

"When you determine the probability of successful resistance, don't try to remedy a lifetime of unmet ego needs that the attacker has brought with him to the assault."

The fears of the resisting victim are over-emphasized and exaggerated. Certainly confrontive situations are frightening but remember, it takes more than one person to engage in a confrontation. Each party has fears; most of them are similar. Both the attacker and the resistor fear pain, harm, loss and failure. The attacker's fears are double because he can lose and fail immediately in a unsuccessful attempt, and he can lose and fail in the long run because he also has fear of detection and punishment.

Fear may reduce your effectiveness, especially diffused and nebulous psychological fear. Fear for your immediate safety and for your life may assist your effective escape because it will activate physiological reactions.

"Remember your immediate goal is simply escape; the attacker's goals are complex."

Remember **your** immediate goal is simply escape; the attacker's goals are complex. His immediate goal is gaining control, securing time and place, completing an act of violence and then escaping. His fears are complex and diffused. Your fears, if not complicated by learned psychological fears, should be simple and focused on escape.

According to Groth's research of convicted rapists, the majority are married or have a primary sexual relationship. All rapists in Groth's studies had sexual involvements and opportunities and did not need rape as a purely sexual outlet. Groth has effectively desexualized the crime of rape and isolated the rapist's needs and motivations to those of expressing control, dominance, anger and frustration which ultimately, even if twisted, involve the need to win. We can conclude that most rapists have something to lose in their need to win. It is a psychological advantage for you if you fully understand this.

The following are the psychological factors which affect assailants. If you understand these factors, you will realize that the assailant is fearful and you can exploit this fear.

- **Fear of failure - the loss of ill-gotten self-esteem**

  Think about the kind of man who needs to attack women to feel powerful. What if he chooses the "wrong" victim and fails to abduct or overpower her? This will undermine his future attempts because he will fear failure. He has already failed to build healthy self-esteem, so he fears failing in his secret methods to experience control and power even more. Many famous rapist/murderers have expressed fear of failure and said they gave up when a woman resisted. They also reported "practicing" on easier targets and escalating the degree of violence as they gained confidence from successful attacks on especially vulnerable victims, the old, very young, weak or crippled.

- **Fear of pain**

Does this surprise you? Even if a rapist could indisputably overpower and had the time and situational advantages on his side, everyone fears being struck, even accidentally. An attacker's soft parts, his eyes and/or testicles are always in danger in a struggle. Have you ever wrestled around with a guy and accidentally banged his groin or jabbed an eye? Even if the attacker believes you don't know how to fight, he can't be sure you won't flail around and cause him harm.

- **Fear of detection**

This may be the dominant fear the attacker is experiencing in an attack situation. This is why he so carefully controls for situational advantages; why he tries to ensure his chosen victim will not resist. Resistance and opposition take time and time is precious for any kind of criminal. The faster a crime is committed, the less opportunity for detection and capture.

- **Fear of loss**

An attacker fears being caught in the act and captured. Then he will lose control; he will lose physical integrity, social approval, social standing, security and possibly his existing relationships.

- **Fear of punishment**.

An attacker who is caught and captured in the act will face punishment and possible incarceration.

All of these fears are present during most attacks and are most prominent in the initial stages before the attacker has gained control. In the first stages of the encounter, he is still unsure that he will be able to complete the assault at a **minimum of risk** to himself.

Think about these factors for a moment. What does a woman fear about rape and violent encounters? What is the major

116

difference in a woman afraid of rape and a man about to commit rape?

A woman's fear of violation and loss of bodily integrity is the only major difference and this is related to fear of loss and fear of failure in avoiding, defending against or preventing rape. I find it inconceivably puzzling that no one mentions the rapist's fears in an attack situation. He is the one committing the crime and taking the risk. Probably he's been successful before when he's hit, run and escaped; **but he couldn't relax** until he was safe and under cover.

Frederick Storaska, author of *How to Say No to a Rapist and Survive,* hammered this one point home - with an entirely different philosophy behind it. He urged women to remember that "The Rapist Is A Human Being." Storaska wanted women to remember this because the "poor guy" had feelings and he was raping to fulfill emotional needs.

I want you to remember that the rapist is a human being so you won't ever forget that whatever fears you have, he has. An attacker feels the same fear and anxiety experienced by a resistor in the initial stages of the attack.

You're shocked at being attacked? He could be shocked by your committed resistance.

You're afraid of being raped? He's afraid of getting caught.

You're afraid he's crazy? He's afraid you might be.

You're afraid of getting hurt? Like any human being, he's also afraid of pain.

If he does not seem particularly anxious or fearful, your actions can activate his fears.

Remember your immediate fear in this case is loss of bodily integrity and loss of control. Your **immediate** fears, as opposed to the attacker's fears, are minimal. In the long run, women often suffer other losses besides loss of bodily integrity as a result of rape, such as loss of confidence, psychological security, injury and even loss of primary relationships. Yet in an actual assault, the immediate fear is physical violation and fear of death and mutilation, which is largely erroneous. Remember Brownmiller's rape/murder calculation of .2 percent of reported cases. So remember this. Acting on your immediate fear, you only have one simple goal: escape and report. The attacker's fears and goals are more complex.

To reemphasize, the rapist generally has a lot to lose psychologically and socially. These fears are with him at all times and are intensified in the first stages of an attack. It's only when he easily gains power and control that he feels safe. It is essential to remember that a rapist has a lot to lose, especially in a known-assailant situation. The word "rape" and the realization that a rape is going to occur is rarely understood or mentioned in the beginning stages of a known-assailant assault. This is not because of the sexist joke that "she changed her mind" afterward. It is because of the victim's delayed-threat perception and the mistaken belief that protest and polite struggle will make an impression on this "friend." Control is lost by the time the victim realizes rape is inevitable or in progress.

Situational Advantages

Now that you know all the rapist's fears and you can manipulate psychological advantages, what situational advantages do you need to be more effective? Where does most rape occur? What time is rape most likely to occur? According to my survey and the general body of information available on rape, it is most likely to occur in a familiar area, often a residence, between 7 p.m. and midnight.

What are situational advantages and how do you use them to exploit the attacker's fears?

- **Familiar attack area such as neighborhood or home**

  You may be familiar with escape routes or persons in the area. Your own home is an advantage because you are on your own territory. Have inside push-type locks on your bathroom door, study and bedroom. Have a phone extension in at least one extra room that also has a push-type lock. Think about inconspicuous weapons available in your environment, such as a rock collection, pictures, plants, door stoppers, vases. Think about outdoor materials such as dirt, gravel and objects such as trash cans and car hoods that make noise if you strike them.

  Create time and distance by any method possible and use **multiple strategies**. Bombard the attacker with one action after another and with rapid behavior changes and reverse the stress and fear factors.

- **Environmental objects and barriers to create noise or refuge**

  In an apartment, hotel or motel, bang on walls; run out into hallways; knock over garbage cans; pull fire alarms; break windows; bang on car hoods. In other situations, run to lighted areas or convenience stores; stop traffic; create noise and disturbance by those methods and any other available option.

- **Environmental obstructions**

  Inside, get behind any environmental barrier. In a residence, use tables and chairs. The best barrier is behind a locked door where you can open windows and yell or escape. Outside, use vehicles or any possible barrier to evade capture and create time, distance and noise.

- **Evaluate the attacker**

  Can you feel his fear, nervousness, exhaustion? In a random-attack situation, the attacker has probably waited a long time for a chance victim to come along or waited for a particular victim for a long time. In either case, the attacker is likely to be depleted and weakened by fear and anticipation. Most planned rapes by unknown attackers involve the attacker having to wait until late at night or having to get up at 2 or 3 a.m. to carry out the plan.

In premeditated attacks where selection of the victim is left to chance, the attacker has already experienced bursts of fear and charges of adrenaline. It is very unlikely that an attacker will approach committing a violent crime without fear or anxiety.

When considering situational advantages, realize that there is some element in every situation that might work for you. One woman in my study was taken to a secluded area by two attackers who stopped to "help her" with car trouble. When there was no way to repair the car, she accepted their offer of a ride. She felt secure because they were accompanied by a young boy. The attackers pulled off onto a secluded area and then sent the little boy into the woods so they could carry out the rape.

She used trickery by exploiting the same element used to exploit her. She pretended to become frightened that the little boy would get lost. She diverted the attackers' attention to the edge of the woods and then ran. She climbed a mud bank and escaped back to the highway and flagged down a passing motorist.

If possible, utilize all situational advantages, attempt to buy time and divert the assailant or attract attention.

Also consider this. Do criminals attempt to maximize their degree of risk to themselves in committing a crime? Of course not. Wherever possible a criminal will attempt to minimize the risk. Sometimes crimes against property are carried out by desperate people to feed themselves or their family or a drug habit.

Rape is not a crime of desperation; it is a crime of calculated opportunity. Realize that a rapist, known or unknown, will attempt to gain control of all the advantages. If you are not in an area safe for him to carry out a rape, assault, or robbery, don't go with him to a safer area and expect to have a better chance to escape. Don't ease his fears or help him gain psychological control, interaction power and more advantages. Only resort to these tactics as a resistance-survival strategy when you face a weapon, have no possibility of defense or no possibility of immediate escape because of your vulnerable location or the number of attackers.

"Rape is not a crime of desperation; it is a crime of calculated opportunity."

118

Technique
Section

What experience in self-defense training does not prevent, it can help heal.
James S. Johnson

Chapter VI

Self-Defense Techniques

The actual techniques which are shown in this section are founded on six basic principles. These are 1) using your instinctive reaction in an attack, 2) using the attacker's involuntary reaction to pain and shock, 3) unbalancing and redirecting the attacker, 4) circular redirection and downward leverage on the attacker, 5) resisting and then redirecting the force of the attack and 6) using your most effective body weapons.

Your full understanding is important, especially if you intend to act as your own instructor.

The **most** important aspect of your training is your belief in yourself. But no matter how you choose to learn, you **cannot physically learn techniques** without a partner. The second most important aspect is your choice of a partner or instructor. If you practice with your husband, boyfriend or a male or female friend who **does not believe** a woman can learn to defend herself, you may be defeated before you start.

A women's self-defense foundation called Chimera Inc., has a main office in Chicago, Illinois. The Chimera (Ki-MERE-ah) is a mythical beast with the head of a lion, the body of a goat and the tail of a serpent. Its name has come to be associated with imaginary fear.[1] The Chimera organization is dedicated to defeating the fear that women are helpless to defend their own security.[2] Based on research, they strongly believe in the effectiveness of physical resistance and they teach excellent techniques. Chimera has trained instructors in nearly every major city in the United States. To locate a Chimera instructor, call (312) 332-5540 or write Chimera Inc., 10 S. Wabash #602, Chicago, Illinois, 60603.

Chimera instructors teach any organized group, small or large. They are the best option for women's self-defense training when instructors are available in your area. Some large cities have self-defense schools exclusively for women, an excellent option for a woman interested in a specialized course.

If you want to go into the martial arts for long-term study, you should go to your library, a bookstore or a martial arts supply store and look through the book and magazine racks to find information about the diverse martial arts styles and choose one that's best for your abilities and preferences.

"If you practice with your husband, boyfriend or a male or female friend who does not believe a woman can learn to defend herself, you may be defeated before you start."

In the long run, your choice of instructor is far more important than which martial arts style you choose. Though very little information will be given over the phone, your next move is calling the schools in your area to get as much information as possible. You will have to make appointments and meet the instructor face to face to determine whether you can work with that instructor.

To give you some advantages in choosing a martial arts school or self-defense class, determine if an instructor is concerned or open-minded enough to consider some of the issues presented in this book. If not, it is doubtful that he or she could effectively teach you.

I think every martial arts school should offer a self-defense course for the public with a special emphasis on courses for women. A course for women usually should be taught by a woman with men acting as "attackers" not necessarily as authority figures. The facilities for teaching self-defense exist all over the country; the instructors are qualified. Why then is a self-defense course for women so hard to find? In some cases, instructors do not give any priority to the issue of self-defense for women, while others do not have the time to devote to specialized programs for women. With a little research and

preparation, a head instructor could arrange for a qualified female instructor/student to teach such a program.

If you do want long-term study and cannot find a specialized self-defense course, you should join any type of martial arts school for at least six months to learn basics and to have a qualified instructor help you decipher these techniques and experience them. An instructor may have minor or major disagreements with my approach. The only aspect that matters is that the instructor believes women can overcome helplessness and develop more skill in physical defense. Although your own beliefs are most important, any type of psychological sabotage can delay your progress.

Following are the six major principles of the self-defense techniques which are illustrated in this section. The principles employ 1) using first instincts, 2) using the pain/shock method for restraint escape, 3) unbalancing and redirecting your attacker's weight, 4) using circular redirection and downward leverage, 5) resisting and redirecting and 6) using the most effective body weapons.

First Instinct

Most self-defense techniques should be taught to begin with an instinctive reaction. An instinctive reaction will happen anyway regardless of what is taught. The first instinctive reaction when a person has been grabbed or restrained is to reduce physical stress or pain. The first reaction to a choke is to obtain oxygen. The first thing a person will do when a body part is injured is grab that part with his or her hands. If a person is being choked, he or she will claw or grab the throat.

This grabbing reaction should be taught as a first step in a self-defense technique, even though it is an instinctive reaction. Then, in the event of an assault, it will act as an **internal cue** and trigger the body's trained reactions. If the instinctive response is not reinforced as part of a

122

resistance technique, an attacked woman may start to struggle or grasp and she may be more likely to lose control or panic because she will think she forgot what she was trained to do. Panic causes the mind to "go blank" and the body goes on "automatic." This is why the **first instinct** should be taught as the first step to any technique. Then one step follows another.

Pain/Shock Method
for Restraint Escape

In many cases, a restraint cannot be broken unless the attacker has been stunned with pain.

A wrist grab is a good example. If an attacker gets a good grip on your wrists or applies a complete hold, it's difficult to effect a release with tricky little moves. The major reason most wrist-release escape techniques would ever work is the element of surprise or suddenness of the reaction before the attacker has time to clamp down or apply strength. When you practice restraint-escape techniques, you will see what I mean. All wrist grabs are based on breaking out through the thumb and forefinger. When there's no space, it's hard to create it.

In order to create space in a simple limb restraint or a compound restraint of the limbs and body, you must cause sharp pain or shock to cause the attacker to react briefly.

What is the body's reaction to pain? When you feel sharp pain, your hands involuntarily open. What happens when you pick up something that's burning hot? You drop it. If you were carrying a bag of groceries and something fell on your instep or painfully banged your kneecap or shin, what would you do? You would most likely drop, or nearly drop, what you were carrying. There is a brief "letting go" action that occurs as a reaction to physical pain and this can be momentary or prolonged, depending on the intensity of the pain.

Unbalance and Redirect

Restraint-escape techniques must often incorporate pain/shock methods to facilitate the involuntary release action. Pain/shock methods can also be used to unbalance and redirect the attacker; or in other words, get him off you so you can escape.

A good example is any restraint in which only your feet are free. If you stomp the attacker's foot, what will happen? He will take his weight off that foot, making it easier to cause him to fall in that direction. When a foot or leg is hurt, a person takes the weight off that leg and uses the hands for balance. When a person is suddenly unbalanced, the hands involuntarily flail for balance and attempt to cushion a fall. The body's involuntary reactions are the basis of the pain/shock unbalance and redirect method of restraint escape.

When your upper body is restrained, you stomp or back kick your attacker's knees or rake down his shins to get the pain compensation reaction, then you escape during his recovery period. Don't ever wait around for even one second. Pain makes some people very angry, and after the initial immobilizing shock, the attacker could be much harder to control. Anger can desensitize pain reactions.

The whole point is to effect release from a restraint and **create time** to escape.

"The whole point is to effect release from a restraint and create time to escape."

A man can be **destablized** more easily than a woman. How could this be when they are stronger and heavier? Well, I'm sure you've heard the saying, "The bigger they are, the harder they fall." It's an old catch phrase, but here are the reasons it's true.

Men carry more weight in the upper body, which is a distinct balance disadvantage. If they fall, this increased weight is compounded by gravity. A heavier object does not fall faster, but it hits the ground harder. Women have a lower center of gravity and carry more weight in the lower body. Have you ever seen a paper weight with a narrow, light bottom and wide, heavy top? This would be inefficient and unstable. Since this is the way most men are built, you can see how it is easy to unbalance a man. If you can disrupt his balance, you have created time to escape.

Circular Redirection and Downward Leverage

Choking from the front and grabbing clothing, arms, shoulders and wrists are the two most common and most important types of restraint to escape from immediately. All of these are most effectively broken by circular redirection and downward leverage. Downward leverage, or pushing down, is the strongest leverage position because it utilizes bodyweight and gravity. The circular motion used with these techniques creates speed and the element of surprise because many circular motions are below or outside vision perimeters.

Resist and Redirect

This principle is like the door trick you've seen in cartoons or maybe have used yourself when you were a kid. You're holding off a person or persons on one side of the door and, when they are pushing their hardest, you step away as they fly through, stumble and fall. This principle is important because many attackers try to drag and pull a woman away after she initially resists. It usually starts with the attacker grabbing a woman's wrists. She immediately tries to get away. The attacker can't release her or she'd run, so he ends up trying to drag her like a mule.

The principle of resisting and redirecting is resisting just until the attacker gets a footing and really starts to pull.

124

Then you can use the force of his pulling to fly into him with a knee to the groin or knock him backwards, causing him to break his grip. With this technique principle, you use the attacker's force against you and redirect it to compound the force of any blow you use for defense.

The Most Effective Body Weapons

You have a time limit in any specialized self-defense program. Since it can take several years to teach a person to punch correctly, open-handed techniques are far more versatile and easier to learn. Open-handed strikes with the side of your hand and heel of your hand can utilize your power more effectively. To test this concept, do a heel palm or a chop to a hard surface, then punch the same surface. As you can **feel**, the punching is more painful and risky - for you.

A side-heel palm to the neck can practically knock a head off its axis and it can cause intense pain by disturbing the alignment of the spine and wrenching the muscles on either side of the neck. If you have ever suddenly wrenched your neck and suffered whiplash, you know what I'm talking about. It is nearly impossible to prevent neck injury when a sudden forceful movement occurs.

The neck **can** be strengthened through exercise with an additional benefit. Have you ever seen a body builder with a wrinkly neck and hanging jowls? Building muscle builds the neck and you will be able to defend against strangulation plus everyday neck pain and tension caused by weak, unused muscles. Nevertheless, if someone twists your head suddenly or hits you with a side-heel palm, you will suffer trauma; but so will an attacker when you do the same to him, even a heavily muscled one.

Open-handed strikes make sense for another reason. The hand is made of numerous small bones; the head is large and solid. In fact, the jaw bone is the hardest bone in the body. Even though there are sensitive areas on the head, such as the base of the nose, the nerve center under the nose is protected by cartilage. In order to knock someone out with a punch from a closed fist, you must hit him hard enough to affect the nerve center. An upward heel palm under the nose could hit the nerve center without having to use nearly as much power and it will not break your hand.

Open-handed techniques include gouging, grasping and twisting suitable for soft part destruction. The other effective bodily weapons use "hard parts," such as fingers, knees, elbows, front and back of the head and the heels of the feet and hands.

A general rule is to use hard parts for soft part destruction and to strike areas with concentrated nerves. Soft parts of the body include eyes, genitals, tongue and lips.

The only exceptions to this rule taught in courses reduced to the most effective techniques are stomping insteps, stomping out knee joints and using a knuckle rap to the back of the hand, another area of concentrated nerves. The exception to open-handed techniques is the hammer-fist blow. The hammer-fist acts as a "hard part" when applied correctly.

To maximize effectiveness, all strikes should be directed at vital areas, either primary or secondary targets.

Primary Targets

- **Temple** - Use the edge of your hand, your elbow or knee for striking the temple. If struck hard enough, the blow can cause unconsciousness or death.

- **Ears** - Using both your hands, slap both ears with open, slightly cupped hands with a clapping motion. The blow can cause his eardrums to burst. Edge of hand, fist, elbow or hard objects can be used to strike ears.

- **Eyes** - Attack eyes forcefully with two-finger thrust or thumb gouge. Pokes, jabs and pressure can cause temporary blindness. Excessive force can cause permanent blindness.

- **Nose or Philtrum** - This refers to the nerve center on the upper lip and under the nose. This area can be struck with the edge of the hand, heel of the hand, front of the head in a close hold or with the back of head in a bear hug from rear. A severe blow can cause unconsciousness or death.

- **Throat** - Use a hammer-fist, side of your hand or your elbow to strike his throat. Explosive force to the windpipe (Adam's apple) can cause it to collapse. The windpipe itself can be crushed by grasping it forcefully, digging in with the thumb and encircling it and squeezing with all four fingers.

- **Testicles** - Vulnerable to grab-pull-and-twist, this is described in Last-Resort Techniques. Testicles can be struck with an underhanded blow and knee-lift techniques. Blows to testicles can cause severe pain, swelling and temporary incapacitation. Pulling and twisting the testicles can cause shock or death.

- **Solar Plexus** - A hard blow to the stomach just under the rib cage can cause temporary loss of wind or unconsciousness. The elbow is generally most effective as a strike to this area used from a rear-grab position. Another good weapon to stab this area would be an environmental weapon, such as a broom handle.

- **Kneecap** - Use side kick or knee-stomp kick to attack the kneecap. The object is to break or dislocate the knee or cause the attacker to lose his balance to create escape time.

Secondary Targets

- **Jaw/chin** - Strike with the side of your palm, the heel of your palm, elbow or forehead. This causes the whiplash effect to create escape time.

- **Shin** - Use the side of your foot or back of your heel in a scraping motion, kick directly or back kick when your back is to the attacker to cause the pain/shock reaction to release a wrist grip, arms, front or rear-bear hug.

- **Instep** - Use a stomping action on his instep to effect your release. Your total body weight must be used for the power to break the arch.

- **Lower abdomen** - Attack with your elbow or knee. For serious damage, hard and forceful blows are required.

- **Back of the hand** - Use your fist or knuckle rap to the nerve center on the back of the hand to effect hand release. Any dull or sharp object can be used to strike the back of the hand.

- **Elbow joint** - Vulnerable to arm twisting and breaking methods.

The following is a brief summary of important points to remember and elements that would increase your successful application of your physical strategy.

Top Physical Resistance Strategies

- **Running**

- **Yelling**

- **Fighting**

How to Maximize Effectiveness of Strategies

- **Whenever possible, react quickly and assertively.**

This decreases interaction time and decreases the possibility that the assailant can restrain or injure you or gain psychological control.

- **Exploit the element of surprise.**

This is the most effective aspect of an attack. The assailant surprises a victim which may wipe out the victim's effective reactions and thought. Reverse this surprise element. Use all forms of immediate resistance including running, yelling, fighting and using environmental objects for noise, barriers or weapons.

- **Remember the three D's of strategy: Distraction, Distance and Delay.**

All resistance strategies are used to create distance and time in order to escape. Distraction may involve physical pain/shock techniques and psychological ploys to create distance. Once distance has been established, you have created delay - escape time. **Remember** - the most important point of **any** resistance strategy is to escape with minimal interaction and injury from the assault attempt. Physical techniques are not methods of retaliation. They are methods to create space, time and escape possibilities.

- **Use multiple strategies to maximize effective resistance.**

Change rapidly from one strategy to another to confuse and frighten the assailant. Multiple strategies reverse the stress bombardment and have been shown through several studies to be a major element of successful resistance.

Top Avoidance Strategies

- Decrease interaction time with any unwanted approach.

- Increase impersonal social distance.

- Establish and maintain a larger social zone with any non-intimate contact.

- Use assertive verbal and non-verbal communication.

> **"Physical techniques are not methods of retaliation. They are methods to create space, time and escape possibilities."**

How to Practice

I have tried to make the basics and techniques self-explanatory so that you would not require an instructor, but the addition of a formal instructor will help with motivation and proper execution of techniques.

If you intend to practice on your own or with a group, there are only a few important suggestions left.

- You need uninterrupted time several times per week for at least one hour.

- Wear comfortable clothing at first, and later schedule practice in "street clothes." Wear an outfit that is ready for the dry cleaner.

- You need space in order to work out, so you may have to move furniture.

- You need padding if you intend to practice the unbalance and redirect techniques in this section. A futon mattress is fine. You can also buy foam padding that is at least four-feet wide and six-feet long for a few dollars at a foam outlet store. Your practice partner can hold a rolled-up sleeping bag for protection while you practice knee lifts. You can have your partner hold one or more pillows against the wall and practice heel palms (heel of hand) and chops (side-of-hand strikes).

Time, space, commitment and a partner are all you really need. You can improvise on-the-floor padding but be extremely careful. I can guarantee one thing; you will have fun and will learn a lot about yourself and the people you work out with. In order to maximize the experience, realize that you can also improve your fitness level, become competent in self-defense and more confident in your life.

Another very important point to remember is to choose your practice partner carefully. You can be easily deceived by a partner who claims to want to be helpful but subconsciously or secretly is trying to sabotage your efforts.

Often in martial arts classes, we would practice simulated attack situations to demonstrate our defense skills. We would be grabbed or restrained in some manner and would demonstrate the first part of any serious escape attempt by "softening up" the attacker through pain and momentary incapacitation. The "victim" would throw a fake kick to the knee, an instep stomp or a knee lift to "soften" up the attacker for the restraint escape. The "attacker" would usually totally ignore a move that would have undoubtedly affected his ability in a real-life situation and continue to hold the defender in a tight restraint or a vice grip on the wrists. Usually, such a person would be emoting an intense competitiveness or grinning with perverse satisfaction that this woman could not escape.

The same problem exists with students who go home and try techniques with their husbands or other male partners. They come back and report with dismay, "I tried X and I couldn't get away!" I ask them, "Did you **really** stomp out his knee? Did you actually knee-lift his groin with full power?" The answer, of course, was **no**.

This reaction on the part of the "attacker" is not always meant as a sabotage of your efforts. It is sometimes due to a lack of awareness. When you point this out to your partner, he or she will learn to "react" to compensate for the pain and injury which would be inflicted if you actually carried out your practice techniques.

Basic Techniques

• Primary Strikes   Secondary strikes

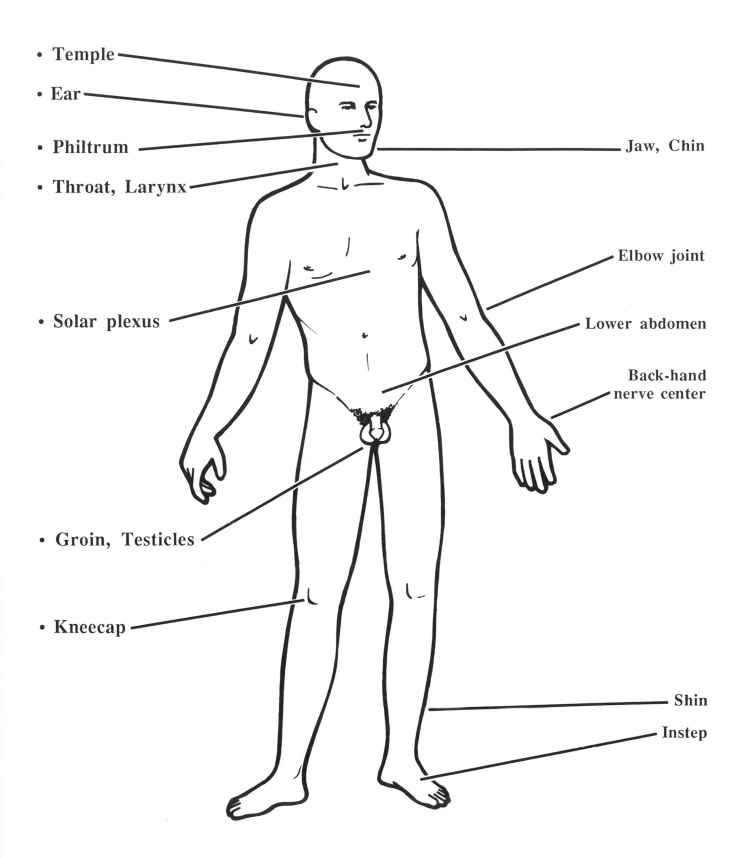

• Temple

• Ear

• Philtrum   Jaw, Chin

• Throat, Larynx

                                                    Elbow joint

• Solar plexus   Lower abdomen

                                                    Back-hand
                                                    nerve center

• Groin, Testicles

• Kneecap

                                                    Shin

                                                    Instep

Basics Section, Part 1: Hand Techniques and Blocking

Heel-Palm Strike

1A. The illustration shows the proper position of the hand for the heel-palm strike with the thumb tucked.

1B. In a low-risk situation, apply the heel of your hand under the attacker's chin to push his head back. This can wrench his neck and temporarily obscure his vision.

1C. In a high-risk situation, you can slam the heel of your hand under his nose at the philtrum and shock the nerve center concentrated in the upper lip area.

The Claw

1D. This is a claw-hand position. It can be used for a throat grab causing a crushed larynx or a testicle grab and twist.

1E. Applying the claw-hand position as an eye gouge can create tearing of the eyes and temporary blindness to gain escape time.

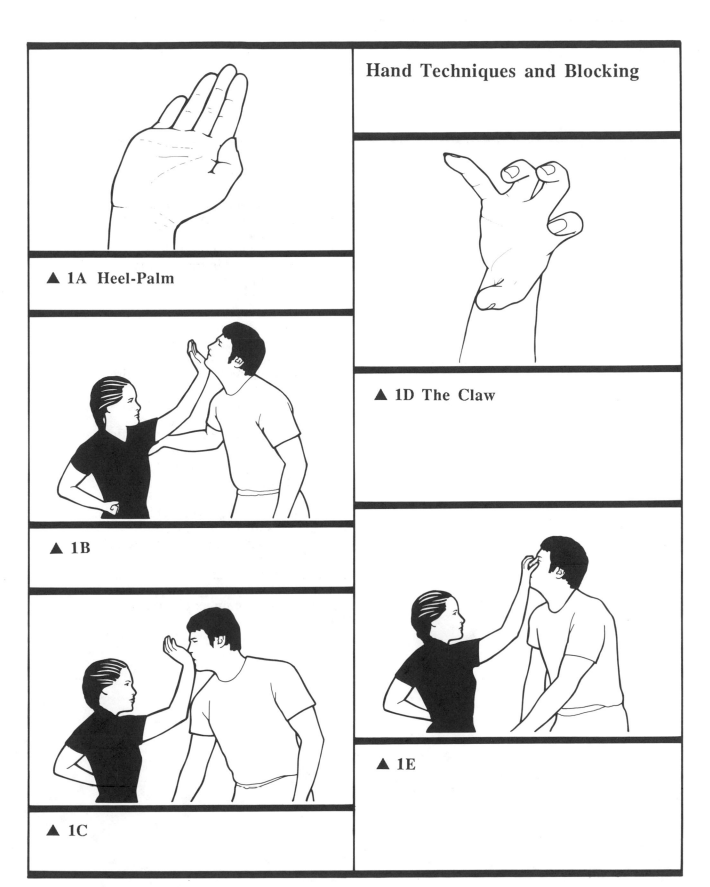

Hand Techniques and Blocking

▲ 1A Heel-Palm

▲ 1B

▲ 1C

▲ 1D The Claw

▲ 1E

Hammer-Fist Blow

2A. The proper hand position for the hammer-fist blow is shown with the thumb tucked close to the outside of the closed fist. This is the only closed-hand technique used in this section. Punching techniques are risky and difficult to learn.

2B. In a front-bear hug, reach up under the attacker's arms and grab his hair and jerk his head back. You can smash his larynx with the hammer-fist blow.

2C. In a simple low-risk release technique, you can use the hammer-fist as you rap your knuckles **hard** against the back of the attacker's hand and above his knuckles.

2D. In a rear-bear hug, step behind the attacker's legs throwing him off balance, then slam a hammer-fist in the attacker's groin as he lurches backward. This unbalancing technique is demonstrated in the Technique Section, situation number eight, page 159.

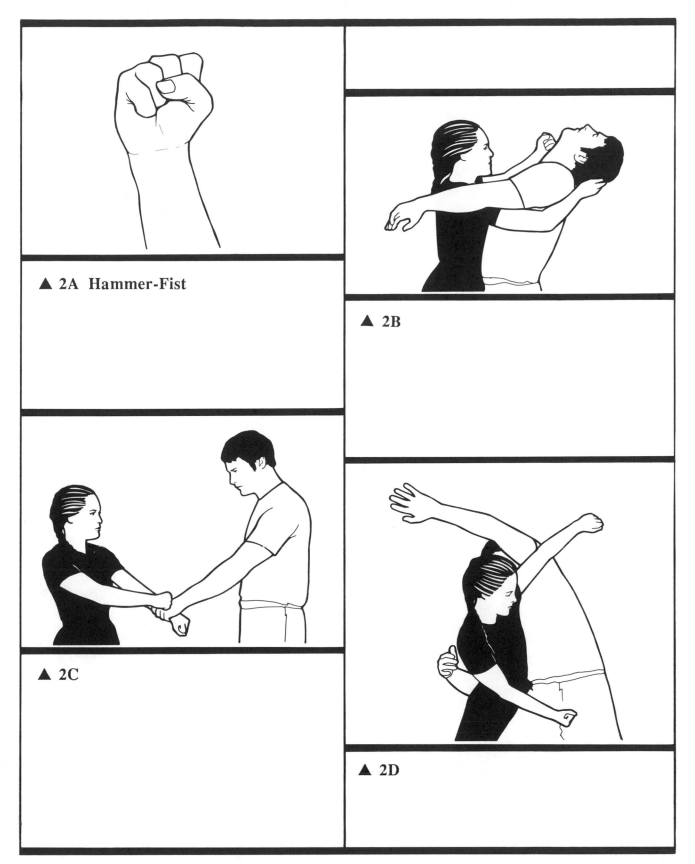

▲ 2A Hammer-Fist

▲ 2B

▲ 2C

▲ 2D

Fear or Freedom by Susan Smith ©1986

Open Hands and Fingers

3A. Basic-Blocking Technique

I consider this the all-time best basic-blocking technique. It's simple, low risk, effective, and best of all, instinctual. Note the body and hand position. You can unwind from this position and execute a heel-palm strike to the attacker's philtrum, the concentrated nerve center under the nose.

3B. Thumb Gouge

The thumb gouge is another simple and effective technique. Note that the thumbs are against the bridge of the nose. This can be done with one hand also. The attacker can be blinded permanently if this technique is done forcefully enough, but even if not, it will temporarily blind him long enough for you to escape.

3C. Eardrum Breaking

It is possible to break both eardrums by cupping the hands slightly and slapping them hard over the ears. This can create pain, shock, temporarily incapacitation and tearing of the eyes.

Open Hands and Fingers
Basic Blocking

◀ 3A

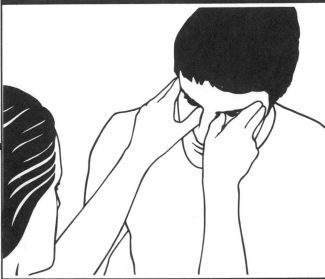

▲ 3B Thumb Gouge

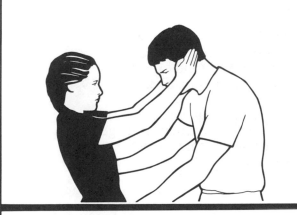

▲ 3C Eardrum Breaking

Basics Section, Part 2: Body Weapons - Hard Parts

Hard parts include knees, elbows and the head. These are the most effective bodily weapons.

1A. Straight-Rear-Elbow Strike

Use the straight-rear-elbow strike for a blow to the solar plexus. Keep your elbow close to your body. Bring it straight back forcefully into the solar plexus or drop your knees to get lower and slam an elbow strike into the groin.

1B. Downward-Elbow Strike

If the attacker uses a lunge-body tackle or, in the course of a struggle, gets bent over so that his spine and neck are exposed, push the head down further and drop a downward-elbow strike to the base of his neck or spine.

1C. Reverse-Turning-Elbow Strike

If the attacker grabs you from the rear but leaves one or more of your arms free, turn your body and execute a reverse-turning-elbow strike.

Note: The elbows can be used to strike in every direction within their range of motion. These are only a few examples.

▲ 1A Straight-Rear-Elbow Strike

Body Weapons - Hard Parts

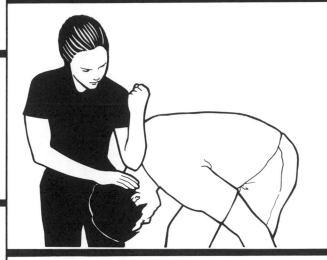

▲ 1B Downward-Elbow Strike

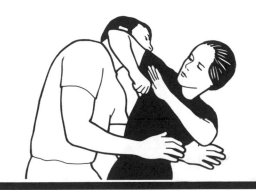

▲ 1C Reverse-Turning-Elbow Strike

Fear or Freedom by Susan Smith ©1986

2A. Front-Head Butt

The front-head butt is using the front of your head to strike the top of the forehead, the bridge of the nose or the top of the lip.

2B. Rear-Head Butt

The rear-head butt is using the back of your head when the attacker grabs you from behind. You can do this and hit the same face locations as in the front-head butt.

You can also combine this with instep stomps and rear kicks.

2C. Outward-Elbow Strike

The elbow strike can be used by bringing your elbow down or in toward your body or throwing it outward straight into the attacker's head or body depending upon his position.

2D. Upward-Elbow Strike

The upward-elbow strike is not an obvious means to use for defense, yet it can be very effective at close range. It is also difficult for the attacker to see it coming.

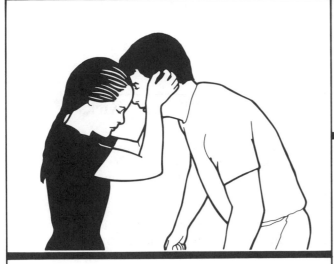

▲ 2A Front-Head Butt

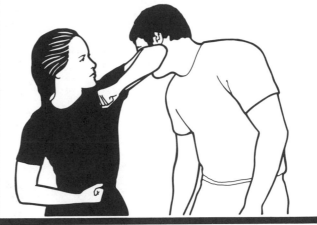

▲ 2C Outward-Elbow Strike

▲ 2B Rear-Head Butt

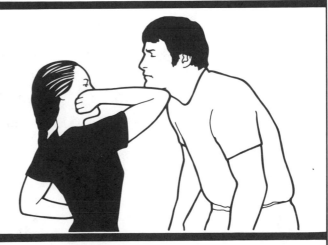

▲ 2D Upward-Elbow Strike

Basics Section, Part 3: Knee Lifts and Kicks

Note that all kicks with the foot are used below the waist. There are many high kicks in the martial arts but for effective self-defense, low, powerful kicks to the knees, which are the primary targets for kicks with the feet, are the most effective. Trying to kick the groin with your foot is dangerous. Knee kicks are more effective for attacking the groin.

1A. Front-Knee-Stomp Kick

Using the knee-stomp kick, aim for the top of the attacker's knee. Catch it with the side of your foot and scrape down to dislocate his kneecap.

The proper preparatory position for the stomp is to bend your knee up close and across the front of your body so that you are ready to aim with the outside of your foot - **never** your toe. This is illustrated in the Technique Section on page 149.

1B. Rear-Knee-Stomp Kick

This kick could be executed at closer range. It can also be used to scrape down the shins and end in an instep stomp. You can use repeated rear-stomp kicks if the attacker holds you from the rear.

Knee Lifts and Kicks

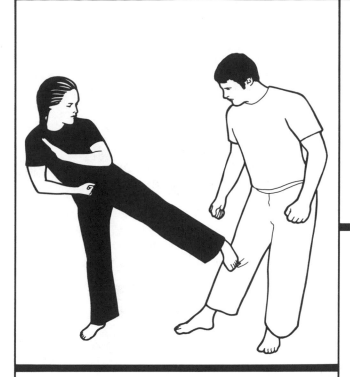

▲ 1A Front-Knee-Stomp Kick

▲ 1B Rear-Knee-Stomp Kick

2A. Knee Lift to the Groin

If the attacker grabs you from the front, stomp on his instep and when he moves his foot, jam a knee lift into his groin.

2B. Stomp

In a rear grab or a bear hug, stomp on his instep or rake the side of your foot down on his shins.

2C. Knee Lift

If the attacker attempts a lunge tackle on you, meet him with a knee-lift on any available target.

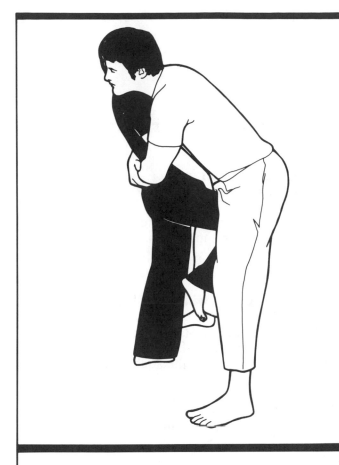

◀ 2A Knee Lift to the Groin

▲ 2B Stomp

◀ 2C Knee Lift

Fear or Freedom by Susan Smith ©1986

Illustrated Techniques

1. Aggressive Front-Upper-Arm Grab

Technique Principle:
**Circular Redirection and
  Downward Leverage**

1A. The attacker or social aggressor roughly grabs your upper arms.

Low risk

1B. Step out slightly with either leg. (The right leg is illustrated here.) Bring your left forearm on the **outside** of the attacker's right elbow and your right forearm on the **inside** of the attacker's left elbow.

1C. As you step down, simultaneously use a forceful circular downward motion with both hands to release the grip.

High risk

First jam your knee into his groin.

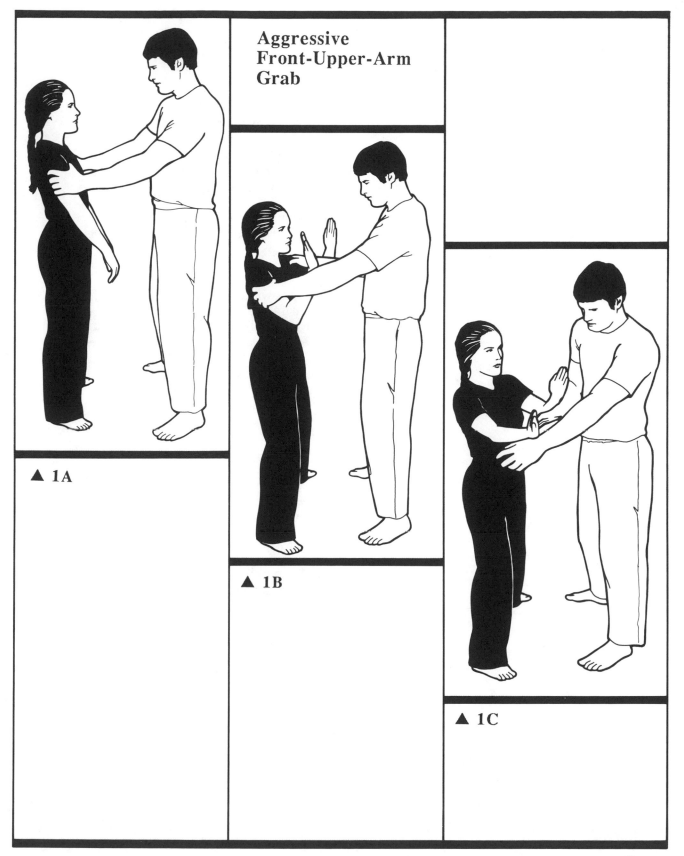

Aggressive Front-Upper-Arm Grab

▲ 1A

▲ 1B

▲ 1C

2. Side-Shoulder-Arm Grab

Technique Principle:
**Circular Redirection and
   Downward Leverage**

2A. The attacker aggressively grabs
your clothes, arm or shoulder.

Low risk

2B. Step towards attacker slightly. In
this illustration the defender steps left
because the left arm is grabbed. If your
right arm is grabbed, step right.

Bring your arm up in a tight circle as
you step and bring it down on the
attacker's wrist with a forceful circular
motion to break the hold.

High risk

In this case, your right arm could follow
through with a heel-palm strike to the
philtrum. (This is the nerve center
concentrated in the upper lip area under
the nose.)

Your knee to his groin is also a good
follow-up move.

Side-Shoulder-Arm Grab

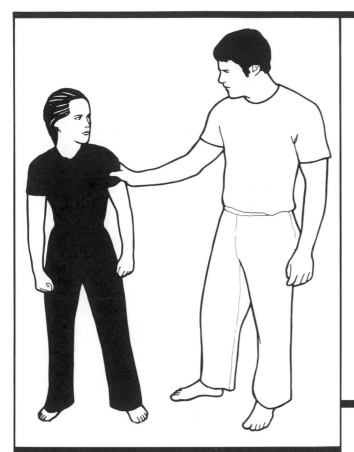

◄ 2A

2B ▶

Fear or Freedom by Susan Smith ©1986

3. Two-Hand-Wrist Grab on Both Arms

Technique Principle:
First Instinct: to pull away
Pain/Shock

3A. The attacker grabs both your wrists.

Low risk

Step back and snap your arms up keeping your elbows close to your body for power.

High risk

3B. If the attacker fails to let go, do a knee stomp.

This illustration shows the proper preliminary position for a knee-stomp using your right leg. This position will utilize the full power of your hip and body weight.

3C. Stomp your attacker's knee catching the kneecap at the top with the side of your foot and then putting your weight on it. This causes dislocation of the kneecap.

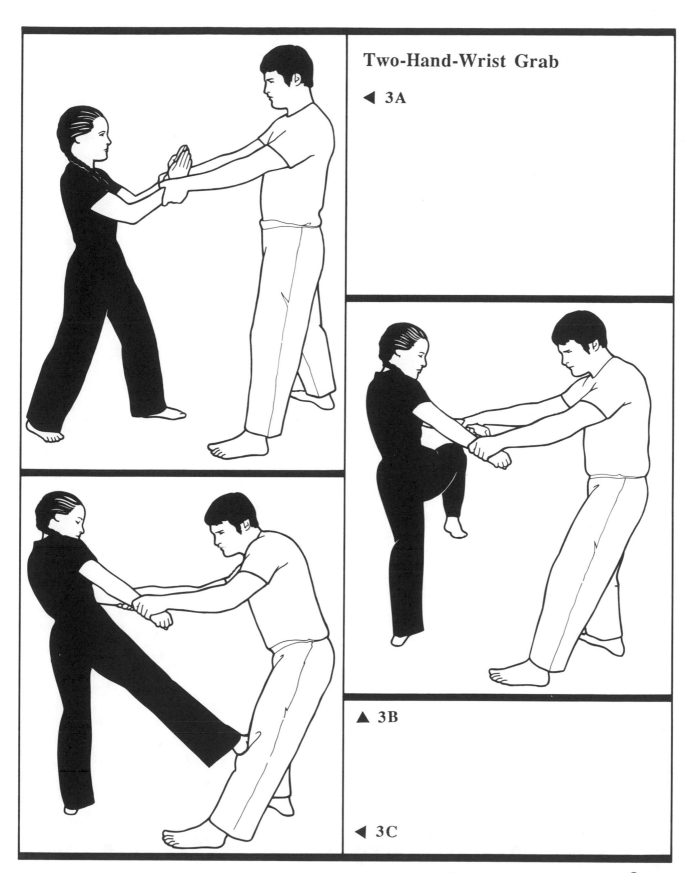

Two-Hand-Wrist Grab

◀ 3A

▲ 3B

◀ 3C

Fear or Freedom by Susan Smith ©1986

4. Two-Hand-Wrist Grab on One Arm

Technique Principle:
First Instinct: to pull away
Pain/Shock

4A. The attacker grabs one of your wrists with both hands.

Low risk

Reach through your attacker's hands and grab your own hand.

4B. Step back while simultaneously pulling your hand out.

High risk

If you don't get free, step back and do a knee-stomp kick to the attacker's front knee.

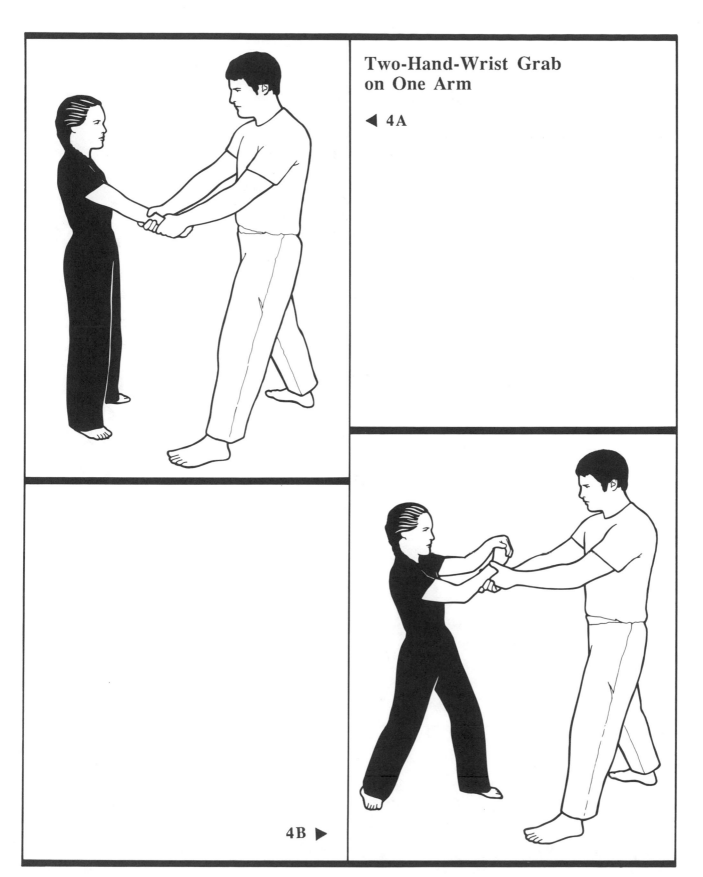

Two-Hand-Wrist Grab on One Arm

◀ 4A

4B ▶

5. Diagonal- or Cross-Hand-Wrist Grab

Technique Principle:
First Instinct: to pull away
Resist and Redirect
Pain/Shock

5A. The attacker grabs your wrist.

Low risk

Follow your first instinct to pull away as the attacker expects. Resist just long enough to get your footing and to get your attacker to attempt to drag you.

5B. Turn suddenly. Step forward and into the attacker causing him to lose his balance and lurch in the direction he was pulling.

High risk

In this illustration, as the attacker lurches off balance, your right knee is in a position to execute a knee lift to the attacker's coccyx (tail bone) which can be extremely painful and incapacitating.

Diagonal-Wrist Grab

◀ 5A

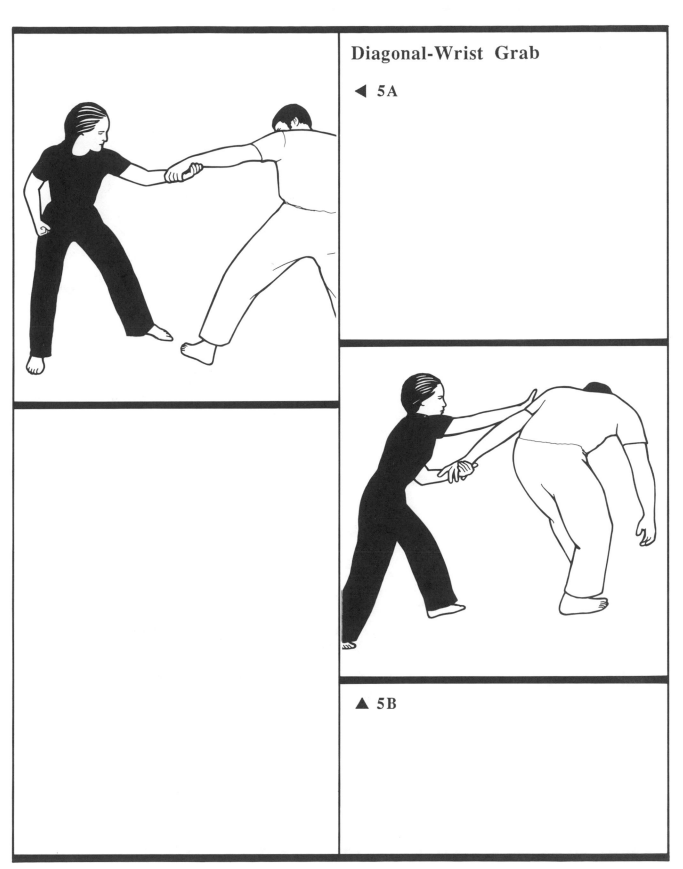

▲ 5B

6. Two-Hand-Front Choke

Technique Principle:
**First Instinct: to grab the
attacker's hands with your
hands to obtain oxygen
Circular Redirection and
Downward Leverage**

6A. The attacker grabs you with a two-handed front choke.

Low risk

6B. Following your instinctual reaction, reach up and grab one of his wrists or hands to create breathing space. This action acts as an internal cue for your next move.

6C. Bring your other arm up and over the attacker's arms crashing down on his forearms. For maximum inpact, 1) step out slightly to the right or left, the right step is shown here, and 2) turn your body to utilize your shoulder and body weight.

High risk

Hang onto the attacker's wrist or hand. The downward-elbow strike then rebounds up deflecting off his forearms and into his neck or temple.

Follow with your knee to his groin.

Front Choke

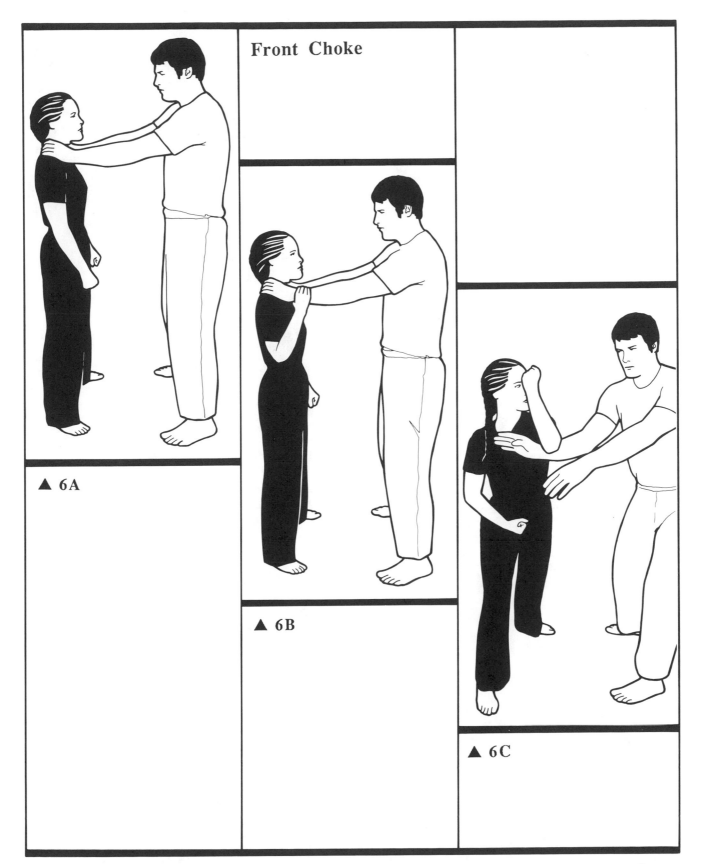

▲ 6A

▲ 6B

▲ 6C

Fear or Freedom by Susan Smith ©1986

7. Two-Hand-Rear Choke

Technique Principle:
**Circular Redirection and
    Downward Leverage**
Pain/Shock

7A. The attacker grabs you in a choke hold from behind.

Low risk

You can turn either way but the right handed illustration is used here.

Immediately step slightly behind your right foot with your left foot while bringing your left arm up in an elbow-strike position.

7B. Pivot on the balls of your feet, about a 180-degree turn, to face your attacker. Continue your elbow up and over your attacker's arms and crash down sharply on his wrists as you turn.

High risk

7C. Immediately after crashing down on the attacker's wrists, jam a knee-lift into his groin before he frees his arms.

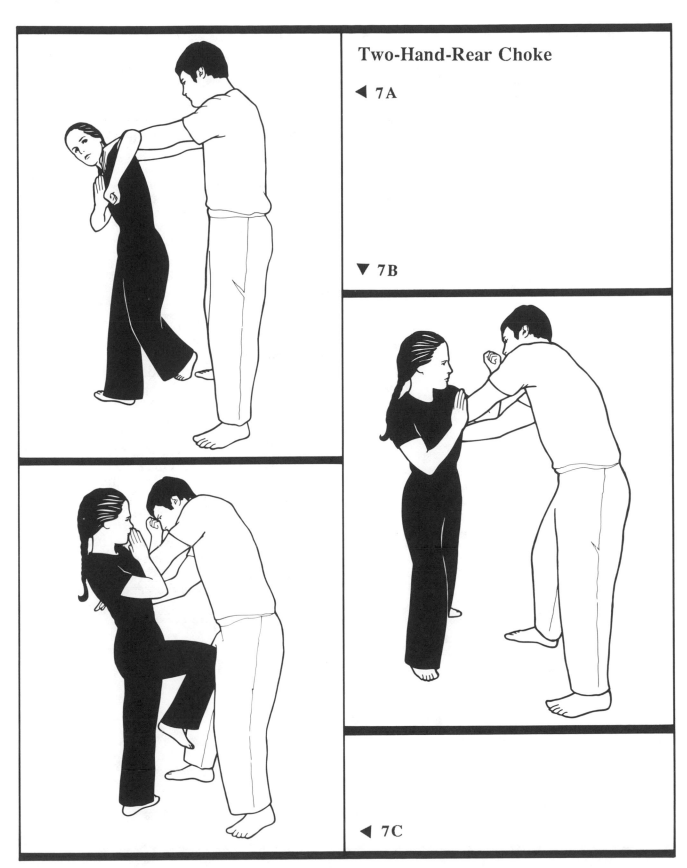

Two-Hand-Rear Choke

◀ 7A

▼ 7B

◀ 7C

Fear or Freedom by Susan Smith ©1986

8. Rear-Bear Hug with Arms Pinned

Technique Principles:
**First Instinct: to create breathing
  space**
Pain/Shock
Unbalance and Redirect

8A. The attacker grabs you in a bear hug.

Low risk

Your first instinct in a bear hug is to struggle for breathing space. Don't struggle. **Create** space by remaining calm and rolling your shoulders forward, collapsing your trunk inward.

High risk

8B. Step outside of the attacker's legs or away to either side to shift the attacker's balance. Then step around and behind the attacker's legs with your inside leg. Jam multiple elbow strikes to his groin.

8C. Stand up straight and throw your arms up. This knocks your attacker's body off of you to get him to fall backwards. Get your leg out of his way and escape.

Rear-Bear Hug

◀ **8A**

▼ **8B**

◀ **8C**

9. Rear-Hair Grab

Technique Principle:
Note: This technique will work from any angle. The rear position is the best position to learn the technique because it is the most difficult.
First Instinct: to reduce stress on your scalp
Pain/Shock

9A. The attacker grabs you by the hair.

Low risk

Follow your first instinct to reach up and grab at his fingers in your hair. Dig your fingers into the back of the attacker's hands.

High risk

9B. If he does not let go, take the stress off your scalp by closing the distance between you as you bend over. This sudden downward motion is unexpected because victims usually try to pull up and away.

9C. Step into the attacker and jam your elbow into his groin. You should be close enough to stomp hard on his instep.

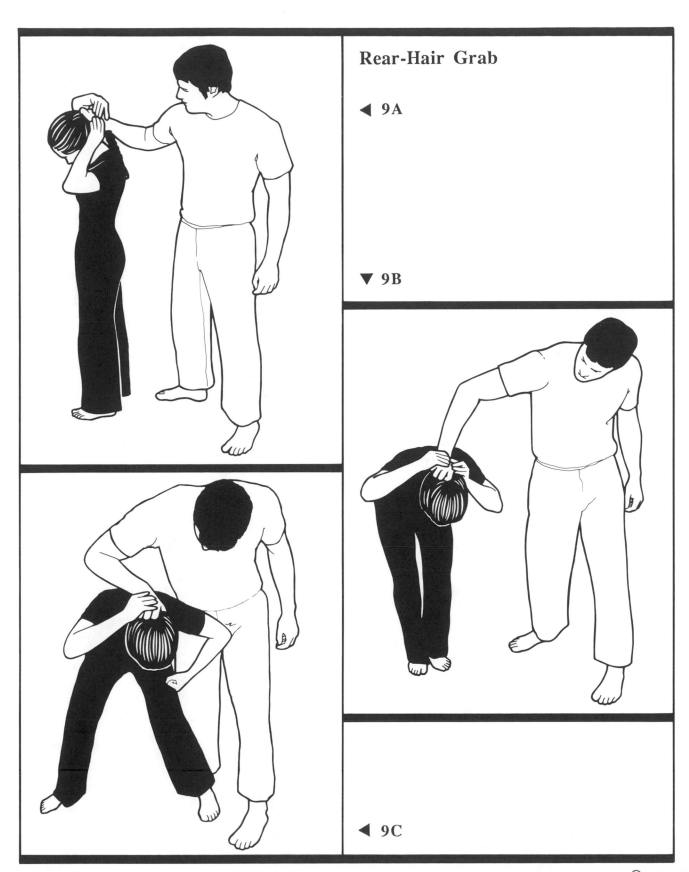

Rear-Hair Grab

◀ **9A**

▼ **9B**

◀ **9C**

10. Two-Hand-Wrist Grab from the Rear

Technique Principle:
Unbalance and Redirect
Pain/Shock

10A. The attacker grabs your wrists from the rear. (For clarity this illustration shows distance between the attacker and the defender. The attacker would probably be closer, which makes the technique more effective.)

Low risk

10B. Step between the attacker's legs, as shown, slamming your hips into his abdomen and knocking the wind out of him. Simultaneously throw both arms straight forward to release his restraint on your wrists.

High risk

10C. After stepping into the attacker, look back, aim and stomp out his knee or turn in either direction and slam into his neck with your elbow. This is demonstrated in the Basics Section under Body Weapons - Hard Parts.

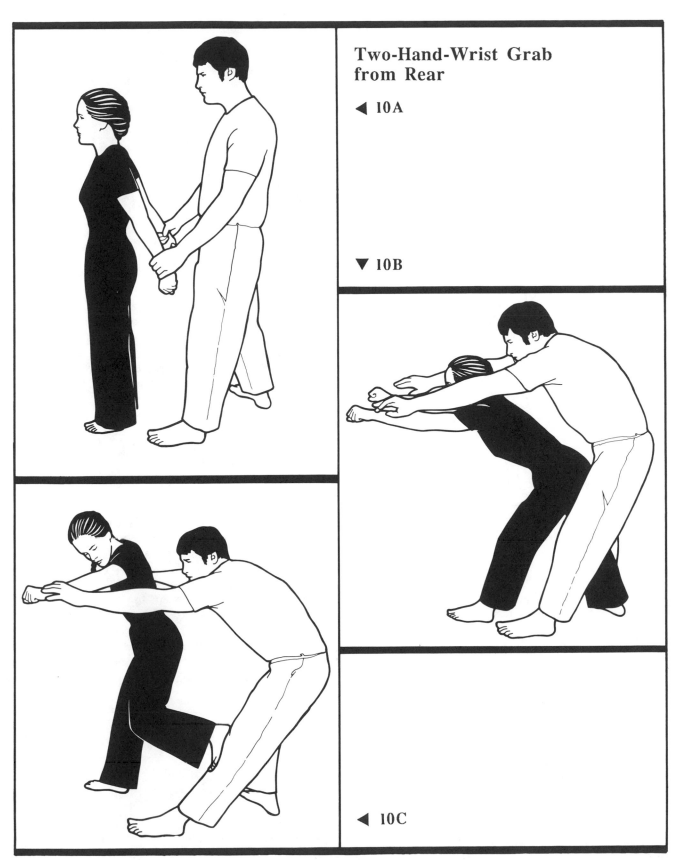

Two-Hand-Wrist Grab from Rear

◀ 10A

▼ 10B

◀ 10C

Fear or Freedom by Susan Smith ©1986

11. Forearm Choke

Technique Principle:
**First Instinct: to reduce stress on
  your neck
Unbalance and Redirect**

11A. The attacker grabs you with one
arm around your neck.

Low risk

11B. Follow your first instinct to
reduce stress on your neck and obtain
oxygen. **Immediately** tuck your chin
as deeply as possible under the crook of
his elbow. Pull down on his arm with
both hands. When you are stabilized,
step back beyond your attacker's legs
on the side his weight is concentrated
on because of his restraint on you.
This will throw him off balance.

High risk

11C. If he still doesn't let go, hold on
to his arm with both your hands, turn in
place 180 degrees while bending at the
waist. Stomp his instep if you can. Be
prepared for the attacker to fall
backwards. Either move your leg or
roll his bodyweight over your leg.
(This is not as difficult as it seems and
can be learned with practice.)

When the attacker falls backward,
escape.

Forearm Choke

◀ 11A

▼ 11B

◀ 11C

Fear or Freedom by Susan Smith © 1986

12. Flank Headlock

Technique Principle:
First Instinct: to obtain oxygen
Pain/Shock
Unbalance and Redirect

Someone places an arm across your shoulders.

Low risk

You can remove his arm quickly and firmly by grabbing his wrist and ducking out of his hold.

12A. If he becomes more aggressive, he may grab you in a headlock.

High risk

Your first instinct is to obtain oxygen. Turn your head **towards** the attacker's body and tuck your head into his side to create breathing space.

12B. Reach up and grab and pull the attacker's testicles or use a hammer-fist blow to the groin to loosen the attacker's grip with a pain/shock reaction. Step behind the attacker's leg if you are not already in this position.

12C. After the blow or blows to the groin, use your outside arm to grab the attacker's arm. Reach up and over the attacker's arm and simultaneously 1) grab his hair close to the hairline, 2) knock his knee forward with your knee behind his and 3) jerk his head backwards. As his body follows his head backwards and he falls, escape.

Flank Headlock

◀ **12A**

▼ **12B**

◀ **12C**

13. Arm Twisted behind the Back with a Wrist Grab

Technique Principle:
**Unbalance and Redirect
Pain/Shock**

13A. The attacker grabs your right arm and twists it behind your back while holding your left wrist. The attacker would probably be closer, but distance is shown in the illustration for clarity.

Low risk

13 B. 1) Stomp the attacker's instep to ensure his legs will be separated, 2) step back with your left leg, 3) slam your hips into the attacker and 4) shoot your left arm straight out to free it.

13C. Stomp the attacker's knee. If he still has you held with one arm behind your back, use the technique on pages 170-1 to get free.

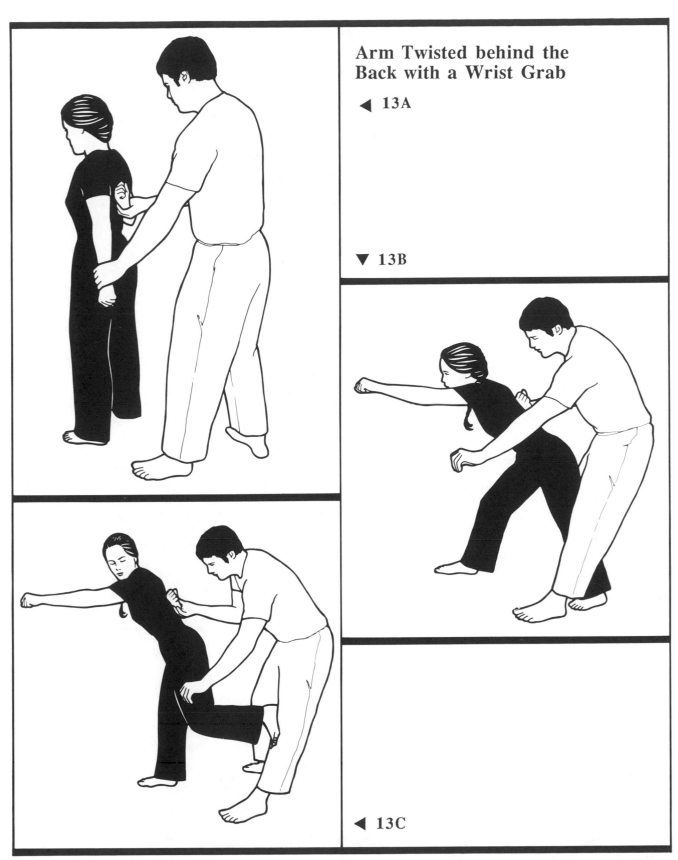

Arm Twisted behind the Back with a Wrist Grab

◀ 13A

▼ 13B

◀ 13C

14. One Arm Twisted behind the Back

Technique Principle:
**First Instinct: to relieve the
    stress on the arm**
Pain/Shock

14A. The attacker twists your arm
behind your back.

High risk

14B. Bend over slightly to take the
stress off your arm and turn away.

In this bent-over position, your inside
leg nearest the attacker can stomp out
the attacker's knee or stomp his insteps
repeatedly.

14C. If he still hasn't let go, follow
through by turning around to face the
attacker and deliver a hammer-fist blow
or knuckle rap to the back of the
attacker's hand. The attacker probably
would not be standing up straight as
shown here if he were kicked in the
kneecap, had his shins raked and his
insteps stomped.

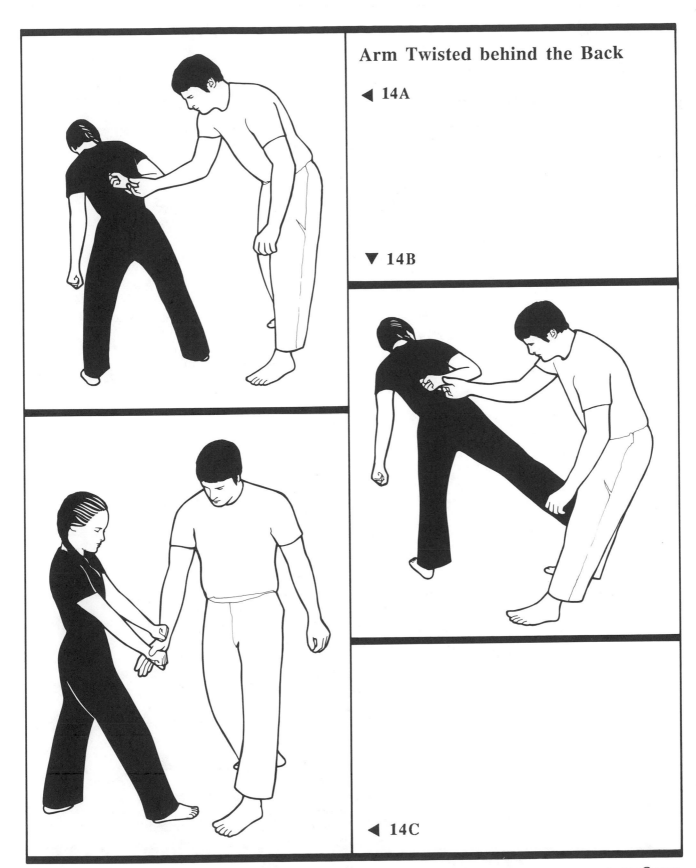

Arm Twisted behind the Back

◀ 14A

▼ 14B

◀ 14C

Last-Resort Techniques

The Testicle Twist

1A. Lock

Lock your thumb and forefinger around the top of the attacker's testicles.

1B. Twist

Once your thumb and forefinger are locked, you can twist and squeeze the testicles. This amount of pressure could be sufficient to cause great pain and shock to the assailant, particularly if the assailant has a tight scrotum sac. At this point, a strike with the heel-palm of your hand, a hammer-fist blow or any hard, sudden impact will incapacitate the attacker.

1C. Jerk

When the attacker has a looser scrotum, you should lock your fingers and twist the testicles to separate them and then jerk hard to create the necessary pressure to cause pain and shock.

1D. Divide and Conquer

If there is a struggle and you cannot get your thumb and forefinger properly around the testicles as in 1A, you might effectively grab the scrotum anyway. Dig your fingers into the scrotum between the testicles to separate and create pressure. Then you may jerk them and/or strike them as in 1B.

Other Last-Resort Techniques

The thumb gouge is illustrated and described on pages 134-5. The upper-lip bite technique is not illustrated. See pages 178-9 for a description.

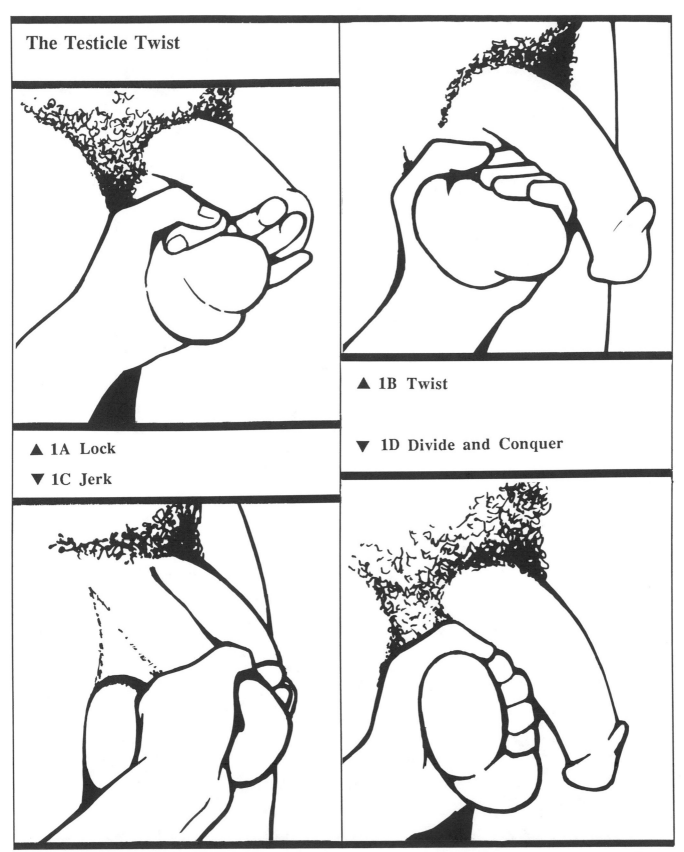

The Testicle Twist

▲ 1A Lock

▼ 1C Jerk

▲ 1B Twist

▼ 1D Divide and Conquer

Fear or Freedom by Susan Smith ©1986

Last Resort Techniques

Whether you be man or woman, you will never do anything in this world without courage.
It is the greatest quality of the mind next to honor.
James L. Allen

In great straits and when hope is small, the boldest counsels are the safest.
Livy

Chapter VII

Last-Resort Techniques

When to Use Last-Resort Techniques

The majority of the physical techniques in this book are designed for defense in the initial encounter in the hope that you will remain on your feet and escape with a minimum of interaction and injury from the assault attempt. It would be catastrophic not to discuss "last-resort" techniques because the circumstances of many violent encounters require that you apply certain physical techniques beyond those possible at the outset of the attack.

Last-resort techniques are to be used when you, the resistor, perceive no other possible options. Last-resort situations represent the extremes in terms of degree of violence, threats or implied threat. Abductions, gang attacks or the presence of a gun or knife represent situations in which the resistor may have less control and fewer options. Depending on the situation, it **is** possible to defend yourself or escape if you are threatened with a knife or gun, abducted or threatened by more than one assailant.

Physical Last-Resort Techniques

A physical "last-resort" technique is a simple but extreme method to incapacitate the assailant in order to escape. These techniques would rarely be used unless the resistor faces a high degree of threat and has no logical choice but to submit temporarily in the initial stages of the attack. Temporary submission allows you to get into the position to use a last-resort technique because you must be close to the attacker to accomplish this.

The three most effective incapacitating techniques to use at the last minute are 1) pulling and twisting the testicles, like wringing a chicken's neck with one hand; 2) gouging the eyes with the thumbs from the inner corner, pressing out; and 3) biting the upper lip, which is an area of concentrated nerves.

All of these techniques can result in shock and temporary paralysis after several seconds, and possibly death after a longer period if the shock is not treated. These techniques are all possible during a rape.

One of the women in my study used her head, in more ways than one, during assault. She reported that she was abducted at gunpoint and taken to a secluded area. The rapist threatened to kill her and brandished his weapon to render his "victim" helpless.

Like many rapists, he was unable to get an erection. He dragged her from the car, shoved her down on the desert floor and commanded her to "blow" him. This rapist, like most attackers who carry weapons, put his gun down because he felt in control; his victim quietly "went along" until she could safely react.

She complied with the rapist's orders long enough to gain his trust and divert his attention, then she took a bite. She bit his penis close to the base, then grabbed a testicle and twisted and squeezed. She did not let go until she was sure the attacker was incapable of retaliation. If she had stopped before this point, she might not have been able to leave him clutching his groin, immobilized in the very spot where he might have left her dead. She took the car keys and drove safely away.

You might be wondering why he didn't start beating her or pick up the gun and blow her brains out. He absolutely couldn't! The pain and shock were so intense, the would-be rapist couldn't think and was immobilized by pain.

Although biting the penis is a good start, the effectiveness of this technique is in the testicle twist. After twisting the testicles, it takes approximately five seconds before the assailant passes out or goes into shock. Again, women ask, "What is the guy doing during those five seconds?" He would very likely be rigid from the intensity of the pain. He would not be functional enough to rain blows on your head. Any movement on his part could increase the pain and injury. He can't pull away and in all probability would not be moving at all if you use the technique correctly.

In order to incapacitate an attacker with a testicle twist, you must enclose it from the top between your thumb and forefinger and twist or pull down. Study the illustration on page 173 to learn the correct way to do this. Maintain this hold for five to seven seconds or until the assailant goes limp and passes out.

"What power women can have in knowing that there is one technical but simple, no-fail defense for rape!"

What power women can have in knowing that there is one technical but simple, no-fail defense for rape!

Another effective technique to use during or prior to a genital rape is the thumb press. Put your hands on both sides of the rapist's face during the assault and use your thumbs to gouge his eyes from the inner corner or bridge of his nose. Again, this technique is one that can be done without signaling your intentions; should you change your mind, the attacker will never know. The thumb press or gouge will result in shock in a matter of several seconds. See the basics section for an illustration of this technique.

The eyes may be more accessible during a genital rape, although your chances are about fifty percent that the rapist will force oral sex because of his inability to get an erection. If this happens and you feel you are in a last-resort situation, don't struggle, cry, scream or beg. If you comply initially, you will be in a position to execute the no-fail technique.

Don't misunderstand the previous statement. I am not saying you should comply with a demand for oral rape under any circumstances, only in those attacks in which all other defenses appear to pose a threat to your life or seem impossible to carry out successfully.

Biting down on the attacker's tongue or

upper lip can also be effective prior to or during a rape. The nerves concentrated in these areas make this technique extremely painful. Five to ten seconds can put the attacker into shock or cause him to pass out. Again, an attacker wouldn't be able to hit you effectively, even if he could move. Movement would increase the pain and trauma for the would-be rapist.

Psychological Last-Resort Techniques

A psychological defense is generally a form of trickery. This type of ploy is a secondary measure to use when you feel resistance would be impossible or if you waited too long to resist and you find you have lost physical control.

Psychological trickery is used to accomplish two objectives. If there are no escape routes, you would pretend submission until you could find an opening to use physical resistance. If you could escape, you would identify with the attacker and comply to convince him you're no threat so that you could manipulate yourself increasingly out of his control to get to an escape route.

During a self-defense presentation to a women's group, one of the members recounted this story. One of her friends was dragged into a dark alley by a rapist wielding a gun. He held the gun and demanded she take off her clothes. Without argument she immediately loosened her pants and pulled up her blouse. Then she stopped in surprise and asked innocently, "Aren't you going to take off your clothes?" The rapist was so surprised and relieved that he'd found a willing victim, he put the gun down and pulled down his pants. His "victim" ran.

Remember, when the rapist feels sufficiently in control, it is quite likely he will put his weapon down. This woman gained control by thinking fast and never signaling her intention to resist. This can be the key to escape when you face a weapon or are faced with any situation in which you must use trickery. Never signal your intentions. Think fast and wait for or create the opportunity to escape.

"Never signal your intentions. Think fast and wait for or create the opportunity to escape."

You must convince the attacker you are no threat to him and that you are willing but you have **personal** preferences. This can surprise the attacker if you realistically institute the dynamics of a **social encounter** or **consenting sexual encounter**. You could say you would love to have sex, but you always take a bath first. You can claim any one of a number of activities that should occur **first**. The idea that you want to prepare for sex implies that you want to make it better for both of you. This is thought by psychologists to be a rapist's fantasy.

Using the word "first" implies your willingness, conjures illusions of sexual submission and lulls the attacker into the false belief that he has already conquered you. He may become careless once he feels he has control and allow you to leave the room. Then if you have a lock on the inside of any door, your bedroom or bathroom, and a phone extension there, you could use it. You could also open a window and escape.

A. Nicholas Groth explains in his study of sex offenders that except for the anger rapist, who does not fantasize about rape and whose assault is more likely to be impulsive and unpremeditated, even extremely violent rapists have a fantasy script that involves the victim responding to their advances. This means nearly any rapist is vulnerable to trickery which follows his fantasy script. Trickery and bargaining must be used to buy time or escape. This is not the same as suggesting that a woman comply to avoid injury; compliance is not necessarily safer than resistance. And remember that resistance is

179

an internal commitment not to participate in violence against your person or in society.

Gang Attacks

The gang attack is another situation which requires last-resort techniques. Gangs are primarily groups of teenagers, although this is not always the case. In every gang attack, there is a group leader who is usually easy to identify. In gang attack accounts reported to me, the women easily identified the leader with no problem. Women often reported that several of the attackers hung back and seemed to be reluctant; but once the attack began, they followed through.

Often the leader subjects the other members of the group to peer pressure. One of the common ways a leader tries to diffuse responsibility is to coerce reluctant members of the gang to commit the rape first. This is another way to determine the leader. He is the one goading the other members or overriding any protests from the group. It is a rare group that does not contain at least one reluctant or uninitiated member. This seems to be part of the thrill of gang rape - to initiate and introduce another male to his first rape.

This is another situation where trickery is required. Often a gang rape is accomplished by implied threat of sheer numbers. According to Menachem Amir's 1971 study, the chances of physical force increase with the number of attackers. The individuals in the group get carried away by the power of the group. Their responsibility for their crime is diffused. When a woman is faced and surrounded by a group, it is difficult to resist and resistance is easily overcome in most cases. Physical resistance can rapidly escalate the situation to multiple rape and assault because the chaos of action takes the pressure off the group to decide what must be done or how to go about it. It also increases the physiological arousal of the rape participants so that their conscience and their fears are temporarily forgotten.

In a gang rape, a victim is procured either by trickery or abduction. A gang usually has a leader who has raping experience and social dominance of this group. The leader is the initiator who controls the action and the procedure. In other cases, there may be rivalry and a preliminary discussion phase. The preliminary discussion phase is when the possibility of escape by trickery is most likely. An initiator will emerge during this stage if the leader has not already been determined. If the resistor can appeal to the initiator's or the leader's ego and separate him from the group, she may be able to use the techniques described earlier: the testicle twist, eye gouge and press, or biting down on the tongue or upper lip.

Again, I must state that any attempt to escape must take into account situational advantages. Many gang rapes have occurred at house parties, parks or on deserted school grounds which are relatively public places. In these situations, if the leader is separated from the group, rendered helpless to commit the rape and to control the group, it is more than likely that the group members will panic and run or come to their senses.

". . . if the leader is separated from the group, rendered helpless to commit the rape and to control the group, it is more than likely that the group members will panic and run or come to their senses."

If an abduction has occurred and the location is totally secluded, then "taking out" the leader may be riskier. However, manipulating the situation to a one-on-one encounter with any group member could make escape easier.

If the attack occurs outside after an abduction by car, getting into the car with the driver could pay off. Use trickery, ego appeals, oral sex, etc., to gain his trust and then execute an incapacitating technique. Lock the doors and drive away if you have the keys or continuously honk the horn if you are within hearing range of others besides the group members. You will attract attention and the group is more likely to disperse and flee.

The Situational Variables of Defending against a Knife or Gun

Let's analyze some specific situations if a knife is the weapon used. Two possibilities are a street assault or any attack in which the assailant has a knife.

How do you determine if it's safe to defend? First consider proximity. If the attacker is several feet from you, don't comply with his demands or allow him to get close. If there is any possibility of escaping or attracting attention, do so **before** the attacker gets close enough to harm you. You must maintain distance and if you have to use a physical defense, attack the assailant's knees with the kick shown in the technique section.

If the attacker(s) pulls up beside you in a car, shows a knife and says, "Get in!" Don't do it. Run immediately. This exact approach has been used and many victims who complied have been stabbed to death.

My students often protest, "But he might throw the knife!" Knife throwing is **not** a well-developed skill in our society. It is also very difficult to hit a moving target; so if you are running, you would be almost impossible to hit. If you were hit while running away, the knife would probably not penetrate deeply nor would it be likely to strike a vital organ. In order to kill with a knife, a major artery must be cut, a vital organ pierced or victims must be stabbed so many times they die from loss of blood or shock from numerous wounds.

In *Unarmed against the Knife,* Oscar Diaz-Cobo identifies another variable to look for: whether the knife fighter is using

". . . overhead stabs or straight stabs to the abdomen with occasional wide slashes to the face, throat or abdomen."[1] These highly visible attacks with wide, sweeping motions can be avoided and more easily controlled than economical, deceptive movements which would characterize a skilled knife fighter.

I am not attempting to instill a false sense of security about defending against a knife, but from the reports of women in my study, very few of the rapists or muggers showed skill or experience with a knife. The closest thing to "skill" was when a rapist would enter a woman's home while she was sleeping, put the knife to her throat and **then** wake her up. What he did was eliminate the possibility of resistance by utilizing every possible physical and situational advantage over his prey.

Diaz-Cobo describes the psychology of the knife fighter which is exactly what I eventually came to understand through my interviews conducted for this book. He states, "Since the unskilled knife fighter's main weapons are confidence produced by possession of his knife and the fear of his adversary, you can gain the psychological edge by demonstrating no fear . . . his confidence will be weakened. He will then become more manageable."[2]

"A rapist who uses a knife needs to hide behind the weapon to bolster his courage."

Remember this about an armed attacker. A rapist who uses a knife needs to hide behind the weapon to bolster his courage. A rapist who sneaks up on a sleeping woman with a knife has demonstrated one attribute very clearly; he is deeply afraid of resistance. This type of rapist must reduce all possibility of resistance by preparation or "control for advantages." He must stalk his prey; he must find a woman who leaves doors or windows unlocked; he must know when she is alone or when the household is sleeping. It can take weeks or months waiting for the "safe" time to attack.

One woman in my study reported this exact scenario. She woke up and a rapist wearing a ski mask was lying on top of her with a cold blade on her throat. He said, "I've been watching you." This woman involuntarily yelled loudly. In fact, she said she used the "Karate" yell and the man fled immediately. She said she didn't have any idea of what to do next but she had learned to yell in a Karate class and when the would-be rapist scared her, it "just came out."

I'm not guaranteeing this is always a safe reaction, but it is probable that the rapist is as scared as you are since he's taken great pains to avoid resistance. A loud, deep yell is not part of his plan, and he may run like a scared rabbit.

Another variable to look for is the kind of knife the attacker holds. If it is a pocket knife, kitchen knife or any knife with a short, one-sided blade, you'll know that the attacker probably is **not** skilled and needs the knife for intimidation and false courage. A four- to six-inch blade, particularly a two-sided blade **could** signal an experienced attacker or at least an attacker with a knife that could more easily maim or kill than would a kitchen knife or pocket blade which is, at best, an afterthought to frighten a naive victim.

A knife is intimidating because it is shiny, sharp and draws blood. However, it is not easy to kill someone with a knife. Why do you suppose you always read accounts of multiple stabbings where, in case after case, the victim does not die? It is because the person struggled and fought back, fending off the knife and taking superficial cuts in other parts of the body. In most fatal stabbings, the victim dies from loss of blood or shock, not from one fatal blow like in the movies or on television.

It is important to know that if you are stabbed, it is **highly** unlikely that you will drop dead. If you can keep your wits about you and if you believe you are entitled to

act in defense of your life, there is nothing to prevent you from using the most effective techniques possible. You can gouge, stomp, kick and bite. Just don't freeze up and eventually sustain so many stab wounds that you die from loss of blood.

The variables for defending against a knife are the same for a known-assailant attack or a random attack. You must consider proximity of the assailant and keep your distance whenever possible. Do not voluntarily put yourself closer to the weapon because of the attacker's verbal threats or orders. It is highly unlikely that the attacker can hurt you from a distance.

Evaluate the attacker. Is he skilled or unskilled? Is he obviously scared or nervous? Does he look like he needs to hide behind the knife or does he look like he is absolutely confident of his ability to use it?

Evaluate the knife. Is it sharp and long with a two-sided blade or is it a pocket knife or kitchen knife?

For more information about the variables for knife defense, read Oscar Diaz-Cobo's book, *Unarmed against the Knife.* This book is often available in bookstores or martial arts supply stores. If you do not have a martial arts supply store in your area or a bookstore that can get you the book, write to the publisher, Paladin Press, Inc., P.O.Box 1307, Boulder, Colorado, 80306.

Self-defense against a gun is a much more difficult proposition. A gun **is** a long range weapon so keeping your distance does not necessarily ensure your safety. However, if the attacker(s) pulls up beside you in a car, levels a gun out the window and orders you to get in, the same rule applies as in the knife situation. This scene does happen with both a gun or a knife and the victim often complies, not realizing that to run immediately at least ensures a fifty/fifty chance of escape.

Look at it this way. An attacker who is

crazy enough to shoot you in the back if you run away would be likely to be a sadistic maniac once he gained control over your body. Complying with an armed and violent criminal when you **still** have an escape option is a bad survival strategy. If an armed attacker attempts to abduct you in public, your best defense is to run immediately. It is quite possible that you are facing a power rapist who is only using a weapon to gain control. You could also be cooperating with a sadistic murderer because the mode of operation of a power rapist and sadistic recreational killer are the same. They both need a conscious victim; they need control; they need time and a safe place to carry out the crime.

The fantasy script of a recreational killer involves slow and ritualistic torture; in some cases the victim is kept alive for days, even weeks. In other cases, once the victims are transported to a secluded place, they are murdered and the rituals and mutilation are acted out on the corpse.

If someone tries to intimidate you with a weapon and there is any chance to escape, take it. Do not be led to your death thinking, "I'll just get my rape and go home."

"Do not be led to your death thinking, 'I'll just get my rape and go home.'"

When a person holds a trigger-cocked gun in both hands in a straddle stance a safe distance from you, there is **no** possible defense technique you can learn or can implement. You can only take a chance. Can he shoot and get away with it? What is his degree of commitment?

If you are interested in gun defense, you should read *In the Gravest Extreme: The Role of the Firearm in Personal Protection* by Massad F. Ayoob. This book is available from the Police Book Shelf, P.O.Box 122, Concord, New Hampshire, 03301.

Available Weapons

In many women's self-defense publications, women are told hair spray, rattail combs and spray perfume can be used as defense weapons. Chemical sprays are often touted as the ultimate in self-defense for women. In fact, makeshift weapons can be found everywhere, in a woman's purse and in common indoor and outdoor household items. Most of these makeshift weapon ploys, including chemical sprays, should be considered temporary devices to slow down the attacker and never used as an absolute deterrent or "ultimate defense."

Let's discuss chemical sprays. Unless you are prepared to defend yourself physically, a chemical spray should **not** be your only means of defense. The effective use of a chemical spray is based on ideal conditions. To be effective, it must be assumed that the attacker will approach you head-on and signal his intentions to attack. It must also be assumed that your arms will be free and you will be able to activate and aim the spray. A chemical spray delivers a small stream, so nothing must divert your aim from his face.

These assumptions will not protect you from the facts.

The majority of attackers utilize verbal targeting and then a sneak approach without signaling their intentions to attack. After the initial approach, they often leave and sneak up behind their target if they are satisfied that she is not prepared to resist. After being attacked and during the struggle, you can't use your spray if you don't know how to get out of a restraint. You may not be able to step back and aim the spray at his eyes. As with any weapon, you must get to it and keep the attacker from using it on you. Unfortunately the only time I heard of an effective use of a chemical spray, the attacker used it on the victim. I am not saying a chemical spray is not effective, but you must realize that conditions must be ideal and you are only slowing the assailant down. You must be prepared to defend physically and/or escape immediately.

Many women buy a **chemical** spray because they fear **physical** resistance will make the attacker angry. I actually heard a chemical spray salesperson say this to a group of women as part of the sales pitch. This is ridiculous. If you attempt to spray a burning liquid in someone's eyes and fail, don't you think **that** would make him mad? Chemical sprays don't last very long; after a few months the spray often won't work anyway.

So let's say all conditions are ideal. You grab your spray, aim at the assailant's eyes and depress the atomizer. Nothing happens or a weak stream shoots out a few inches and drops. Then what? If you're like many women who believe they possess the ultimate self-defense tool and haven't learned self-defense, you've blown your main defense. A chemical spray must be checked periodically every month and changed frequently, every six months even if you don't use it. You would be better off to invest your money in a good self-defense course.

Makeshift weapons are limited only by your imagination; however, all items suggested as makeshift weapons are not the ultimate in self-defense either and should be thought of as temporary measures or threat and distancing ploys. Consider the hairspray and perfume spray idea. These items could temporarily blind an attacker but you must escape immediately. If these items are not available, you must be prepared to execute physical techniques. The problem is you must get to these items in your purse or somewhere else. Thinking about items instead of using your bodily weapons, mental resources and situational advantages can waste valuable time.

Some weapons that could be used to **poke** and **stab** at an assailant as a means of buying time and keeping distance are rakes, shovels, brooms and mops. Any

tool or item with a long handle can be used temporarily to hold an assailant at bay while you work your way to the nearest escape route.

Household items that can be used include any appliance with a cord such as an electric alarm clock. You can swing an item like this around by the cord over your head to prevent the assailant from getting close to you while you back towards an exit. If the assailant grabs any item you are using to create and maintain distance, use the old cartoon trick. Resist briefly and let go; the attacker will fall backwards while you escape.

". . . any appliance with a cord such as an electric alarm clock. You can swing an item like this around by the cord over your head to prevent the assailant from getting close to you while you back towards an exit."

Several items that you are likely to have in your hand at the time of an assault could be a flashlight or a telephone receiver. You may have heard a noise and are checking outside with a flashlight. Use it to jam upwards under the assailant's nose or smash it into his temple. Try to control the impulse to hit him **over** the head. An overhead strike can be most easily seen and blocked. A phone receiver can be used as a swinging weapon to keep the assailant at a distance, and it can also be used to strike temples or jam into an attacker's upper lip or under the base of his nose.

The idea that a rattail comb is a good defensive weapon is based on two elements. First, an item like this can be gripped tightly and you're not likely to drop it. Second, it can be used effectively for only one defense and it is a deadly one; gouging the attacker's eyes. If you are prepared to stab an attacker in the eye or gouge his eyes, a pencil, pen, eating utensil handle, pocket knife or any similar item will do; but then, so will your thumbs or fingers.

Another blinding technique is using dirt or sand. In the home, you could back up against a houseplant and grab a handful of dirt to throw or smash into the assailant's eyes. If you are in the kitchen, a handful of red cayenne or black pepper could be rubbed or thrown at close range into the attacker's eyes. If the attack occurs outside, a handful of dirt or sand could be thrown or smashed into the assailant's eyes.

As I said before, available weapons are limited only by your imagination. Look around your home. Do you have a lot of plants, a rock or mineral collection, lots of books, heavy ash trays? Anything, even pictures or plaques on the walls, can be used to throw or the edge could be jammed into his throat or under his nose.

". . . available weapons are limited only by your imagination."

Keep in mind that available weapons are a means to buy time, create distance or momentarily stun or blind an assailant so you can escape screaming, "Fire!" It is possible to incapacitate an assailant with a well-placed strike or stab to a vital area with any available weapon from your household or environment. However, you should be thinking in terms of creating the possibility of escape - not avenging the attack.

The Surreptitious Resistor's Revenge

The decision to defend against a lone rapist or a gang, armed or not, depends on many factors. Your situational advantages, your perceived probability of success, the presence of weapons, your mental, physical and emotional state must be considered.

Another last-resort technique involves complying or "going along" for the sake of survival and then gathering or leaving evidence. Assuming that nothing can be done at the time of the attack, the resistor decides to comply as a means of avoiding further injury.

The "surreptitious resistor" can leave clothing fibers, an earring or other jewelry and hair on the site of the rape. The assailant's hair and clothing fibers can be left on the site or taken from each assailant and concealed on the resistor. This does not involve ripping handfuls of the assailant's hair. If you run your hands through his hair, several strands will come out. It won't carry much weight if you leave it in his cruising car or in his residence. In the assailant's car or residence, your own hair and clothing fibers should be left behind. Put the assailant's clothing fibers or hair in your pockets or shoes to use as evidence later.

If the rape occurs outside the car, leave evidence at the site of the rape in addition to inside the vehicle. You can take "dirt samples" under your fingernails, even make small holes in the ground with your fingers or dig your heels into the ground to leave identifying marks. The dirt under your fingernails or ground into your shoes could be compared to the dirt on the rape site or in the attacker's car. If you are carrying a purse or personal items in your pockets, you could leave some items under the seat of the car or anywhere that the assault occurred.

If you are wearing fingernail polish, here is a risk-free suggestion. Peel off your polish and leave fragments in the assailant's car. You could also leave fingernail fragments. The presence of fragments of polish or nails prove you were in the car or at other sites. It proves you were trying to leave evidence which may be important to your defense. If you are taken to a home or apartment, try to leave an identifying mark, such as a tooth impression on any yielding surface or leave clothing fibers, hair, or any personal item concealed somewhere.

Women who reported being abducted by a lone rapist or by a gang and forced onto the floorboards of the car had no way of knowing where they finally ended up. This is the time to leave strands of hair, fingernail fragments, fingernail polish and clothing fibers. If your hands are tied behind you, you can still pull off clothing fibers or leave fragments of polish or fingernails. If you do not know where you have been taken, you may never be able to lead police to the site of the rape and you may not know your situational advantages. You may be a half block from help; you may be miles.

Immediately begin thinking survival, then begin gathering or leaving evidence. Memorize as much about the situation and the assailants as possible.

Women in the study reported they were often unable to name the make and model of the car in which they were abducted. The model of a car is often inside on the door panel or dashboard. Look for any distinguishing features that could help you identify the vehicle later. You can also make small tears in the upholstery or leave bite marks that will last on vinyl or leather.

If you end up in a residence, try to leave evidence or identifying marks somewhere. Also attempt to determine where you are by surreptitiously looking at papers or envelopes that might be scattered around. If you can get into the bathroom, you might be able to get names and addresses off prescription medication. If there is any item available to safely leave a tooth impression on, then do it. You might also smear toothpaste on the underside of a cabinet or scratch your initials in a concealed place. Tell detectives about all of your attempts to leave evidence.

The Truth About Self-Defense

When a gun is pointed at your head or a knife is at your throat, physical techniques may be impossible to use in the initial stages of an assault. This is where psychological ploys must be used. If psychological attempts are successful, it may be possible to escape or to use incapacitating physical techniques. The goal in any situation is to survive, and you must determine second by second the probability of reacting safely.

Now I am going to tell you a shocking truth about self-defense. There is basically no "right" way to react in an assault situation. Anything you do could be right; anything you do could be wrong. There are **no** absolutes in self-defense. There is no simple risk-free method that works every time. All survival strategies from passivity to last-resort techniques have situational validity. There is no general reaction which could be termed safest or most likely to be effective.

"You can only prepare yourself by knowing your options."

You can only prepare yourself by knowing your options. You must trust your ability to read behavioral and situational cues and have faith in your judgment to apply self-defense techniques and strategy. Knowing more about the dynamics of rape and assault situations will improve your ability to make the **right** choices, which means **situationally appropriate** choices.

Many people have successfully escaped from violent situations without prior training using absolutely no logic. They trusted an innate feeling that they were not going to die even in the face of "apparent reality:" i.e., weapons, threats or gangs. The "experts" would have told them that such reactions are suicidal but the outcome proved otherwise.

An example of this is one woman's story, as reported in my survey for this book. She was abducted at knifepoint by three men. Two men held her in the back seat of a car while the other drove. One man held the knife and the other kept telling her what they were going to do to her when they got her to a secluded area.

Suddenly she started struggling wildly and screaming repeatedly, "God knows what you're doing! God can see you!" They were still in the city and other motorists could see this wild activity going on the backseat of the car. Two men struggling with one frantic woman looked suspicious. They were unable to control her. The driver became agitated and pulled over saying, "Let her go! She's crazy!" They kicked her out of the car and pulled away.

This woman did not evaluate the safety of reacting, but without "logic" she took advantage of the situation. The attackers had their script figured out; a woman flanked by two men with a weapon would meekly accept her fate. This woman was "crazy" because she didn't play her part. By these rapists' standards, women who submit to multiple rape and possible death are "sane." We should all be so crazy!

This is a "self-defense" book, but what is the definition of self-defense? A wide range of activities and beliefs fit under the heading of "self-defense."

"My definition of 'self-defense' is having an internal commitment to resist and not to comply unnecessarily with anyone who intends to harm, humiliate or dominate you."

My definition of "self-defense" is having an internal commitment to resist and not to comply unnecessarily with anyone who intends to harm, humiliate or dominate you. This commitment covers everything from day-to-day social interaction all the way to violent assault. A "resistance strategy" is any action or reaction originating from an internal sense of control, whether that reaction be passivity or extreme resistance. The concept of self-defense encompasses any action, reaction or non-action in an effort to escape, reduce injury, survive or save the life of another person.

You have read the "successful resistance stories" involving many women. One woman escaped multiple attackers with a knife by wildly resisting. One woman outwitted an attacker with a gun by waiting for an opening and fearlessly following through with a physical last-resort technique. One woman tricked an armed attacker into putting down his gun and pulling down his pants. There are many ways to resist and escape, even in the face of weapons and/or multiple attackers.

The Most Important Rule of Self-Defense

The single most important rule in self-defense is to heed your intuition and follow your survival instincts. In simple terms, **trust yourself.** Women have had the experience of being tricked by **apparent reality** when their instincts, "psychic" alarms or intuition told them something was wrong. Human beings, the most physically vulnerable of all creatures, have not survived millions of years without almost foolproof instincts and intuition. When some internal cue tells you that all is not well or right, you should heed it - no matter what the reality appears to be.

The Law and Self-Defense

You may need to concern yourself with the legal implications of defending yourself successfully. We have all heard horror stories of attacker turned victim; stories in which a rapist or robber is severely injured and sues the defender. In spite of the publicity and visibility of these cases, it is a rare occurrence. Yet, the issue is a valid concern and must be addressed.

In cases where the intended victim injures the attacker or kills the assailant, the law wants proof that death or grave bodily harm to the assailant occurred because the potential victim faced **unavoidable** danger of death or grave bodily harm. In several states, a citizen can shoot an offender caught in the course of any felony. In other states, you must be in deadly jeopardy before you pull the trigger or use lethal force.

American laws generally condone homicide only when undertaken to escape imminent and unavoidable danger of death or grave bodily harm. If you intend to shoot to kill in defense, even in your own home, it would be wise to know the laws in your state. Americans often believe they can shoot a fleeing criminal or attack and restrain a criminal to bring him to justice. This is not always true. Once the threat of harm is passed, shooting or attacking to stop or detain a criminal will no longer be considered self-defense. There is only one loophole. The moment the assailant turns away and the moment he ceases the assault are not necessarily the same. He may be **running to get a weapon**. If there is reason to believe the attacker intends to continue the assault, you are within your rights to continue the physical defense or shoot the attacker, not as he flees but as he runs to get a weapon or for better cover in order to regroup and continue the assault. Remember this difference because it could be crucial to your defense if you use deadly force to save your life.

If you have decided to obtain a gun for self-defense and/or become skilled in physical defense, you have taken on a responsibility to act within the law of your state. If you obtain a gun, it would be practically worthless to you unless you also take a firearms training course.

The laws are different in every state so I can only mention the general information that will apply.

Simply stated these are the following:

- Homicide is condoned only when undertaken to escape **imminent and**

unavoidable danger of **death or grave bodily harm**.

- You cannot shoot or physically attack a fleeing criminal unless you are absolutely sure he intends to continue the assault.

- If you shoot and injure or kill an assailant, your first phone call should be an ambulance, the second to an attorney, the third to the police. Expect to be arrested for murder. Make no statement whatever to the police or press without legal counsel. It seems unfair and unbelievable somehow that a woman who kills in self-defense would be arrested and charged with murder, yet this situation is not the time for righteous disbelief. The law states that self-defense is justifiable homicide, but the police have no way of immediately determining justifiable homicide.

When I inform my students there are many legal complications to self-defense, they often say, "Well, if a man attacked me on the street and I knocked him out, I wouldn't wait around to see if he was all right. I'd just take off and not report it." I really can't give you any advice here. Anything I say would be either moralizing or incriminating. The choice is yours. Just be sure that you have acted within the law when you do report.

In many cases, a rapist goes free because of the victim's statements, even though a violent rape took place. By the same type of statements, you could be convicted of murder or be prosecuted as the aggressor in defending against a deadly assault on your life.

How could this happen? Very simply. In court you cannot make statements such as, "I thought he would kill me" or even, "He said he would kill me". **Thinking** is not enough, neither is a threat. You must state that you were absolutely certain the assailant **intended** to carry out the threat and was **capable** of carrying out the threat.

What If You Become a Victim of Rape?

Because of the social consequences of remaining silent, I urge you to report. There are often also personal consequences for the victim, such as the rapist returning or continuing to successfully assault other women.

One woman in my study suffered great personal guilt for not reporting a known-assailant rape. Five years later the same assailant was arrested for the rape and murder of a sixteen-year-old girl. The original victim said she often wondered how many women had been victimized by this man and if reporting would have helped keep him off the streets.

You can report to the police without prosecuting the rapist and going to court if that is your choice. The important factor is that the rapist has been described or identified and is on record.

"Reporting a rape is to the police what seeing a cockroach in your kitchen means to the exterminator; if you see one roach, hundreds are hiding."

Rapists are known to be repeat offenders. Reporting a rape is to the police what seeing a cockroach in your kitchen means to the exterminator; if you see one roach, hundreds are hiding. A man accused of one rape is probably guilty of many more. Reporting a rape is no guarantee of arrest or conviction but it is a step towards personal protection, social responsibility and aiding the police in ferreting out these criminals.

If you have been raped, do not touch anything on the scene if you remain there. Call the police immediately. Then call a friend or the rape crisis center in your area and ask for an advocate. Do not change your clothes, bathe or douche. An advocate will accompany you during the police questioning, medical examination and court proceedings. It is your legal right to have someone with you all times for advice and moral support.

Do not withhold any information about the assault when talking to the police or during the medical exam. If you were raped anally, you must report it. Semen samples or smears from your anus or vagina must be taken for evidence. In many cases, the rapist does not ejaculate. In cases when there is no semen, there may be other evidence of assault. If you have bruises or other injuries, make sure photos are taken. The police will also want to keep torn clothing, sometimes your underwear and even the bed sheets if the rape occurred there.

Try to give the most complete description possible paying close attention to characteristics that cannot be changed. Hair styles, colors and facial hair can be altered to dramatically change appearances. In addition to height, weight and build, try to identify these factors.

- Facial oddities: birthmarks, scars, moles, freckles, pimples, harelip, receding or protruding chin

- Eyes: crossed, missing, slanted, color

- Ears: pierced, protruding, cauliflower, large, small

- Nose: crooked, hooked, upturned, flat, small, long

- Tattoos: arm, hand, fingers, chest, neck, pictures, designs, names, words, initials

- Speech: impediment, accent, stutter, refined

- Deformity: leg, arm, hand, limp, bowlegged

- Teeth: false, caps, missing, gold, broken, stained, decayed, irregular

There are many more specifics that you could state if you recall them. Every identifying factor should be recorded.

After the ordeal of reporting is over, you may need to seek counseling and support. If you live in a large metropolitan area, you can seek aid at a rape crisis center. Some smaller communities now have centers. Many women have resolved fear, anger, guilt and helplessness with the help of such agencies.

I cannot summarize this entire book with a final concluding paragraph. I have said what I believe needs to be said, most of which has not been said within in the context of self-defense for women. I think the best and simplest example which describes my message is Marshall McLuhan's statement from *The Medium is the Massage:* "There is absolutely no inevitability as long as there is a willingness to contemplate what is happening."

This expedient method
Is not the way
To physical power
Or supreme confidence.
These gifts are already yours
Although they may dwell within you
Unawakened and unrealized.
This method will provide the tools of knowledge
And remove obstacles
To facilitate the progress of the student.
A student is always committed to learning
And deeper understanding.
There is never a point of mastery,
Only degrees of understanding.
People often come to me with tales
Of martial arts masters who jump six feet
Or destroy ten attackers.
They admire the invincible,
Believe in the mystique,
Aspire to the legend,
But manifest the negativity
About their own physical reality
And boredom when instant gratification
Cannot be obtained.
Internal commitment cannot be destroyed
By the worst of circumstances,
Just as it can not be created
By the best of circumstances.
The highest goals of self-defense training for women
Are to open the individual's mind
To the option of increased physical mastery through learning
And to realize the existing strength
Of the body, mind and spirit.
With the tools in this book,
I hope that each person
Will be inspired to allow
Her natural awareness and confidence
To become a reality.

Susan Smith

Footnotes and References

Arranged by Chapter and Section

Footnotes, Chapter 1, Self-Defense for Women: A Positive Social Trend and an Opportunity for Personal Growth

[1] S. L. Bem, "Sex Role Inventory (BSRI)" 1974 in Carole Beene, *Women and Women's Issues - A Handbook of Tests and Measures* (San Franciso: Jersey Bass Publishers, 1979).

[2] "Anorexia, The 'Starving Disease' Epidemic," *U.S. News and World Report,* August 30, 1982.

[3] Dr. John A. Moran, President, Phobia Society of Arizona, telephone interview, December 13, 1985.

[4] Ronald C. Mewborn and Ronald W. Rogers, "Effects of Threatening and Reassuring Components of Fear Appeals on Physiological and Verbal Measures of Emotion and Attitudes," *Journal of Experimental Social Psychology*, 15 (1979), p. 245.

[5] Christopher Peterson, Martin Seligman, E.P. "Learned Helplessness and Victimization," *Journal of Social Issues*, No. 2 (1983), pp. 113-116.

[6] Berle Lieff Benderly, "Rape Free, Rape Prone," *Science Magazine,* 1982, p. 40.

[7] Susan Brownmiller, "Rape!" Phonotape, *Encyclopedia Americana/CBS News, Audio Resource Library* 10751 (Grolier Educational Corp., New York 1975).

[8] Ibid., Peterson and Seligman.

[9] Jane Roberts, *The Nature of Personal Reality* (New York: Bantam Books, Inc., 1974), p. 210.

[10] Nathaniel Branden, *The Psychology of Self-Esteem* (New York: Bantam Books, Inc., 1969), p. 110.

[11] Ibid., Jane Roberts, p. 308.

[12] Allan Please, *Signals* (Toronto, New York, London, Sydney, Auckland: Bantam Books, 1984), p. 26.

Additional References, Chapter 1

Andersen, Kurt. "Private Violence," *Time*. September 5, 1983.

Bart, Pauline. *Avoiding Rape: A Study of Victims and Avoiders*. Chicago, Illinois University at the Medical Center, August 1979.

Dowd, Maureen. "Rape: The Sexual Weapon," *Time*.

Ekman, P. "Universals and Cultural Differences in Facial Expression of Emotion," *Nebraska Symposium on Motivation*. 1971, 18, pp. 207-233.

Hall, J.A. "Gender Effects in Decoding Non-Verbal Cues," *Psychological Bulletin*. 1978, 85, pp. 845-857.

Henley, Nancy A. *Body Politics: Sex, Power and Non-Verbal Communication*. Englewood Cliffs, New Jersey: Prentice-Hall, 1977.

Holiday, Laurel. *The Violent Sex: Male Psychobiology and the Evolution of Consciousness*. Guerneville, California: Blue Stocking Books, 1978.

Magnuson. "Child Abuse: The Ultimate Betrayal," *Time*. September 5, 1983.

Montague, Ashley. *The Natural Superiority of Women*. Collier Books, Division of MacMillan Publishing Company, Inc. New Revised Edition, 1974.

"Mr. Goodbar Is Not Dead Yet," *Arizona Woman's News*. (Interview with James Jarrett, Director of Phoenix Firearms Training Center, May 1983).

Olson, Kiki. "Stop Thief," *Woman's Day Magazine*. May 22, 1984, p. 80.

O'Reilly, Jane. "Wife Beating: The Silent Crime," *Time*. September 5, 1983.

Restak, Richard M., M.D. *The Brain: The Last Frontier*. New York: Warner Books, 1979.

Storaska, Frederick. *How to Say No to a Rapist and Survive*. New York: Random House, 1975.

Sourcebook. Nature and Distribution of Offenses from data provided by the U.S. Department of Justice, Bureau of Justice Statistics, 1981.

Woman Protect Yourself. Crime Prevention Bureau, Las Vegas Metropolitan Police Department. (Pamphlet)

Zimbardo, P.G. "The Human Choice: Individuation, Reason and Order Versus Deindividuation, Impulse and Chaos." In W.J. Arnold and D. Levine, *Nebraska Symposium on Motivation*. Lincoln: University of Nebraska Press, 1970.

Footnotes, Chapter 2, Social Mythology

1 Phil Gunby, "Sexual Behavior in an Abnormal Situation," *JAMA Medical News*, January 16, 1981, Vol. 245, No. 3, p. 215.

2 Susan Brownmiller, *Against Our Will: Men, Women and Rape* (New York: Bantam Books, Simon & Schuster, ©1975 by Susan Brownmiller. Reprinted by permission of Simon & Schuster, Inc.), p. 293.

3 A. Nicholas Groth with H. Jean Birnbaum, *Men Who Rape: The Psychology of the Offender* (New York: Plenum Press, 1979), p. 13.

4 Ibid., p. 13.

5 Diana Russell, *The Prevalence of Rape and Assault*, Rockville, Maryland: National Institute of Mental Health, August 1979, p. 28.

6 Aric Press with Ann McDaniel and Elaine Shannon in Washington; Martin Kasindorf, Susan Agrest and Tessa Namuth in New York; Richard Sandza and George Raine in San Francisco; Monroe Anderson in Chicago; Linda Prout in Miami and bureau report, "Rape and the Law," *Newsweek*, May 20, 1985, p. 64.

7 Mary P. Koss and Cheryl J. Oros., "Sexual Experiences Survey: A Research Instrument Investigating Sexual Aggression and Victimization," *Journal of Consulting and Clinical Psychology*, 1982, Vol. 50, No. 3, p. 455.

8 Ibid., Diana Russell, p. 28.

9 Ibid., Susan Brownmiller, p. 216.

10 Pauline Bart, "A Study of Women Who Both Were Raped and Avoided Rape," *Journal of Social Issues*, Volume 37, Number 4, 1981, p. 123.

11 S. L. Bem and D. J. Bem, "Case Study of a Non-Conscious Ideology: Training the Woman to Know Her Place," *Beliefs, Attitudes and Human Affairs* (Belmont, California: Brooks/Cole, 1970), p. 97.

Additional References, Chapter 2

Brownmiller, Susan. *Femininity*. New York: Linden Press/Simon & Schuster, Inc., 1984.

Chernin, Kim. *The Obsession: Reflections on the Tyranny of Slenderness*. New York, Cambridge, Philadelphia, San Francisco, London, Mexico City, Sao Paulo, Sydney: Harper Colophon Books, 1981.

De Beauvior, Simone. *The Second Sex*. New York: Vintage Books, A Division of Random House, 1974.

Diamond, Jared. "Everything Else You Always Wanted to Know About Sex," *Discover Magazine*. April 1985.

Friedan, Betty. *The Feminine Mystique*. The Dell Publishing Company, 1972.

Goldberg, Herb, Ph.D. *The New Male-Female Relationship*. New York: A Signet Book, New American Library, 1983.

Hall, Edward T. *Beyond Culture*. Garden City, New York: Anchor Press/Doubleday, 1977.

Harragan, Betty Lehan. *Games Mother Never Taught You*. New York: Warner Books, 1977.

Heilbrun, Carolyn G. *Toward a Recognition of Androgny*. New York, Hagerstown, San Francisco, London: Harper and Row, 1974.

Langley, Roger and Richard C. Levy. *Wife Beating, The Silent Crisis*. New York: A Kangaroo Book, Pocket Books, 1977.

Montague, Ashley. *The Natural Superiority of Women*. New York: Collier Books, A Division of MacMillan Publishing Company, Inc., 1974.

Morgan, Robin. *Sisterhood is Powerful - An Anthology from the Women's Liberation Movement*. New York: A Vintage Book, a division of Random House, 1970.

Steinem, Gloria. *Outrageous Acts and Everyday Rebellions*. New York and Scarborough, Ontario: A Plume Book, New American Library, 1983.

Webster's Seventh New Collegiate Dictionary. Springfield, Massachusetts: G. and C. Merriam Company, U.S.A., 1972. (Consulted for definition of "socialize.")

Footnotes, Chapter 3, Results of the Four-Part Survey

Part I: Known-Assailant Attack

[1] Pauline Bart, *Avoiding Rape: A Study of Victims and Avoiders* (Rockville, Illinois: National Institute of Mental Health, 1979), p. 25.

[2] Frederick Storaska, *How to Say No to a Rapist and Survive* (New York: Random House, 1975), p. 95.

[3] Late Night America, May 3, 1985, (Interview with Pat Collins, CBS Movie Critic, Arts and Entertainment Director).

[4] Ibid., Pauline Bart, p. 19.

[5] Susan Brownmiller, *Against Our Will: Men, Women and Rape* (Bantam Books, 1975), p. 277.

[6] Ibid., p. 228.

[7] Ashley Montague, *The Natural Superiority of Women* (New York: Collier Books, A Division of Macmillan Publishing Company, Inc., 1968), p. 114.

[8] Smith Survey conducted in Phoenix, Arizona, Interviews with Successful Resistors. (August 1982 through July 1983)

Additional References, Chapter 3, Part I

Graphs and charts taken from the computer sheets that illustrate the four-part survey can be obtained by sending $2.00 (for postage and copy costs) to **Strictly Self-defense for Women**, P.O. Box 15224, Phoenix, Arizona, 85060.

Burt, Martha. *Attitudes Supportive of Rape in American Culture*. Prepared for National Institute of Mental Health, Rockville, MD. Minnesota Center for Sociological Research, September 1978.

Carolyn, J. Hursch, Ph.D. *The Trouble with Rape*. Chicago: Nelson-Hall, 1973.

Fisher, J. D. and D. Byrne. "Too Close for Comfort: Sex Differences in Response to Invasions of Personal Space," *Journal of Personality and Social Psychology*. 1975, 32, pp. 15-21.

Goffman, Irving. *Interaction Ritual*. Garden City, New York: Anchor Books, Doubleday and Company, Inc., 1967.

Lesse, Stanley, M.D., Med. Sc. D. "The Status of Violence Against Women: Past, Present and Future Factors," *American Journal of Psychotherapy*. Vol. XXXIII, No. 2, April, 1979, pp. 190-200.

Medea, Andrea and Kathleen Thompson. *Against Rape*. Farrar, Straus, Giroux, Inc., 1974.

Offir, Carole Wade. "Don't Take It Lying Down," in The Health Advisor, *Woman's Almanac: 12 How-to-Handbooks in One*. Compiled and Edited by Kathryn Paulsen and Ryan A. Kuhn. Philadelphia and New York: J.B. Lippincott Company, p. 61.

Selkin, James, Ph.D. "The Mind of the Rapist," also from *Woman's Almanac*. pp. 58-60.

Sanders, William B. *Rape and Women's Identity*. Bevery Hills, London: Sage Publications.

Schurr, Cathleen. "Victim as Criminal," *Know, Inc.* Pittsburgh, PA, 15221: P.O. Box 86031, 1972.

Footnotes, Chapter 3, Part II: Random or Stranger Attack

[1] R.D. Clark, III and L.E. Word, "Why Don't Bystanders Help? Because of Ambiguity?" *Journal of Personality and Social Psychology*, (1972), 24, pp. 392-400.

[2] Robert A. Wallace, *The Genesis Factor* (New York: Berkley Books, 1975), pp. 93-95.

[3] A. Nicholas Groth with H. Jean Birnbaum, *Men Who Rape: The Psychology of the Offender* (New York: Plenum Press, 1979), p. 13.

[4] Ibid., p. 14.

[5] Ibid., p. 25.

[6] Ibid., p. 27.

[7] Ibid., p. 30.

[8] Brad Darrach and Joel Norris, "An American Tragedy," *Life*, August, 1985, pp. 69-70.

[9] Ibid., p. 70.

Footnotes, Chapter 3, Part III: Successful Resistance

[1] Susan Brownmiller, *Against Our Will: Men, Women and Rape* (New York: Bantam Books, 1975), p. 227.

[2] Nancy A. Henley, *Body Politics: Sex, Power and Non-Verbal Communication* (Englewood Cliffs, New Jersey 07632: ©1977 by Prentice-Hall, Inc.), p. 14. Reprinted by permission of Prentice-Hall, Inc.

[3] M. J. Lerner, D. T. Miller and J. G. Holmes, "Deserving Versus Justice: A Contemporary Dilemma, *Advances in Experimental Social Psychology*, L. Berkowitz. Ed., (New York: Academic Press, 1976).

[4] Timothy Beneke, *Men On Rape* (New York: St. Martins Press 1982), pp. 110-111.

[5] Ibid., p. 105.

Additional References, Chapter 3, Part III

Aynsworth, Hugh and Stephen G. Michaud. *The Only Living Witness*. Canada: A Signet Book, 1984.

Bart, Pauline B. and Patricia H. O'Brien. *Stopping Rape: Successful Survival Strategies,* Elmsford, New York: Pergamon Press, Athene Series, 1985.

Block, R. and W. Skogen. *Resistance and Outcomes in Robbery and Rape.* Center for Urban Affairs, Northwestern University, 1982.

Buckley, William T. "How to Sway Decisions: A New Psychological Study Turns Up a Simple and Surprising Technique," *Self Magazine,* May 1985.

McIntyre, J. *Victim Response to Rape: Alternative Outcomes.* Rockville, Maryland: National Institute of Mental Health, 1981.

Queen's Bench Foundation. "Rape-Prevention and Resistance: Interviews and self-report questionnaire from 108 women recruited via media and public," unpublished 1976; in *Resistance Strategies.* Chimera Inc., 1982.

Rule, Ann. *The Stranger Beside Me.* Canada: A Signet Book, 1981.

Russell, Diana E.H., Ph.D. *The Prevalence of Rape and Assault.* Rockville, Maryland: National Institute of Mental Health, August 1979.

Zuckerman, Miron. "Belief in a Just World and Altruistic Behavior," *Journal of Personality and Social Psychology.* (1975), Vol. 31, No. 5, pp. 972-976.

Additional References, Chapter 3, Part IV: Assaults

Abrahamsen, David, M.D. *The Murdering Mind.* New York, Evanston, San Francisco, London: Harper and Row, Publishers, 1973.

Bowles, Billy and Brian Flanigan. *The Man Who Murdered Women.* Detroit Free Press. August 22, 1982.

Clark, R.D., III and L. E. Word. "Why Don't Bystanders Help? Because of Ambiguity?" *Journal of Personality and Social Psychology.* (1972), 24, pp. 392-400.

Darrack, Brad and Joel Norris. "An American Tragedy," *Life.* August, 1984.

Stack, Andy. *Lust Killer.* New York: A Signet Book, New American Library, 1983.

Footnotes, Chapter 4, Attack Deterrents

1 Mark Snyder and William B. Swann, Jr., "Behavioral Confirmation in Social Interaction: From Social Perception to Social Reality," *Journal of Experimental Social Psychology,* Vol. 14, (1978), p. 148.

2 M. E. Shenab and K. A. Yahya, "A Behavioral Study of Obedience in Children," *Journal of Personality and Social Psychology,* (1977), 35, 530-536. [Quotation from synopsis of several related studies in *Social Psychology: Understanding Human*

Interaction, Third Edition, by Robert A. Baron and Donn Byrne, (Boston, London, Sydney, Toronto: Allyn and Bacon Inc., 1974), p. 253].

3 Elton B. McNiel and Zick Rubin, *The Psychology of Being Human,* 2nd Edition, (San Francisco: Canfield Press, 1974), p. 472.

4 Nancy A. Henley, *Body Politics: Sex, Power and Non-Verbal Communication* (Englewood Cliffs, New Jersey: Prentice Hall, 1977), p. 13.

5 Ibid., p. 12.

6 Mary Brown Parley, "Conversational Politics," *Psychology Today,* May 1979, p. 52.

7 Ibid.

8 Ibid., Nancy A. Henley, p. 16.

9 Ibid., p. 16.

10 Jim Nail, "How Muggable Are You?" *Black Belt Magazine,* October 1981, p. 44.

11 Ibid., p. 44.

12 Ibid., p. 46.

13 Smith Survey, conducted in Phoenix, Arizona 1982-1983. Confidential phone survey of women in the martial arts, questionnaire (52 questions), 63 responses from women who had taken or were currently involved in various martial-arts styles.

14 Timothy Beneke, "Male Rage - Men Talk About Rape," *Mother Jones,* (1982), p. 14.

15 Ibid., Henley, p. 175.

16 *People Magazine,* December 23, 1985. p. 53.

17 Ibid., p. 53.

18 Susan Brownmiller, *Femininity* (New York: Linden Press, Simon & Schuster, 1985), p. 34.

19 Ibid., p. 34.

20 Ibid., p. 35.

21 Ibid., Nail, p. 46.

22 Ibid., p. 46.

Additional References, Chapter 4

Aric Press with Ann McDaniel and Elaine Shannon in Washington; Martin Kasindorf, Susan Agrets and Tessa Namuth in New York; Richard Sandza and George Raine in San Francisco; Monroe Anderson in Chicago; Linda Prout in Miami and Bureau Reports. "Rape and the Law," *Newsweek*. May 20, 1985.

Argyle, M., V. Satter, H. Nicholson, M. Williams and P. Burgess. "The Communication of Inferior and Superior Attitudes by Verbal and Non-verbal Signals," *British Journal of Social and Clinical Psychology*. 1970, 9, pp. 222-231.

Every Woman's Car Care Handbook. Akron, Ohio, 44317: The Firestone Tire & Rubber Company, 1200 Firestone Parkway.

Givens, Dr. David B. *Love Signals*. New York: Pinnacle Books, Madonna, 1983.

Goffman, Erving. *Encounters: Two Studies in Sociology of Interaction*. Indianapolis, New York: The Bobbs- Merrill Company, Inc.

Hall, E.T. "A System for the Notation of Proxemic Behavior," *American Anthropologist*. 1963, 65, pp. 1003-1026.

Hall, Judith A. "Gender Effects in Decoding Non-verbal Cues," *Psychological Bulletin*. 1978, 85, pp. 845-857.

Henley, Nancy. *Status and Sex: Some Touching Observations*. Bulletin. Psychonomic Society, 1973, Vol. 2.

Johnson, Ray. "Making Your Home Burglar-Proof," *New Woman*. May, 1985.

Key, Mary Ritchie. "Linguistic Behavior of Male and Female," *Linguistics*. 1972, 88, pp. 15-31.

Key, Mary Ritchie. *Male/Female Language*. Metuchen, N.J.: The Scarecrow Press, Inc., 1975.

Kitch, Carolyn. "Myths about Crime that Could Put You in Danger." *McCalls*. August 1985.

Booth, Cathy and Denise Worrell. "Madonna Rocks the Land," *Time*. May 27, 1985.

McLuhan, Marshall and Quentin Fiore. *The Medium is the Massage. An Inventory of Effects*. New York, London, Toronto: Bantam Books, 1967.

Milgram, Stanley. "Behavioral Study of Obedience," *Journal of Abnormal and Social Psychology*. Vol. 67, No. 4, pp. 371-378.

Morgan, Ellen. "The Eroticization of Male Dominance - Female Submission - The Sexist Turn On That Castrates Self, Love and Sex," *Know, Inc*. 1975.

Pease, Allan. *Signals: How to Use Body Language for Power, Success and Love.* Toronto, New York, London, Sydney, Auckland: A Bantam Book, 1984.

Ryan, William. *Blaming the Victim.* New York: Vintage Books, A Division of Random House, 1976.

Strom, Jolen C. and Ross W. Buck. "Staring and Participant's Sex: Physiological and Subjective Reactions," *Personality and Social Psychology Bulletin.* 1979, V. 5, No. 1, pp. 114-117.

Tschirhart, Linda and Ann Fetter Sanford. *In Defense of Ourselves.* Garden City, New York: A Dolphin Book, Doubleday and Company, 1979.

Zweigenhaft, Richard L. "Personal Space in the Faculty Office: Desk Placement and the Student-Faculty Interaction," *Journal of Applied Psychology.* 1976, Vol. 61, No. 4.

References, Chapter 5, Degrees of Threat/Degrees of Resistance Application of Strategies

Ayoob, Massad F. *The Truth about Self-Protection.* Toronto, New York, London, Sydney: Bantam Books, 1983.

Bloom, Lynn Z., Karen Coburn and Joan Pearlman. *The New Assertive Woman.* Dell Publishing Co., Inc., 1975.

Backhouse, Connie and Ray Brophy, Alice Friedman, Martha Hooven, Beth Johnson, Freada Klein, Margaret Lazarus, Anne Lopes, Lynn Rubinett, Kate Swann, Denise Well, Wendy Sanford, Editor. *Fighting Sexual Harassment: An Advocacy Handbook.* Boston, Massachusetts: Alyson Publications, Inc. and The Alliance Against Sexual Coercion, 1981.

Delacoste, Frederique and Felice Newman. *Fight Back! Feminist Resistance to Male Violence.* Minneapolis, Minnesota: Cleis Press, 1981.

Groth, A. Nicholas with H. Jean Birnbaum. *Men Who Rape: The Psychology of the Offender.* New York: Plenum Press, 1979.

Hall, Edward T. *Beyond Culture.* Garden City, New York: Anchor Press/Doubleday, 1977.

Lakoff, Robin. *Language and Woman's Place.* New York, Evanston, San Francisco, London: Harper Colophon Books, Harper and Row Publishing, 1975.

Langley, Roger and Richard Levy. *Wife Beating: The Silent Crisis.* New York: Kangaroo Book, Pocket Books, 1977.

Maughan, William L. and Richard H. Nagasawa, Ph.D. *Resist! Women's Guide To Escape Assaults.* Scottsdale, Arizona: W.L. Maughan, 1978.

Storaska, Frederick. *How to Say No to a Rapist and Survive.* New York: Random House, 1975.

Footnotes, Chapter 6, Technique Section

[1] *Webster's Seventh New Collegiate Dictionary* (Chicago: R. R. Donnelley and Sons Company, The Lakeside Press), p. 144.

[2] Chimera, Inc., *Resistance Strategies* (Chicago, IL, 60603: Chimera, Inc., 10 S. Wabash #602), p. 2.

Additional References, Chapter 6

Guilfoil, John. "Iron Palm Breaking," *Inside Kung-Fu.* December, 1982.

Gray, Henry, F.R.S. *Gray's Anatomy.* Philadelphia, Pennsylvania: Running Press, 1974.

Hosey, Timothy. "Winning Streetfights with the Street," *Black Belt Magazine.* 1980.

Kazoroski, Ron. "Women's Self-Defense: Training the Untrained for Survival," *Karate Illustrated.* June, 1983.

Lee, Eric. *Fight Back, Your Guide to Self-Defense.* Hollywood, CA: Unique Publications Inc., 1982.

Siverio, Manual. "The Streetfighter's View of the Arm," *Karate Illustrated.* August 1983.

Wedlake, Lee. "The Elbow," *Inside Kung-Fu.* June, 1983.

Footnotes, Chapter 7, Last-Resort Techniques

[1] Oscar Diaz-Cobo, *Unarmed against the Knife* (Boulder, Colorado: Paladin Press, 1982), p. 3.

[2] Ibid., p. 3.

Additional References, Chapter 7

Amir, M. *Patterns in Forcible Rape.* Chicago: University of Chicago Press, 1971.

Ayoob, Massad, F. *In the Gravest Extreme, the Role of the Firearm in Personal Protection.* Massad F. and Dorothy A. Ayoob, Publishers, 1980.

Bart, Pauline. *Avoiding Rape: A Study of Victims and Avoiders.* Rockville, Illinois: National Institute of Mental Health, 1979.

Conroy, Mary. *Every Woman Can: The Conroy Method to Safety, Security and Self-Defense.* New York: Grosset and Dunlap, 1982.

Delacoste, Frederique and Felice Newman. *Fight Back: Feminist Resistance to Violence.* Minneapolis: Cleis Press, 1981.

Groth, A. Nicholas with H. Jean Birnbaum. *Men Who Rape: The Psychology of the Offender.* New York: Plenum Press, 1979.

Mashiro, N. Ph.D. *Black Medicine II, Weapons At Hand.* Boulder, Colorado: Paladin Press, 1979.

Mashiro N. Ph.D. *Black Medicine III, Low Blows.* Boulder, Colorado: Paladin Press, 1981.

Stack, Andy. *True Crime Annals: Lust Killer.* A Signet Book, New American Library, 1983.

Organizations and Agencies

Chimera, Inc.
6 East Monroe 1502
Chicago, IL 60603
Phone: (312) 332-5540

Chimera (Ki-MERE-ah) is a women's self-defense foundation dedicated to defeating women's fears of defending themselves. Chimera has trained instructors all over the United States who go into the community to teach groups of women. They are a non-profit organization so all donations are tax-deductible.

Know, Inc.
Box 86031
Pittsburgh, PA 15221-0031

Know is a non-profit organization dedicated to making known the needs brought about by changing roles in society. Primary concerns are discrimination, particularly sex-role stereotyping and discrimination based on sex. Most of the papers distributed by Know are written by women. The average price is $.50 to $1.50. The quality of the publications are excellent.

PGH Action Against Rape, Inc. (PAAR)
P.O. Box 10433
Pittsburgh, PA 15234

This organization distributes a free booklet, *Every Woman's Guide to Personal Rape Prevention.* The short term goal of the organization is to provide compassionate, effective treatment of rape victims by society's institutions and the long range goal of eradication of rape in our society. Single membership fee is $5. Organization membership is $25.

Project on the Status and Education of Women
Requests, Box C
Association of American Colleges
1818 R. Street, N.W.
Washington, DC 20009

This organization distributes a report that includes a list of resource publications and organizations. Copies are $3. (Author's note: This is well worth sending for. This organization distributes extensive information on just about every issue of special interest to women.)

Kings County Rape Relief
305 South 43rd Street
Renton, WA 98055

You can get booklets that deal with child sexual abuse, *No More Secrets* and *He Told Me Not to Tell*, from this organization.

U.S. Department of Health and Human Services
National Center for the Prevention and Control of Rape (NCPCR)
National Institute of Mental Health
5600 Fishers Lane
Rockville, MD 20857

If you write to this agency, you will reach the National Clearinghouse for Mental Health Information. This is a national center for the collection, storage, retrieval and dissemination of scientific information in the area of mental health. They will send you a complimentary copy of the following publications and provide you with a price list for additional copies.
How to Protect Yourself against Sexual Assualt
National Directory: Rape Prevention and Treatment Resources
Public and Private Sources of Funding for Sexual Assault Treatment Programs
Rape and the Older Woman: A Guide to Prevention and Protection
He Told Me Not to Tell

The Eisenhower Foundation for the Prevention of Violence
1666 K Street, N.W.
Washington, DC 20006
Phone: (202) 783-6215

Information and referrals to neighborhood patrol organizations.

National Organization for Victims Assistance (NOVA)
918 16th Street, N.W.
Washington, DC 20006
Phone: (202) 265-5042

Victim assistance and national clearinghouse for victims.

National Association of Criminal Victim Compensation Boards
Worker's Compensation Bureau
c/o Richard J. Cross
Highway 83, N. Russel Building
Bismarck, ND 58505
Phone: (701) 224-2700

Literature on victim compensation.

Fichet, Inc.
P.O. Box 92
Halesite, NY 11743

Copies of the *Home Security Checklist* can be obtained free from this company.

National Technical Information Service
5285 Port Royal Road
Springfield, VA 22161
Phone: (703) 487-4650

This information service distributes the final report summaries of research grant studies of the Rape Prevention Center. Write for a list of papers pertaining to rape. The papers cost between $5 and $8.

Women's Institute for Freedom of the Press
3306 Ross Place, N.W.
Washington, DC 20009

Distributes an annual index directory of women's media publication to aid networking among women, women's organizations and women's media, both nationally and internationally. The directory is $8.

The First World Congress of Victimology
Program Chair
109A South Columbus Street
Alexandria, VA 11314
Phone: (703) 549-7239 or 549-7953

The First World Congress of Victimology was held August 20-24, 1980 in Washington, D.C. The Congress is open to professionals, practitioners, volunteers and scholars from throughout the world. It focuses not only on the victims of crime but on other types of victims as well, like victims of a natural disaster. The congress sponsors eight awards recognizing professionals who have made outstanding contributions to the field of victimology, including awards for original research and evaluation, innovative programs and services, training and audiovisual materials and technological or architectural innovation. Nominations are invited for all categories. Futher information about the annual conference, entering the awards competition, the scholarly paper submission and professional and media presentations is available from the above address.

National Institute on Rape
P.O. Box 2325
Berkeley, CA 94708

Publications and papers on rape are available.

Center for the Study of Women and Sex Roles
CUNY Graduate School and University Center
33 West 42nd Street
New York, NY 10036

The Center for the Study of Women and Sex Roles is set up to foster a high level of interdisciplinary scholarly research and graduate education and to facilitate the growth of knowledge in this area through conferences, seminars, lectures and course work. Its research and course-related interests include the psychology of sex roles, cross-cultural studies of sex-role learning, the role of women and the law, women's history, sex biases and stereotypes in education and women in the arts.

Programs in Sex Roles and Social Change
Columbia University
Center for the Social Sciences
420 West 118th Street
New York, NY 10027

This program encourages and facilitates empirical research among social scientists in four main areas: the labor force, the family, the law and higher education. It has a special interest in emerging areas in the sex role field and international comparisons and the interaction between social science research and the law. The Center's activities have stimulated interdisciplinary communication among scholars within the university community and plans include expansion of this network to the larger intellectual community of New York.

International Center for Research on Women
1010 16th Street, N.W. Third Floor
Washington, DC 20036

The International Center for Research on Women is one of two international centers concerned with the impact of the development process on the roles and status of women. The Center conducts work aimed at not only understanding and improving the lives of women in developing countries but accelerating the socioeconomic development of those countries by including women as active participants. Projects range from research on poverty as a women's issue and the impact of migration on family structure to women-headed households and the conditions of rural women in several countries.

International Research and Training Institute for the Advancement of Women
Office of the Assistant Secretary-General
Center for Social Development and Humanitarian Affairs
One United Nations Plaza, Room DC-1026
New York, NY 10017

The Institute promotes the goals of the United Nations Decade for Women through research, training and the collection and exchange of documentation/information within the context of national, regional and international plans of action. The Institute works closely with intergovernmental, governmental and non-governmental agencies with similar aims, and with the Voluntary Fund for the United Nations Decade for Women.

Center for Continuing Education for Women (CCEW)
University of Michigan
328-330 Thompson Street
Ann Arbor, MI 48109

This center has three inter related functions: service, advocacy and research. Since 1964, the Center has offered a wide range of direct and indirect services to help women (and men) whose education is or may be complicated by family and/or the need to work. It has been an advocate for individual students and for more sensitive institutional responses throughout the schools and departments of the University. To some extent, it has had an impact on other institutions of its kind.

Institute for Social Research
University of Michigan
Panel Study of Income Dynamics
Institute for Social Research
Ann Arbor, MI 48106

The Institute's Panel Study of Income Dynamics is an extensive investigation of the causes and consequences of peoples' changing economic fortunes over time. The study follows 5,000 families (17,000 individuals), shedding light on a variety of social issues relating to women's family roles. Findings over the nine years so far have been presented in six volumes of interest to economists, demographers, sociologists, social policy makers and others interested in poverty, job discrimination and the social economics of the American family.

Center for Human Resource Research
Ohio State University
National Longitudinal Surveys of Labor Force Behavior (NLS)
Columbus, OH 43201

The Center is concerned with a wide range of contemporary problems associated with human resource development, conservation and utilization and has acquired pre-eminence in the fields of labor market research and manpower planning. The largest project of the Center, the National Longitudinal Surveys of Labor Force Behavior, has been conducted since 1965 for the Department of Labor. Sample data are collected on a continuing basis for four groups of the U.S. population. The groups are men 45-59 years of age; women 30-44 years of age; men 14-24 and women 14-24. Monographs and special reports, as well as data and tapes for public use, are available from this agency.

Center for Research on Women (CROW)
Stanford University
Polya Hall
Stanford, CA 94305

The Center for Research on Women sponsors research undertaken by the Stanford faculty on the changing roles of women and men within their own disciplines and interdisciplinary teams and facilitates the sharing of findings with students and interested members of the wider community. The research program includes research scholars, seed money research grants, the center's group activities, research seminars and a research conference. A major study underway is concerned with the biology and psychology of sex differences. The educational programs include course development, a lecture series and other public events.

A Program of Policy Research on Women and Families
Urban Institute
2100 SM Street N.W.
Washington, DC

The program represents a significant extention of the research agenda of the Institute to cover new developments in sex roles and life styles. Objectives are to analyze and interpret ongoing changes in women's aspirations and status and the implications of these changes for individuals and social institutions, to identify and anticipate the range of public policy options for responding to these changes and to provide the conceptual and factual basis for choosing among the alternatives. Projects range from the tax treatment of two-earner families to the effects of recession on the employment of women and the need for new financial arrangements for the support of children in cases of divorce, separation or out-of-wedlock birth.

Women's Studies Research Center
University of Wisconsin
Madison, WI 53706

The Women's Center maintains linkages with other centers and institutes on the Madison campus with isolated scholars engaged in research on women and women's community groups and state agencies whose mission is to transform research into policy. Activities such as monthly colloquia, grant-writing competitions and celebrations further these goals. Research efforts focus on four areas: women's studies pedagogy; the concept of motherhood; women and health; and theoretical and methodological debate between traditional approaches to the social sciences and humanities and more recent considerations of what constitutes knowledge and knowing.

Fifty States Project
Office of Public Liaison
Old Executive Office Building, Room 436
Washington, DC 20500
Phone: (202) 456-7896

The project assists state governments in identifying and correcting legislation and statutes which discriminate against women. The Governor's office in each state has a representative to the project.

Department of Education
Women's Educational Equity Act Program
400 Maryland Avenue, S.W. Room 2031
Washington, DC 20202

WEEA gives grants and contracts to non-profit organizations for the purpose of developing model programs and products which enhance educational equity for women and girls and which address the most persistent barriers to educational equity.

Inter-American Commission of Women
Organization of American States (OAS)
General Secretariat
17th and Constitution Avenue, N.W.
Washington, DC 20006
Phone: (202) 789-6084

The commission serves as an intergovernmental agency which seeks to improve the status of women in OAS member countries.

Federal Women's Program Division
Office of Personnel Management
1900 East Street, N.W., Room 7H17
Washington, DC 24015
Phone: (202) 632-70

The aim of the division is to advance and enhance employment of women, including minority women.

International Women's Programs
Department of State
Bureau of International Organization of Affairs, Room 4334-A
Washington, DC 20520
Phone: (202) 632-2560

The programs office deals with international issues concerning the status of women within the context of the UN Decade for Women.

Women's Bureau
Department of Labor
200 Constitution Avenue, N.W., Room S3002
Washington, DC 20510
Phone: (202) 523-6611

The bureau works to improve the economic status of women by developing policies, standards and program initiatives which enhance services for women in employment and training and address the concerns of women with special employment-related needs.

Office of Women's Business Ownership
Small Business Administration
1441 L Street, N.W.
Washington, DC 20416
Phone: (202) 653-6074

The office seeks to increase the strength, visibility and profitability of women-owned businesses by enhancing equal access to and greater opportunity for participation in government and private sector resources and programs.

Executive Women in Government
Consumer Product Safety Commission
1111 18th Street, N.W.
Washington, DC 20207
Phone: (202) 634-7740

The group serves as an informal network for upper-level female employees in all branches of the federal government.

Interagency Committee on Women's Business Enterprise
1441 L Street, N.W.
Washington, DC 20416
Phone: (202) 653-6074

The committee, made up of a presidentially appointed chair and representatives from each federal agency, works to promote women-owned businesses.

Task Force on Legal Equity for Women
Department of Justice
10th and Constitution Avenue, N.W., Room 5114
Washington, DC 20530
Phone: (202) 633-2701

Implements decisions made by presidential and cabinet council on how to best ensure that federal laws contain no provisions discriminatory to women.

Gender Discrimination Agency Review Group
Department of Justice, Coordination and Review Section
Civil Rights Division
320 First Street, N.W.
HOLC Building, Room 832
Washington, DC 20530
Phone: (202) 724-2240

Searches federal code, statutes, regulations, practices and policies for cabinet council on legal policy.

Afterward

It is essential that any instructor of self-defense for women be strongly committed to the concept of feminism. Aside from a fraction of feminist supremists, extremists and separatists (all of whom have important messages and contributions), I interpret feminism as actually a departure from extremism.

A society in which one half of the population (males) have rights and powers that the other half (females) do not have is an extremist society. A feminist should have a commitment to integrate female participation and independence at every level of society and to affirm the interdependence and importance of **all** human beings. We are making statements about history, humanity and possibilities - all in an attempt to integrate not separate.

The feminist movement has always attempted to bring balanced and healthy equity to women's existence. Feminism has attempted to right the wrongs of an extremist society in which women first had to struggle for the right to vote and are still struggling for social and economic equality.

Women are sometimes bitter because it takes so much to accomplish so little. Yet we have been encouraged by the slightest glimpse of a world where we matter as people and our contributions in non-traditional and traditional roles are recognized and valued rather than automatically devalued because "they're made by women."

In my commitment to feminism and justice, I must take a firm stand on the many issues pertaining to self-defense. While being committed to non-violence, I must teach aggressive defense techniques. This is not a contradiction. It is an acknowledgment of reality and idealism. The more prepared you are to resist or cope with violence and inhumanity, the less likely you are to have to use defensive knowledge. Yet if it must be used, your will have a choice of physical and psychological weapons, tactics and strategy.

Then, a person who believes in non-violence and justice can continue to live in peace because that person can and will defend, to the best of her ability, her right to life, peace and freedom.

I cannot agree with the concept of non-violence as non-action against violence. This concept supposes that the peaceful must concede to physical, social and psychological slaughter. We must be committed to peace by protecting our rights. We must always realize the matter of choice and the influence of knowledge on choice. Every step of the way, we can chose - to the best of our understanding and abilities - fear or freedom.

Susan Smith

Susan Smith has a first degree black belt ranking under Shifu D.G. Isch, 6th Dan in the Shou' Shu Mandarin Chinese system founded in the U.S. by Shifu Al Moore. She currently holds the rank of Yon Kyu under Sensei Michael O. Wall (in photos above), 3rd Dan, Shuri Ryu Okinawan Karate founded in the U.S. by Grandmaster Robert A. Trias, head of the United States Karate Association.

Susan founded a women's self-defense school in Phoenix, Arizona and taught at the school exclusively for several years.

She has appeared on radio and TV talk shows and organized and taught training sessions and seminars at numerous community agencies and groups.

In recognition for being the founder of a system, Susan was granted Sokeship by Shihan Dr. Robert Pavelsky of the American Karate Training Institute. The title "Soke," meaning founder, is granted to independent martial arts practitioners who create traditional style systems as well as dedicated self-defense systems like the one she teaches. Susan calls the system "White Lotus" because it involves an open, evolutionary method of teaching and learning. Instructors remain independent and add to the system both by design and by discovery. Susan is interested in promoting and participating in responsible, effective self-defense programs for women.

As Soke, Susan may issue instructor certificates for the system she teaches. She would like to work with women who are or have been involved in martial arts, law enforcement, military training or the physical fitness field.

For more information about seminars, instructor training or to exchange research and information on self-defense and related social issues, write to Susan Smith at P.O. Box 15224, Phoenix, AZ 85060.

 **Mother Courage Press**

In addition to *Fear or Freedom* by Susan Smith, Mother Courage Press also publishes

Why Me? Help for victims of child sexual abuse (even if they are adults now) by Lynn B. Daugherty. This book was written to be read by survivors of child sexual abuse who are now teenagers or adults. It is also intended for counselors or other people who want to understand and help these survivors. It was chosen for the Editors Choice Award for Young Adults in 1986 by the American Library Association's publication, *booklist*. Its reviewer wrote, "Emphasing the responsibility of the abuser, the fact that abuse is a widespread experience, and the dynamics of an abusive situation, Daugherty begins the process of healing psychological wounds."
Paperback, (112 pages) $7.95

Something Happened to Me by Phyllis Sweet. This is a sensitive, straightforward book designed to help children victimized by incest or other sexual abuse. A reviewer for *Young Children,* the Official Journal of the National Association for the Education of Young Children, wrote, "The marvelous introduction and epilogue are written for adults and reveal the extraordinary care that the author, a school psychologist, has taken to assure the dignity and self-worth of children from troubled families."
Paperback, Illustrated, 8-1/2 by 11, (36 pages) $4.95

Watch for more bibliotherapeutic books (books for healing and helping) from Mother Courage Press.

Coming in the spring of 1987, *NEWS* by Heather Conrad. George Orwell predicted in his novel *1984* that "Big Brother" would be watching us all by then. Yet when 1984 rolled around, the media bent over backwards to tell us this hadn't happened. This novel says "Oh yeah?" More than science fiction, it's a "what if" novel in historical perspective about an action that could have taken place in 1984 and dramatically would have changed the world, and "a bunch of women did it!"

If you don't find them in your local book store, you may order books directly from Mother Courage at 1533 Illinois Street, Racine, WI 53405 . Please add $1.00 for postage and handling for the first book and $.25 for each additional book.